THE NEW MIDDLE AGES

BONNIE WHEELER, *Series Editor*

The New Middle Ages is a series dedicated to pluridisciplinary studies of medieval cultures, with particular emphasis on recuperating women's history and on feminist and gender analyses. This peer-reviewed series includes both scholarly monographs and essay collections.

PUBLISHED BY PALGRAVE:

GENDER AND POWER IN MEDIEVAL EXEGESIS

Theresa Tinkle

GENDER AND POWER IN MEDIEVAL EXEGESIS
Copyright © Theresa Tinkle, 2010.

All rights reserved.

First published in 2010 by
PALGRAVE MACMILLAN®
in the United States—a division of St. Martin's Press LLC,
175 Fifth Avenue, New York, NY 10010.

Where this book is distributed in the UK, Europe and the rest of the world,
this is by Palgrave Macmillan, a division of Macmillan Publishers Limited,
registered in England, company number 785998, of Houndmills,
Basingstoke, Hampshire RG21 6XS.

Palgrave Macmillan is the global academic imprint of the above companies
and has companies and representatives throughout the world.

Palgrave® and Macmillan® are registered trademarks in the United States,
the United Kingdom, Europe and other countries.

ISBN: 978–0–230–10435–8

Library of Congress Cataloging-in-Publication Data

Tinkle, Theresa Lynn, 1954–
     Gender and power in medieval exegesis / Theresa Tinkle.
         p. cm.—(The new Middle Ages)
     Includes bibliographical references.
     ISBN 978–0–230–10435–8 (alk. paper)
         1. Women—Religious aspects—Christianity—History of doctrines—
Middle Ages, 600–1500. 2. Bible—Criticism, interpretation, etc.—
History—Middle Ages, 600–1500. 3. Christian literature—Male
authors—History and criticism. 4. Power (Social sciences)—History—To
1500. 5. Feminist theology. I. Title.

BR163.T56 2010
220.8'30540902—dc22   2010007417

A catalogue record of the book is available from the British Library.

Design by Newgen Imaging Systems (P) Ltd., Chennai, India.

First edition: September 2010

10 9 8 7 6 5 4 3 2 1

Printed in the United States of America.

For Deborah Christine Gregg
and
Susan Jovan Ollis

CONTENTS

ACKNOWLEDGMENTS

I am grateful for the friends, colleagues, and institutions that have supported my work on this book. The College of Literature, Science, and the Arts at the University of Michigan provided a sabbatical and one-term fellowship that allowed me to finish writing. Several scholars responded to the work in progress, helping me refine the argument. Anonymous readers for *SAC, Chaucer Review, JEGP,* and Palgrave offered welcome encouragement and smart suggestions for improvement, while Bonnie Wheeler has been both efficient and helpful. Friends and colleagues commented perceptively on various parts and versions of the argument, and more importantly posed fascinating questions. I am especially thankful to Lisa Lampert, Henry Ansgar (Andy) Kelly, George Hoffman, and Michael Schoenfeldt. As this study was taking form, Ellen Toronto shared her emotional insights and robust feminism with me; she has had a profound impact on my sense of an audience and on my ideas about gender and power. Jill and Tobin Siebers sustained me during my final year of writing with friendship, ice cream, and stimulating conversations about everything from Francis Bacon's art to the latest Onion video. My husband John Kotarski supported me from beginning to end with love and fresh-baked bread. His interest in and keen perceptions about gender and power have challenged me to think harder, to discover the nuances in power relationships, and to find the words that fit my meanings. Warmest thanks to each of you!

This book is dedicated to the memory of my older sister, who did not live to see it but is part of the history that compelled me to write it; and to my younger sister, who inspires me.

PREVIOUSLY PUBLISHED WORKS

Medieval Venuses and Cupids: Sexuality, Hermeneutics, and English Poetry (1996)

The Iconic Page in Manuscript, Print, and Digital Culture, edited with George Bornstein (1998)

Chaucer and the Challenges of Medievalism: Essays in Honor of H. A. Kelly, edited with Donka Minkova (2003)

PERMISSIONS

Part of chapter 2 has been published as "Contested Authority: Jerome and the Wife of Bath," *Chaucer Review* 44.3 (2010): 268–93. It is used with the permission of the Pennsylvania State University Press.

An early version of chapter 4 has been published as "Exegesis Reconsidered: The Fleury *Slaughter of Innocents* and the Myth of Ritual Murder," *Journal of English and Germanic Philology* 102 (2003): 211–43. Copyright 2003 by the Board of Trustees of the University of Illinois. It is used with the permission of the University of Illinois Press

A version of chapter 5 has been accepted as "The Wife of Bath's Marginal Authority," in *Studies in the Age of Chaucer,* for 2010. It is used with permission of the publisher.

ABBREVIATIONS

ELN	*English Language Notes*
JEGP	*Journal of English and Germanic Philology*
PL	*Patrologia Latina,* ed. J.-P. Migne (Paris, 1844–1904)
PMLA	*Publications of the Modern Language Association*
SAC	*Studies in the Age of Chaucer*
SP	*Studies in Philology*

CHAPTER 1

WOMEN ON TOP IN MEDIEVAL EXEGESIS

There is no knowledge without a particular discursive practice; and any discursive practice may be defined by the knowledge that it forms.[1]

The Bible both affirms and contests gender hierarchy. Women are to keep silent in the church and to attend under a veil; for man is the head of woman, as Christ is head of the church. A woman's speech violates divine order. Christ nonetheless appears after his resurrection first to a woman, making her his apostle to the apostles, using her voice to spread his word. Scripture presents women in positions of authority not only as a disruption of ordained social order, but also as the basis of a new order that sets the church apart from dominant culture. As medieval exegetes attempt to decipher scripture's meanings for their own lives, they confront many such contradictions, and they make choices about which passages to privilege, which to accept literally, and which to read for signs of hidden meanings. Through exegesis, writers create the Bible's literary and theological unity out of disparate historical documents. In the process, they normalize ideologies of gender and power for the church.

Although medieval exegetical literature displays considerable formal and conceptual diversity, each work is rooted in the same soil: each is composed in a deeply misogynistic culture, and written in predominantly masculine social contexts, almost exclusively for male readers, in response to that profoundly patriarchal document, the Bible. Despite all these factors, and doubtless contrary to modern expectations, medieval exegesis is not universally misogynistic or patriarchal. Accepting scripture's revolutionary implications, some exegetes reject patriarchal power structures and invent their own subversive authority as feminine. They picture themselves within an inverted social hierarchy: they present themselves figuratively as women on top.

Consider Augustine of Hippo's *Confessions*. His early Genesis commentaries develop a conventionally scholarly and authoritative masculine persona (*De Genesi contra Manichaeos, De Genesi ad Litteram Imperfectus*), but *Confessions* revises that pose. Augustine writes *Confessions* as a newly instituted bishop, in part to articulate his episcopal ideals and the ideology by which he will exercise power. He begins by critiquing the ancient hierarchical structure of society. The man on top appears in his work as a proud and violent sinner, an unredeemed pagan. Augustine rejects paganism, sin, and masculine status together. He defines himself as a bishop by inverting the social hierarchy. Eschewing power, he pictures himself as weak, humble, and dependent—a baby, an untutored child. He fashions for himself a gender identity palpably different from that of pagan Romans. At the same time, he invests feminine figures with spiritual power and authority. He represents his mother Monica as the model for his own priesthood, and he describes God as a mother nurturing and protecting him in his role as bishop. These gender inversions belong, of course, to the realm of the literary imagination and have limited social consequences: he does not abrogate episcopal power, or ordain women as priests. *Confessions* nonetheless challenges Roman structures of civil and domestic governance and suggests a radical Christian ideology (though, as we will find in chapter 3, that is but half the story, and a bit simplified).

As Augustine's work demonstrates, early Christians do not always or inevitably legitimate the status quo of social power—the man on top. Despite the church's heavy patriarchal footprint in medieval culture, early (and later) believers often challenge patriarchal social order and gender hierarchy. Many reject ancient ideologies of power—though they do not necessarily refuse to exercise authority or supremacy in the church.[2] Their redefinitions of power and hierarchy are typically motivated by their understanding of Christianity as born out of paradoxical reversals: the all-powerful deity becomes a dependent infant; life grows from the heart of death.[3] For many in the church, Christianity turns worldly orders upside down. Men therefore repudiate power and pride, the status of the man on top, and identify with women and children, the least in the social order, but greatest in the ranks of the spirit. The trope of women on top represents male writers' humility, powerlessness, and identification with the incarnate, suffering savior. Through this trope men articulate an order for the church that distinguishes it from all other human institutions. In other words, they pointedly refuse to reproduce the pagan social system, or its models for power and domination. Although they never actualize their grand refusal by creating an egalitarian church, they do invent a viable alternative to the ancient ideology of power. They preserve scripture's challenges to gender hierarchy.

Women on top can represent an ideology of spiritual humility, and a rejection of ancient masculine gender roles. When a woman actively usurps a man's position, however, she becomes the bearer of entirely different and more mixed messages. In carnivalesque inversions, women on top typically symbolize the sensual desires that usurp the place of manly reason. By exposing men's inability to rule them, women on top contest the norm of male dominance, and invite other women to join in their rebellion. At the same time, the inversion teaches men to assert themselves more forcefully, to enact their role as superior reason. In this way, the trope subtly confirms the appropriateness of male dominance. Women on top thus have ambivalent implications in carnival contexts, as Natalie Zemon Davis demonstrates in her compelling study of fifteenth- to eighteenth-century British and European culture.[4]

Earlier writers, including some exegetes, occasionally treat women on top in this carnivalesque sense, as a sign of comic misrule. Chaucer's Wife of Bath is often interpreted along these lines, and critics have repeatedly concluded that her mouthy rebellion against her husbands and clerks proves that women's sensual desires overwhelm their reason. In other words, women's innate character makes them inadequate exegetes (if not worse). From this perspective, Alison's risible exegesis only demonstrates her sensual misrule and should be dismissed by a reader attuned to the *gravitas* of Latin exegesis. The trope of the woman on top is inherently ambivalent, however, and argues against our simply dismissing Alison's exegesis. Her *Prologue* is certainly comic, and she does challenge some modes of exegesis. Yet those factors alone do not necessarily invalidate her exegesis, or render her scriptural lessons unpersuasive. It is conceptually possible that her exegesis is, within her particular social setting, as competent as it is confident.

Early manuscripts of the work confirm this possibility. Just as Alison rewrites scripture, so too do fifteenth-century scribes rewrite her text. Many scribes highlight particular passages by adding marginal notes alongside the verse, and many of these notes document Alison's biblical sources. As far as I can discern (recognizing that glossing programs are subject to more than one interpretation), most of the extant manuscripts present Alison as a straightforward biblical expert (so chapter 5 proposes). Whether or not this argument is accepted, Chaucer obviously uses the Wife's marriage sermon to imagine a "feminine" exegesis. Rather than representing a learned man delivering a sermon, authorized by his participation in exclusively masculine institutions—rather than delivering the sermon *in propria persona*—Chaucer attributes the work's exegesis to a lay woman. This fact testifies to a rupture in the historical development of exegesis: biblical authority here flees elite masculine institutions and takes up residence with a lay woman. By examining scribes' responses to Chaucer's work, we may be able to infer whether they find his experiment in feminine exegesis plausible, laughable, or both.

"Woman on top": a trope of gender inversion, a sign of misrule, a sexual position. Woman on top is an ambiguous sign in medieval culture, and therefore also in exegesis. In a culture organized to support male dominance, women on top can always invite scorn. At the same time, more positive attitudes are possible, and even likely, for those who recognize the spiritual power of hierarchical inversions. Scripture can be made to support a broad range of contradictory attitudes.

Discourse, Gender, and Power

It is not self-evident that exegetes from Augustine to Chaucer would need this trope, or that they would bother to represent women speaking of scripture, authoritatively or otherwise. With few exceptions, exegetes are men, and they address other men almost exclusively for most of this period. They define the object of their knowledge as scripture and/or God (an interesting slippage), in ways that keep men in control of the institutional sites of exegesis (monasteries, pulpits, universities), and thus in control of the discourse, that is, the practices that situate knowledge of scripture within a network of social and institutional relations.[5] Yet having excluded real women from the discourse, exegetes continually bring them back through representations: they adopt feminine personae, employ feminine voices, and picture women on top. Why? What is the point of women's absent presence in exegesis?

This book proposes that representations of women on top help exegetes conceptualize their own authority. Through this trope, writers express the hierarchies of power that allow them to distinguish between their own privileged access to God and others' errors, between their competence and others' nonsense.[6] The woman on top may be valorized or discredited, but she is in either case crucial to the invention of asymmetries—between clergy and laity, men and women, learned and lewd—that function to authorize exegetes. By praising and emulating the woman on top, exegetes reject traditional social hierarchies; they identify not with power but with weakness—with the omnipotent deity who allows himself to be crucified, with the children who shall inherit the kingdom, with the women who lack social and ecclesiastical status. By inverting traditional hierarchies, exegetes invent their authority as stemming from their difference within conventional social order (which is, in fact, always a *différance*). The trope represents these writers' Christian virtues. By contrast, those exegetes who disparage women on top affirm a traditionally superior masculine role. The trope allows them to claim a "natural" or inherent authority and power. They depict women on top in order not only to mark their difference from such unruly beings, but also to distance themselves from stigmatized "feminine" traits: irrationality, sensuality, ignorance, subordination, and powerlessness. Women on top represent what these exegetes exclude from their own self-definitions. Whether celebrated or degraded, women on top reveal how exegetes encode relations of power and authority.

If we want to be absolutely precise, a reasonable goal for scholars, exegesis is prediscursive throughout the period covered in this book: not a single system of relations governed by established rules, but a series of dispersed statements only later transformed into the kind of regular system that Foucault would call discourse. Nonetheless, medieval exegesis reveals, just as Foucault's later discourse on madness does, structured relations that grant power, authority, rationality, and knowledge to a selected few, while denying the same to the masses. Women on top can represent the few or the many. In either case, the trope expresses writers' ideologies of religious power. When they represent a woman speaking of scripture, they grant her the capacity and legitimate authority to define this most important cultural object of knowledge—or not. The trope thus defines—with infinite variety—who can speak with authority about scripture, to whom, for what purposes, in what contexts. That women are included among those who can speak with authority, at least in the literary imagination, merits study. At the very least, we may more fully historicize medieval inventions of religious authority, including the actual breaks and reversals in the development and justification of ecclesiastical power, aspects of the discourse sometimes obscured in studies of the exegetical canon.

Comedy, challenges to the status quo, reconfigurations of gender, and ideologies of power are not what many of us expect to discover in medieval exegesis. A half century ago, some scholars did their best to convince their peers that exegesis holds little promise of satisfying desires for aesthetic pleasure and historical nuance, or for a politically and socially engaged, edgy, or theoretically up-to-date medievalism. Much excoriated, those scholars shall pass nameless here. They failed, in any event, to convince their more imaginative colleagues, who discerned that medieval exegesis speaks directly to widespread interests in post-structuralist and feminist theories, gender and Jewish studies, the history of theology and biblical hermeneutics.[7] In the last half century, exegetical studies have proven not just the potential interest of the discourse, but also its connections to the broad cultural movements of the period—asceticism, anti-Semitism, scholasticism, and Lollardy, to name a few flourishing fields of inquiry.

Meanwhile, modern biblical scholarship has undergone a similarly exciting renewal. Recent theoretical approaches to scripture open the work to a far wider range of meaning than seemed possible even a few decades ago. Historical, feminist, and post-structuralist scholars have dramatically changed how we understand scripture. Historically informed feminists have closely examined the contexts within which biblical texts originate, elucidated the meanings and purposes of specific texts within their original contexts, and examined how those texts came to be included in or excluded from the canon. They have demonstrated that both scripture and exegesis arise within specific cultural contexts, and that both change as they enter new contexts. This book is indebted on every page to feminist scholars who resituate scripture in culture; and to those who expand the canon, revolutionizing the history of early Christianity.[8] Though I rarely address the text of scripture directly in this book, I am everywhere indebted to their methodologies and theoretical formulations. By changing my ideas about the past, feminist biblical scholars have altered my sense of possibility for the future.

Feminism is inevitably transgressive—never more so than when feminists use the master's tools to dismantle the master's house, or at least to build new rooms within it.[9] Yet feminist transgression has, I believe, considerable cultural value. Religion functions to legitimate arbitrary relations of power, never more obviously than in the medieval church, but perhaps never more insidiously than in contemporary American "Christian" culture. If political discourse is a reliable guide, Christianity's influence on American culture is not appreciably waning, at least not in respect to women's prescribed social roles and assumed capacities. Nor is the problem for women restricted to a single religion or culture. Fundamentalists in all religions (globally) deny women the authority to interpret religious texts and traditions.[10] Feminists can push toward equality at the deepest levels of their cultures by developing a "counterexegesis," which is to say by "contesting or refuting dominant readings of the Bible" and other religious texts.[11] If this is transgressive, it can nonetheless be an important part of feminists' agonistic struggle with the institutions and ideologies that continue to shape cultures.

Narrow schools of confessional interpretation at present dominate how the Bible and religion are understood by most citizens of our world. Patriarchal readers have the holy books pretty much to themselves. Those who claim to know exactly what scripture means (often without regard for the problems presented by a variable text, by translations, or by relevant histories) are not often enough challenged by academic arguments that complicate the text, point out the gap between current interpretations and historical traditions, or call attention to the hermeneutic difficulties presented by this particular work of literature. Feminist scholars can broaden scriptural interpretation by bringing their perspectives to the Bible and its varied reception; we can at least contest androcentric versions of religious history. Feminists have much at stake in religion, and they can make substantial cultural as well as scholarly contributions by studying and teaching the Bible, its variable historical reception, its strategies for excluding women from certain roles, its overlooked inclusiveness. In other words, historically informed and intellectually rigorous feminist scholarship about the Bible can be a form of ethical social action in the secular arena.[12] Being explicitly activist does not make feminist scholars less objective or legitimate than their peers. All scholarship exhibits bias and particularity; problems arise only from denial of that fact, which leads to universalizing the particular. As an agnostic feminist, I do not claim to represent a universal point of view, but acknowledge my uniqueness while striving to respect and learn from others' viewpoints.

Feminist theory is designed precisely to expose historical constructions of power asymmetry, gender hierarchy, and gendered authority, all of which are central to exegetical literature. Medieval exegetes script power relations, and feminist theory promises to decipher the scripts and tease out their cultural implications. In the process, we may recover constructions of gender and power that are lost in other accounts of exegesis.

Opening the Exegetical Canon

Biblical exegetes are everywhere, and scriptural interpretation one of the most pervasive literary activities of the Middle Ages. Unconstrained by modern scholarly standards, medieval exegetes adopt virtually every literary genre to their purposes. Not only do they turn out academic commentaries, treatises, and sermons; they also interpret the Bible in the course of writing letters (even love letters), autobiographies, drama, and poetry. Modern scholars have spent decades painstakingly establishing the history of academic Latin exegesis, tracing out the development of interpretive traditions, and illuminating exegetes' struggles to interpret the variable and polysemous work they know as scripture.[13] This scholarship constructs a canon that includes works such as Augustine's magisterial commentary on Genesis (*De Genesi ad Litteram*), the monumental twelfth-century compilation known as the *Gloss* (*Glossa Ordinaria*), and Thomas Aquinas's commentary on the Gospels (*Catena Aurea*). These and similar works epitomize the cultural authority of clerks, and they merit study, though perhaps not the reverence they inspired among some twentieth-century medievalists.[14] Recent scholarship uncovers areas of considerable interest in this canon, and exegetes' comments on such topics as gender identity, religious difference, and sexuality remain consequential even (or perhaps especially) now.[15]

If our goal is to understand medieval exegesis, however, the canon is too narrow. The discourse is not in fact restricted to academic tomes. Exegetes themselves employ many other genres, which should logically be included in the canon we study. Augustine, for instance, composes two early, more or less academic commentaries on Genesis, the first to counter Manicheans, and the second an unfinished attempt at literal interpretation. He then unites exegesis with autobiography, producing the hybrid form of *Confessions*. In other words, he revises his earlier approaches to exegesis to connect his life experiences with his interpretations of scripture. He does not treat scripture as a discrete object of knowledge, the focus of objective, scholarly inquiry. Rather, he makes himself one object of knowledge, the pages of scripture another, and his deity the third. Sometimes scripture mediates Augustine's relationship with his deity; at other times the deity mediates scripture, or human and deity commune directly, dispensing with scripture. Human, deity, and sacred book are three sides of a love triangle, and Augustine's desire is not always triangulated through scripture. Meaning is everywhere in Augustine's experience, even within the depths of the human heart, and its origin is always God.[16]

Confessions tells us as much about Augustine's reading of Genesis as do his other early commentaries, but reveals more about how he conceives of his role as exegete, and how he constitutes his object of study. Since Augustine's generic innovation is not accepted into the mainstream, the work does not establish an authoritative origin for the medieval discourse. *Confessions* is nonetheless crucial to a historical understanding of the discourse, for it illuminates the difficulties Augustine confronts as he tries to establish his exegetical authority—and his object of knowledge—in an age before fixed hermeneutic principles arise, before a dominant discourse emerges. The work signals Augustine's frustration with his own earlier experiments; it shows him trying to find a suitable form for his exegesis. *Confessions* witnesses to a break in the formation of medieval exegesis and alerts us to a trajectory the discourse might have taken. Contemporary and later writers could have developed Augustine's hybrid form further; the discourse could have become predominately confessional and intimately personal. Subsequent exegetes (and Augustine himself) do not choose that trajectory. Instead, they cultivate a more objective-sounding, impersonal rhetoric. They invent and standardize rules for exegesis; they devise academic standards for the discourse. They clearly prefer the institutional authority encoded in an academic style over Augustine's prayerful self-exposure. Exegesis becomes academic not for lack of patristic alternatives, then, but because many writers elect to make it so. Although modern scholars should certainly map the well-trodden paths taken by the many, we should also recognize the dead ends, for they signpost the deliberate closing off of alternatives, the self-conscious writerly decisions that shape how the discourse defines its object of knowledge (the text, not the self) and establishes its authority (through institutions, not through a relationship with the deity).

If we open the canon to include such works as *Confessions*, we gain a fuller appreciation of exegesis as a broadly dispersed discourse that is, *pace* the theologians, neither continuous nor unified—even in the works of a single writer.[17] Exegesis exhibits many such breaks with its own past, shifts of emphasis, and reinventions of form as well as method. And it is precisely at such moments of change that we can best perceive what is at stake in exegesis: the cultural work the discourse is expected to do or fails to do (which might involve personal, pastoral, aesthetic, and/or institutional interests); the methods by which exegetes (re)establish authoritative practices; and the strategies by which they authorize their works within particular social and institutional settings.

Modern generic distinctions—between "literature" (autobiography, poetry, drama) and "exegesis"—do not exist in the Middle Ages. Just as Augustine grafts exegesis onto autobiography, so other writers adapt or invent genres in order to convey scripture to their audiences with fresh force. Centuries after Augustine, at a momentous turning point in the history of exegesis, devout writers begin composing biblical plays—most famously, about the Marys' Visit to the Sepulcher—in order to teach audiences what they should know about scripture, and, at least as significantly, how they should feel about the passages brought to life before them. Liturgical drama emerges as an aesthetic form of exegesis. Still later, as vernacular literatures flourish, poets and playwrights retell and comment on biblical texts in their mother tongues, inventing their own biblical aesthetics and literary forms, indebted to earlier forms but also independent from them. Vernacular writers conceive of exegesis by and for the laity. This is a remarkable moment in the history of the discourse; and, since large popular audiences eagerly embrace vernacular biblical literature, these changes have weighty cultural implications. Each form of exegesis advances unique devotional and intellectual values and claims cultural legitimacy within a certain sphere of relations. Each innovation implies dissatisfaction with other forms of exegesis and asserts superiority within its immediate social context.

Exegetical innovation and adaptation continue throughout the Middle Ages, as structures of education and ecclesiastical agendas change, as vernaculars mature into subtle literary languages, and as new genres displace the old. The institutional and social sites of exegesis shift and shift again; so do writers' avowed purposes, audiences, and aesthetic sensibilities. The many forms of exegesis open as many windows on the past, allowing us to glimpse particular historical agents at work within and outside institutions. Each literary form reaccentuates scripture, attributes it to particular voices, and creates its specific cultural resonance.[18] Arguably, poets and playwrights have as great an impact on how the population understands scripture as do the prosers who compile commentaries exclusively for academic audiences.[19] We therefore cannot begin to comprehend the scope or impact of medieval exegesis if we restrict our inquiries to the academic canon. Historical accuracy (if nothing grander) requires us to accept the actual diversity of exegetical literature, and to mark changes in the developing discourse—turning points that reveal the forces of history and human character that shape biblical reception.

Whatever language or genre they choose to write in, exegetes necessarily rewrite scripture, continually forming and reforming their object of study. For the Bible is first of all a text; its meanings emerge only in the interpretations that reinscribe it.[20] Medieval exegetes spin their discourse out of (and sometimes literally around) this text. Foucault aptly describes this kind of discourse, which "must say for the first time what had, nonetheless, already been said, and must tirelessly repeat what had, however, never been said.... [It] allows us to say something other than the text itself, but on condition that it is the text itself which is said, and in a sense completed."[21] This is the paradox of exegesis: it must say only scripture, but say what scripture does not. Exegetes both depend on the Word that authorizes their words and invent meanings that connect the Word to their own lives, that "complete" it for themselves and their audiences. In the process, they reveal their authorial presence, for exegetes, like the rest of us, are "social and embodied beings, and the products of their thought and action bear ineradicable traces of their situations and interests."[22] Exegetes leave traces of themselves in their selection of words and passages for commentary, in the meanings they ascribe to scripture, in the subtle or obvious ways they assert authority.

Exegetes (like other writers) at once hide and express the fact that they are socially situated, enmeshed in structures of power, inhabitants of particular cultural situations. Gabrielle M. Spiegel gives us a useful purchase on this aspect of exegesis when she theorizes the "social logic of the text": "texts represent situated uses of language," and "language itself acquires meaning and authority only within specific social and historical settings."[23] Spiegel's emphasis on texts' local settings and culturally specific meanings can serve as a valuable corrective to some modern "exegetical critics'" ahistoricism.[24] She helps us recognize that exegesis, like any other discourse, advances meanings that are not self-evident, transparent, or transcendent. These are, of course, precisely the values theologians traditionally attribute to exegesis. Historicism nonetheless requires us to read the discourse against the grain, acknowledging a profound hermeneutic suspicion about exegetes' implicit or explicit claims to be transparent mediators of God's Truth.

Exegetes focus so intently on how the Bible works as a text, how it invites and resists meaning, that they divert us from paying attention to their own cultural situatedness. Directing us to gaze always on scripture, they distract us from seeking the personal, social, and institutional pressures that drive their interpretations. We should refuse the distraction. Exegetical works of all sorts—including academic commentaries, sermons, autobiographies, liturgical plays, and epistles—are best approached as socially situated utterances. Jacques Berlinerblau cogently defines this approach as "sociohermeneutics": "a field of inquiry that scrutinizes the interplay that exists between a polysemous sacred text and culturally positioned interpreters."[25] Indeed, the main literary and historical interest of the Christian Bible derives (for me, at least) from the polysemeity that generates a heterogeneous reception, and that eventually supports cultural movements as diverse as patristic asceticism, neo-Platonism, colonialism, racism, feminism, and "family values." While proponents of each movement profess to speak only the text, they discover in it fundamentally different messages. Only by returning exegesis to its local contexts can we recover the interplay between scripture and socially situated commentators.

As social beings, exegetes respond not only to scripture but also to ephemeral cultural forces. They use the Bible to answer challenges to their faith posed by heretics, Jews, or Muslims; they try to restore a status quo threatened by social or economic changes. As time passes, an exegete's work survives the ephemeral particularities of his immediate context and circulates among readers who know nothing about his cultural position, for whom his local references are inexplicable, and his controversies moot or forgotten. Severed from its original social logic, the work must be rewritten for new audiences. (We should note that the same process happens with the Bible, most obviously when Christians reinvent the Jewish holy scrolls.)

Literary packaging does not preclude this historical process: the magisterial Latin tome and the satiric vernacular poem are alike subject to rising and faltering fortunes. As a consequence, exegesis, like scripture, becomes heterogeneous, contradictory, and fragmentary in reception. (This sounds like a fashionable postmodern judgment but is a basic fact about scripture and sometimes recognized in medieval writings.[26])

Augustine, for instance, unfolds his ideas about Genesis in several works; centuries later, brief passages from these works circulate out of context, become part of other commentaries, and end up in massive encyclopedic compilations contributing to meanings he could not have imagined. He appears in the twelfth-century *Gloss* more like Osiris than like himself: the body of his work torn to pieces, the integrity of his thought irrecoverable.

The study of medieval exegesis ideally requires a double historical perspective: attention to the ways in which an exegete discovers meaning in and for particular audiences in specific contexts (sociohermeneutics); and consideration of how his (rarely, her) work is also received and rewritten for new audiences in vastly different contexts (reception study). This book attempts such a double perspective, not for the discourse as a whole (that would be impossible) but for selected works that reveal turning points in the history of exegesis: works that insist we notice something new is happening, either by advancing new conceptions of biblical knowledge or by presenting generic innovations. This is a study of rupture rather than of continuity. I focus on three crucial moments in the development of exegesis: the age of Augustine, the twelfth century, and the age of Chaucer, including his reception in the fifteenth century. The choice of these eras is selective but not arbitrary. Cases could certainly be made for other writers in other places and times. This book does not aim at comprehensiveness, however. It does aim to rethink the relationship between history and exegesis, interrogate the value of the canon, and analyze the formal innovations by which exegetes continually reinvent the discourse, making it accommodate their desires. The eras selected for this study exhibit new forms of exegesis emerging and jostling for dominance. At these moments, exegetes are like poets who estrange us from the familiar in order to render it fresh and vital again.

In its continual reinvention of biblical meanings, exegesis recalls Derridean supplementarity: "the supplement supplements. It adds only to replace. It intervenes or insinuates itself *in-the-place-of*; if it fills, it is as if one fills a void."[27] What any biblical text means depends on which gaps an exegete decides to fill. Since scripture offers infinite possibilities for meaning, every supplement manifests interpretive choices. Throughout the Middle Ages, exegetes interpret selected texts in light of their own distinctive concerns. They translate the Bible's language and interpret its meanings for new audiences; they rewrite it according to their own understanding of how it should determine Christian praxis. As we will see, exegetes' social and institutional contexts, hermeneutic presuppositions, and personal experiences influence how they approach scripture. Through their interpretations, exegetes construct and reconstruct the social meaning of the Bible. As they expose some part of scripture's potential for meaning, they displace the Word with their own words. Their reception of scripture evidences that work's continuing adaptation to new cultural contexts; their reception of each others' works likewise demonstrates the adaptation of earlier works to new contexts. Consequently, the authority of any exegetical work is always provisional, subject to revision and erasure.

Toward a Discontinuous History

This book sets forth case studies of women on top, beginning with scripture, progressing to the age of Augustine, passing next to the twelfth to thirteenth centuries, and ending with the fourteenth to fifteenth centuries. Each chapter analyzes how exegetes use the trope to figure their religious identity and authority over scripture. As my foundational training is in literary study, the texts selected reward close analysis: attention to personae and points of view, to particular strategies of reaccentuating scripture, to the rhetoric of authority, to what is concealed as well as to explicit meanings. Each chapter focuses on specific readerly inventions of biblical meanings rather than on exegetical traditions, though traditional accounts serve as necessary counterpoint. The coherence of this study derives from its pursuit of a single trope through a chronological series of literary treatments. Each work displays how writers ignore or appropriate earlier exegesis into their own biblical supplements, in the process fashioning anew the implications of the woman on top.

"Subversive Feminine Voices: The Reception of 1 Timothy 2 from Jerome to Chaucer" (chapter 2) introduces the historical scope of the book by analyzing a single biblical text diachronically. In 1 Timothy 2, Pseudo-Paul recommends that women should remain silent in church. Feminist biblical scholars argue that the passage records a competition between women teachers and men trying to silence them. Read in this way, the epistle discloses opposing models for Christian leadership. Chapter 2 studies how these opposing models are treated in medieval exegesis, beginning with Jerome's *Against Jovinian* and two of John Chrysostom's sermons, continuing with the twelfth-century *Gloss,* and ending with Chaucer's citation of the epistle in his *Wife of Bath's Prologue.* Each of these works addresses current social and ecclesiastical concerns. Each divulges anxiety about women teaching, as well as a distinct opinion about women's capacity for exegesis. Of course, the contexts of exegesis alter significantly between the fourth and fourteenth centuries. Each work examined in this chapter vividly reinvents the contest between ecclesiastics and women embedded in 1 Timothy 2. By following the biblical text through its historical peregrinations, we can clearly discern changes in the social and institutional sites of exegesis, in the specific cultural issues the text is taken to address, and in the interpretations that support or challenge existing gendered structures of authority. Considered together, these texts imply that women on top do not lack authority; that is the problem with them.

Each of the next three chapters takes up one of these eras in greater detail. "Gender Trouble in Augustine's *Confessions*" (chapter 3) analyzes the author's invention of an exegetical persona in his early Genesis commentaries and proposes that he defines his authority as priest, bishop, and exegete by manipulating traditional and nontraditional gender roles. As suggested earlier, Augustine enacts feminine virtues in order to critique his culture's dominant ideologies of power and authority. This chapter focuses on the ideological implications of Augustine's early episcopal self-fashioning and offers a starting point for reevaluating his later and more influential writings about the union of the church and political power.

"Affective Exegesis in the Fleury *Slaughter of Innocents*" (chapter 4) studies a liturgical play in relation to earlier academic exegesis and other roughly contemporary twelfth- and thirteenth-century discourses. By the time the play is composed, the biblical narrative has accrued a great deal of academic commentary, which typically transforms the supposedly historical characters into allegorized figures. Most exegetes read the slaughtered Jewish babies as Christian martyrs, the soldiers who slay them as murderous Jews intent on killing Christ, and the entire scene as foreshadowing the Crucifixion. The play gives the academic tradition a new twist: it uses the Slaughter to develop the myth of ritual murder—the notion that Jews ritually slay Christian children as a way of commemorating the Crucifixion. Jews clearly represent the Other in this play, the role filled by women in the reception of 1 Timothy 2, and by pagans in Augustine's *Confessions*. In each case, the Other helps negatively to define Christian identity. The Fleury play attributes its crucial exegetical messages to the figures of children, who articulate the theology of redemption, and to a woman, Rachel, who expresses a profoundly affective piety. Children and a woman thus teach the audience how they should respond to the biblical narrative, what it should mean in their own devotional lives. The least in the church become here greatest in disclosing the Gospel's import, exemplifying a variation of the women on top trope. This chapter traces how the play alters the accepted meanings of scripture in response both to actual events and to anti-Semitic discourses.

"The Wife of Bath's Marginal Authority" (chapter 5) follows exegesis into a later vernacular context. In the *Wife of Bath's Prologue,* Chaucer uses a feminine persona to advance a gendered sermon about marriage and sexuality. Although the work is often read as an ironic commentary on women's exegetical incompetence, very little direct evidence of medieval readers' responses to this work have been brought forward to confirm or refute this interpretation. Indirect evidence, in the form of fifteenth-century scribes' Latin notes on the work's biblical citations, could redirect the scholarly discussion. The scribes' notes record their responses to Alison's conclusions about scripture. Most of these notes, I argue, demonstrate the Wife's (Chaucer's) accuracy in citation and translation, and affirm her reliability as a commentator. For these readers at least, a fictional woman can apparently speak with authority about the biblical "woes of marriage." Chaucer's work dramatizes a contemporary contest between the laity and ecclesiastical authority, and the work's scribal reception indicates a surprisingly broad support for the lay side of that contest. In an age of violent controversy over vernacular scripture, Chaucer manuscripts witness to broad acceptance of some "heretical" positions about scripture and lay exegesis.

Authority is always provisional, always contested in exegetical literature. Exegetes constantly rewrite each other as well as scripture. These case studies demonstrate that exegetes often reflect on their own and others' authority by reaccentuating scripture through women's voices, by representing women on top. Opening the exegetical canon to autobiography, liturgical drama, and vernacular poetry can reveal how medieval people actually understand the Bible, which is not necessarily how authorities tell them they should, and how they authorize their interpretations. These case studies disclose the literary strategies by which exegetes of all stripes claim, *mirabile dictu,* to know what God means.

CHAPTER 2

SUBVERSIVE FEMININE VOICES: THE RECEPTION OF 1 TIMOTHY 2 FROM JEROME TO CHAUCER

Scripture has a nose of wax.[1]

"But I suffer not a woman to teach, nor to use authority over the man: but to be in silence": this verse from 1 Timothy 2 asserts a masculine right to prescribe women's roles in the church.[2] Women, like children and slaves, should manifest Christian virtue by submitting to the paterfamilias within the family and to the bishop in the church. In this way, 1 Timothy 2, like other post-Pauline epistles, conceives of Christendom as an Aristotelian social hierarchy. This household code is actually outmoded in contemporary Roman and Jewish society, so the text insists on a power that the context renders insecure. The text is prescriptive rather than descriptive; it does not mirror an existing reality but imagines religion compensating for men's declining social power.[3] In other words, the text exists because women are *not* silent: they are teaching and exercising authority over men, and their taking on these supposedly masculine roles provokes anxiety, at least in some parts of the church. If the text implies women's prior speech, however, it does not report their words or precise teachings. Feminine speech per se—rather than particular theological or doctrinal errors—challenges the Pauline ideal of hierarchical order.[4] "Paul" answers that challenge by repressing the women's words and voices, devising a rigidly univocal text to replace communal heteroglossia.[5] His text bears witness to the social fact of Christian disunity and to feminine speech that precedes and resists his own. By exposing a gap between his own ideals and those of others, he confesses that his authority is open to dispute. Women's speech undermines his performance of masculine authority.

"Paul" seeks further to regulate women's economic, social, familial, ecclesiastical, and reproductive roles, suggesting the broad range of cultural issues linked to women's leadership in the church:

I will therefore that men pray in every place, lifting up pure hands, without anger and contention.
In like manner women also in decent apparel: adorning themselves with modesty and sobriety, not with plaited hair, or gold, or pearls, or costly attire,
But as it becometh women professing godliness, with good works.
Let the woman learn in silence, with all subjection.
But I suffer not a woman to teach, nor to use authority over the man: but to be in silence.
For Adam was first formed; then Eve.
And Adam was not seduced; but the woman being seduced, was in the transgression.
Yet she shall be saved through child-bearing; if she continue in faith, and love, and sanctification, with sobriety. (I Tim. 2: 8–15)

"Paul" connects women's control of wealth, intellectual leadership, and seductive powers, crediting women's "faults" in each of these areas to (woman's) original sin. In this way, he attempts to naturalize masculine economic, intellectual, and sexual dominance and to ground that dominance in theology. Yet he does not take his ability to dominate women for granted, nor does his ideal of hierarchical order look inevitable. Indeed, he portrays women as always already subversive of his agenda: dressing ostentatiously, instructing men, and seducing men. As Elisabeth Schüssler Fiorenza has taught us, such biblical texts express tension between a desire to subjugate women and an awareness of feminine resistance.[6] First Timothy 2 at once inscribes anxieties about "feminine" vices and disobedient women and confesses the fragility of masculine power, its susceptibility to being thwarted by notionally less-powerful agents. The passage makes apparent the contest that attends the articulation of power; it acknowledges a continuing struggle over the hierarchy it seeks to establish and expresses an unresolved tension between masculine authority and feminine subversion.

First Timothy 2 invites readers to side with the apostle, to stand with him in the aura of religious power, but it also tempts readers to dwell imaginatively on those provocative women and to conceive of their unutterable words. This ambiguously double invitation anticipates and to some extent even scripts divergent acts of medieval reception. This chapter examines how four exegetes rewrite this script: Jerome's *Against Jovinian,* two of John Chrysostom's sermons, the *Gloss (Glossa Ordinaria),* and Geoffrey Chaucer's *Wife of Bath's Prologue*. Each writer tries to root his own transient, historically conditioned ideas about masculinity, sexuality, and social order in the supposedly eternal, unchanging soil of scripture. This is obviously a highly selective survey. My goals here are to offer a roadmap to the exegetical territory covered in this book—the changing genres and hermeneutics, institutional affiliations, and social contexts of exegesis—and to suggest the importance of these particular historical eras to the developing discourse of exegesis (subsequent chapters investigate each era in greater depth). These texts do not articulate a continuous, unified interpretive tradition; the discovery of such traditions almost always rests more on theological grounds than on a historical footing. Rather, these works exhibit particular strategies for managing the biblical text's anxiety over religious authority and manifest an awareness of feminine subversion. Taken together, these works exemplify the culturally specific nature of exegesis, the broad range of interpretations possible for a single brief text, and the methods, both subtle and obvious, by which exegetes reaccentuate scripture. Each writer produces meanings that speak to the concerns of his own local culture, which, we will find, have little if anything to do with the interests of earlier or even, in some cases, contemporary exegetes. In the process, each exegete rewrites not only his predecessors but also the Bible.

To study exegesis, we need to recognize infinite possible layers of textual meaning, for the sense of the Word and its attendant commentaries changes each time they are resituated in a new context. First Timothy 2 addresses a controversy over church leadership in the late first century, seeking to establish how Christians will be governed, what roles women will play in religion, and how the church will relate to the dominant social order. Several centuries later, Jerome and Chrysostom select for commentary the textual details that speak to their shared ascetic concerns, yet they choose entirely different details to interpret and arrive at contradictory conclusions about what the passage teaches. Jerome develops a philological argument about one word, while Chrysostom invests his rhetorical energy in the matter of women's dress. (Obviously, both pass over a great many textual details; a New Critic would be appalled at their method.) Monastic exegetes of the twelfth century, compiling the *Gloss,* seize on the details that strike them as crucial, none of which has to do with Jerome's philology or Christian fashion; in fact, the *Gloss* envisions a social order that Jerome would call un-Christian. Finally, Chaucer revoices the text in a bourgeois setting and uses it to invoke Wycliffite controversies specific to his time; as we will discover, he engages Jerome only to reverse his logic. The original social logic of the biblical passage does not transcend these fundamentally diverse sites of literary production, disparate personal interests and institutional contexts, incongruent social agendas, and changing hermeneutic presuppositions. These texts demonstrate the uniqueness of each exegetical work and reveal how the discourse of exegesis is formed and transformed over the course of the Middle Ages.

Through their interpretations, exegetes construct and reconstruct the social meaning of the biblical text, constantly adapting scripture to new cultures, foreign to the original text. The Bible, Jerome's *Against Jovinian,* Chrysostom's sermons, the *Gloss,* and Chaucer's *Wife of Bath's Prologue* elucidate a diachronic sequence in which new fissures constantly open and new supplements emerge. As we will discover, the feminine resistance embedded in 1 Timothy 2 becomes a constantly reopening fissure in reception, a reminder of the unstable and contingent nature of exegetes' discursive power.

Jerome's (S)exegesis

Jerome wrote a commentary on the entire Bible, in the course of which he touches very briefly on 1 Timothy 2, to express his dissatisfaction with the word *sobrietas* ("if she continue in faith, and love, and sanctification, with *sobriety*"). He atomizes the text, focusing on the word in the passage that has potential for ascetic interpretation. He then uses translation to create an opening for that interpretation, substituting the Greek for the Latin text: women are now saved by chastity (*castitas*).[7] (This linguistic variation should alert us to the importance of versions and material texts in the history of Bible commentary: the Septuagint, variant versions of the Old Latin, and Vulgate can support significantly different interpretations.) Jerome represses the biblical idea of women saved by childbearing, replacing it with an ascetic message. He also represses the issue of women teaching: by atomizing the text, he erases women's leadership. He reduces women's role in religion to sexual restraint. His brief commentary forcefully revises the Pauline epistle, significantly narrowing the sense of the passage.

Since translation plays an important role in Jerome's argument, he refers the reader to his earlier treatise *Against Jovinian,* where he takes up the problem in some detail and in a broader theological context. Our understanding of the controversy Jerome engages in *Against Jovinian* is one-sided, for Jovinian's work survives only in Jerome's quotations of it. According to Jerome, Jovinian argued that virginity and celibacy were of no greater spiritual value than marriage; that believers baptized with the Spirit cannot sin; that fasting is not spiritually superior to the thankful reception of food; that all are equally rewarded in heaven. Having spent the better part of his life devoted to an ascetic ideal, living at odds with his own sexual impulses, Jerome responds to Jovinian with a lengthy and remarkably intemperate argument in favor of virgins' superiority (and as a corollary, against wives and marriage), marshalling his considerable knowledge of scripture and hermeneutic ingenuity to support his position. In other words, the Bible serves as one of Jerome's weapons in a battle to define Christian identity. He does not seek impartial, disinterested, balanced judgments but rather evidence to justify asceticism. Arguments ad hominem appear (at least to Jerome) entirely appropriate to the contest. He introduces a passage from Jovinian with the promise that here the "Epicurus of Christianity" ("Epicurum Christianorum") has "discharged himself like a sot after a night's debauch."[8] After quoting Jovinian, Jerome marvels, "Would you not think he was in a feverish dream, or that he was seized with madness and ought to be put into the strait jacket" (I.3.347).[9] Here and throughout the treatise, Jerome seeks to deauthorize his opponent's hermeneutics by discounting his rationality, portraying him as a drunkard, a sot, a madman. As Jerome wraps up the argument, he returns to this theme: "I must in conclusion say a few words to our modern Epicurus wantoning in his gardens with his favourites of both sexes" (II.36.414).[10] Jerome's rhetoric polarizes the issues, acknowledging no middle ground between virginity and debauchery, and thus contradicting his larger argument that virgins, widows, and wives all exhibit degrees of virtue. Since Jovinian does not rank virginity above all, he must license unrestrained sexual pleasure. Elsewhere, Jerome expresses even stronger outrage: "Here our opponent goes utterly wild with exultation; this is his strongest battering-ram with which he shakes the wall of virginity" (I.12.355).[11] The controversy appears closer to rape than academic discussion, and Jovinian's phallic attack on virginity suggests the degree to which his interpretive challenge threatens Jerome's self-definition. For Jerome the issue is of tremendous theological importance, and urgently personal.

Jerome begins *Against Jovinian* by sifting through a good many passages from Old and New Testaments—all of which support virgins' superiority—at length arriving at 1 Timothy 2 and his argument about chastity (*castitas*):

> and he [the Apostle] points out that she who was once tied with the bonds of marriage and was reduced to the condition of Eve, might blot out the old transgression by the procreation of children: provided, however, that she bring up the children themselves in the faith and love of Christ, and in sanctification and chastity; for we must not adopt the faulty reading of the Latin texts, *sobrietas*, but *castitas*, that is, σωφροσυνη. . . . The woman will

then be saved, if she bear children who will remain virgins: if what she has herself lost, she attains in her children, and makes up for the loss and decay of the root by the excellence of the flower and fruit. (I.27.366–67)[12]

The meaning of 1 Timothy 2 once again comes down to a single word, the passage coerced into a strained defense of virginity. Although the biblical text literally insists that women are saved through childbearing, in effect legitimating marital sexual intercourse, as Jovinian apparently argued, Jerome proposes that women are saved only through their children's virginity. This argument illustrates what many critics see as Jerome's predilection for an "unnatural exegesis" that "distort[s] the scriptural record."[13] So he looks to anyone schooled in modern hermeneutics. The interpretive challenge for ascetics, however, is that scripture only tenuously advances their agenda; they create ingenious (if not violent) hermeneutics in order to ground their praxis in scripture.[14] The same argument emerges again in Jerome's treatise, and translation once again serves ideology.[15] Indeed, all scripture (as well as a good deal of pagan literature) is cut to fit the same Procrustean conclusion. As he does in the Bible commentary, Jerome here rewrites the Pauline teaching to make it fit his own narrower social agenda.

Elaine Pagels has demonstrated part of what is at stake in the Jovinian controversy. Contemporary Romans foster the social expectation that every person marry, have a family, and commit to a public role in the state; the worth of the individual derives from fulfilling duties to family and state. Jerome removes the individual from social custom, redefining the value of the individual as resting on his or her spiritual life. Virginity becomes not a mark of shame but the sign of a life devoted to spiritual union with God—a sign of the inherent worth of the individual spirit.[16] From Jerome's perspective, men and women who conform to society by marrying and procreating are inferior in the hierarchy of the spirit: in a very real way, he dissents from social patriarchy.[17] There are, to be sure, limits on his willingness to rewrite social custom, and he elsewhere argues for the strict subordination of a virginal noble woman to her family.[18] Within the immediate historical context, however, his argument shockingly revalues marriage and provokes considerable debate. Many of his contemporaries felt compelled to argue against this extreme representation of the sexualized body, including Augustine of Hippo, though he too was sensitive to the "subtle and perpetual ravages of sexual feeling that so evidently obsessed Jerome."[19] Similar, often intense, disagreements characterize much of patristic exegesis and deliver to later exegetes a rich if potentially confusing record of interpretive alternatives and possibilities for multivalence.[20] Pagels is partly right that Roman cultural norms are an issue in Jerome's treatise, though social change has by his time rendered these norms more past ideals than present realities.[21] Jerome does not, however, actually compare Roman marriage and Christian celibacy. Instead, he distinguishes between marriage under Jewish law and virginity according to the Christian Gospel. Traditional Roman values appear under the guise of "the Jews [who] gloried in children and child-bearing" (I.22.362); marriage becomes one of the "works of the law" by which "no flesh [shall] be justified" (I.37.376).[22] The Gospel displaces Jewish "law":

> I do not disparage our predecessors under the law, but am well aware that they served their generation according to their circumstances, and fulfilled the Lord's command to increase, and multiply, and replenish the earth...But we to whom it is said, "The time is shortened, that henceforth those that have wives may be as though they had none," have a different command, and for us virginity is consecrated. (I.24.364)[23]

The Christian supersedes the sexualized body in precisely the way he does Jewish law. Marriage thus becomes a sign of allegiance to the Old Law of the sexualized and procreative flesh; it becomes nothing less than a departure from Christian identity.[24] Despite his avowed respect for Judaism, Jerome goes on to disparage the "carnal" and "literal" Jew in terms that are already stereotypical: "when we were in the flesh, the sinful passions, which were through the law, wrought in our members to bring forth fruit unto death. But now we have been discharged from the law" (I.37.374).[25] Marriage constrains the individual to a merely carnal existence, aligned with the "oldness of the letter" and the absence of the Spirit (1.37.374).[26] Quite simply, Jerome presents marriage and sexual activity as non-Christian, and in the process he conflates Judaism and paganism. Though he argues in the treatise that marriage is permissible, his ascetic fervor repeatedly undermines his argument. He insists that any compromise with sexual impulses, any conformity with "Jewish" cultural norms, constitutes a betrayal of the faith. What separates the Christian explicitly from the Jew, and implicitly from the pagan, becomes not just doctrine or belief but an ascetic idea of the body and its relation to social order.

Jerome recognizes no middle ground between complete abstinence and ungovernable lust. Far from imagining a moderate exercise of sexual impulses within marriage, he assumes desire is ungovernable:

> The desire to handle other men's persons, and the burning lust for women, is a passion bordering on insanity. To gratify this sense we languish, grow

angry, throw ourselves about with joy, indulge envy, engage in rivalry, are filled with anxiety, and when we have terminated the pleasure with more or less repentance, we once more take fire, and want to do that which we again regret doing. (II.8.394–95)[27]

Physical passion confuses homo- and heterosexual acts, and leads to eroticized madness. To "subjugate our refractory flesh, eager to follow the allurements of lust" (II.7.394), Jerome recommends a spare diet, for lust can to some extent be lessened by ascetic discipline.[28] Even here, though, memory intrudes: "The sense of touch can picture to itself even bygone pleasures, and through the recollection of vice forces the soul to take part in them, and after a manner to practice what it does not actually commit" (II.8.395).[29] Sexual experience is spiritually indelible, and even the memory of fleeting pleasure corrupts the soul.

In fact, Jerome comes close to defining individual worth almost exclusively in terms of physical state, for he assumes that any sexual experience (including rape) corrupts the whole being.[30] One passes immediately from virginity to bestial lust, defilement, and perpetual slavery to the flesh. Peter Brown memorably describes Jerome's experience of sexuality: "the human body remained for Jerome a darkened forest, filled with the roaring of wild beasts, that could be controlled only by rigid codes of diet and by the strict avoidance of occasions for sexual attraction."[31] Jerome's interpretive agenda in *Against Jovinian* derives from his conviction that there can be no compromise with sexual passion, no possibility of taming sexual impulses by anything less than total renunciation. His response to Jovinian therefore broadcasts nothing so much as his inability or unwillingness to imagine a moderate sexual desire or a comfortable governance of carnal impulses. This is, at least, how Jerome represents himself, though we would be justified in suspecting that his heroic battle with sexuality is in fact carefully constructed to advance his reputation as a rigorously ascetic spiritual guide.[32] Since he supposes that virginity precludes the unending cycle of lust, corruption, and regret, he sees virginity as the cure for the disease of sexual desire. Given these premises, he understandably reads 1 Timothy 2 as a mandate for virginity, or at least chastity. He transforms his own sexual experiences and fantasies into discourse: into (s)exegesis.

Jerome's position was controversial in his own time, and he refers to some women countering his emphasis on strict chastity with their own appeals to scripture: "what am I to do when the women of our time press me with apostolic authority, and before the first husband is buried, repeat from morning to night the precepts which allow a second marriage?" (I.47.383).[33] Even if entirely fictional, these women must be plausible to his first readers: women must be claiming the right to interpret scripture for themselves, preferring "apostolic authority" to Jerome's ascetic fervor. Jerome presents their protests in his own voice, inflecting their argument with a weary sarcasm. At the same time, he acknowledges that their prior interpretation resists his own, that his exegesis is debatable. He thus reproduces the gendered contest in 1 Timothy 2. At the same time, he rectifies "Paul's" silence about nonconformist women's words, filling the gap with his own assumptions about women's "carnal" exegesis.

Jerome tries to deauthorize the women's argument in favor of second marriages, in much the way he counters Jovinian, by impugning their "Christian purity" and recommending they conform to nothing more rigorous than "heathen" chastity (I. 47.383).[34] In this treatise, Christian identity persistently reduces to sexual experience. Significantly, Jerome does not address the conflict between his own teachings and "apostolic authority," resolve the apparent contradiction between biblical authorities, supply an ascetic interpretation of the women's text, or otherwise correct the women's understanding of the Bible. Instead, he advances a pagan text as more appropriate for "carnal" women. He proceeds to summarize (in some detail) Theophrastus's book *On Marriage,* which characterizes wives as gold diggers, wantons, and shrews. Against the ancient Roman ideal of matronly virtue, Jerome satirically details matronly vice. Ironically, his satire undermines the distinction he elsewhere draws between Christian and pagan: he offers nothing more than "a Christian continuation of the antifeminism of certain pagan thinkers" and the more "extreme" pagans at that.[35] He appears to forget for the moment that his definition of Christianity excludes pagans and Jews. His endorsement of chastity is never in question, but his ascetic hierarchy gets muddled.

In the process of responding to feminine protests, Jerome implies that women are exegetes in his local context, that they participate in debates over Christian praxis, and that their argument cannot be ignored. Most significantly, the women figure resistance to Jerome's ascetic teachings; their protest, like Jovinian's, gestures toward cultural contests over the definition of Christian identity. Jerome situates his treatise in a vigorous debate between men and women, ecclesiastics and laity, ascetics and moderates. And although *Against Jovinian* single-mindedly advances Jerome's position, it also preserves a record of that debate, and thus of objections, alternative positions, and counterarguments. The treatise stages exegesis as oppositional, a performance before an audience that participates actively in the interpretative process and may well reject the speaker's position. *Against Jovinian* presents Jerome's authority as contested and contestable. This leaves the work peculiarly open to supplements. Centuries later, as we will see, Chaucer's Wife of Bath elaborates the women's dissenting position, and she too prefers apostolic license to Jerome's exceptional rigor. The open quality of Jerome's text may help explain both its generative power for Chaucer (along with other poets) and its popularity in later academic contexts.[36]

Elizabeth A. Clark persuasively argues that "ascetic exegesis...is precisely *about* the creation of hierarchy and distinction": the distinction of sexual renunciation, the hierarchy of virgins over all others, the superiority of ascetic Christians to "carnal Jews."[37] Jerome's *Against Jovinian* demonstrates her point. Here Christian women's desire to remarry locates them at the bottom of the spiritual hierarchy, together with the "Epicurean" Jovinian and all Jews, who, in Jerome's view, similarly resist the new dispensation of the spirit.[38] Jerome brings dissident women into his argument as foils to sharpen the contrast between carnality and chastity. Yet their dissenting presence emphasizes how unstable Jerome's authority is, how vulnerable to reasoned dispute and biblical counterargument. By bringing these women into his treatise, he draws attention to the contingency of his own position. The women witness to a continuing gendered contest over Christian hermeneutics; and their argument, deflected but never refuted, makes it possible for readers to conceive of a credible nonascetic exegesis. The unruly women signal that Jerome's hierarchies remain unsettled; they undermine his assertion of spiritual dominance and authority.

At a more subtle interpretive level, the passage divulges Jerome's veiled unease about those "carnal" biblical texts that talk back to him in "women's" voices; it reveals his awareness of the many verses that resist his ascetic reading strategies. From this perspective, his interlocutors express his own almost repressed doubts about biblical passages that seem to speak another and more "carnal" message.[39] The women highlight a fissure in Jerome's (s)exegesis—one that, centuries later, Chaucer will expand into his own riotous supplement.

Chrysostom's Sexualized Auditors

For Jerome, 1 Timothy 2 signifies the spiritual priority of virgins; for his contemporary John Chrysostom, the text serves primarily to define modest feminine dress. Obviously, the two exegetes focus on entirely different textual details and press scripture's waxen nose into incongruous new forms. Their different social settings explain some disparities in their approaches to the text. Whereas Jerome polemically addresses a reading audience about an ongoing debate in Christendom, Chrysostom speaks as a pastor to his congregation. Like Jerome, Chrysostom was a stern ascetic, yet his sermons are far more temperate than Jerome's treatise

(most writings of the time are). Chrysostom's custom was to preach systematically on consecutive passages of scripture; over time (in Antioch,
386–98, and as bishop in Constantinople, 398–404) he composed a large
body of commentary, including two sermons on 1 Timothy 2. Although
he privileges virginity in theory, in these particular homilies he is far
more interested in defining women's place in the social order. He adapts
his pastoral teaching to his congregation's apparent needs and explicitly
instructs married men and women: not to turn their backs on marriage
and sexuality, but to make their faith visible in their habitus, especially in
the social practices that evidence sexual chastity, economic moderation,
and subordination to higher authorities.[40]

Chrysostom's first sermon explains what it means to pray with a pure
heart ("I will therefore that men pray in every place") and to dress modestly ("In like manner women also in decent apparel: adorning themselves with modesty and sobriety"). He dispenses with men's obligations
quickly in order to dwell at length on women's dress, a topic that much
engages him. For Chrysostom, women's dress can suggest problematic
uses of wealth; further, women's adornments can make them sexually
tempting and thereby contribute to "causing the downfall of otherwise
pious men," as Jacyln L. Maxwell recently put it.[41] Chrysostom begins
with an injunction to women: "Imitate not . . . the courtesans. For by such
a dress they allure their many lovers."[42] He associates courtesans with the
disreputable stage, arguing that women's costly garments recall theatrical
decadence: women dancing and speaking immodestly, men cross–dressing, the staging of immorality.[43] He seeks to draw a bright line between
"courtesans" or "actors" and the faithful, whose dress should signify their
spiritual difference.

Chrysostom expands on what constitutes immodest dress, chas-
tising women not only for gold and jewels but also for more subtle
adornments:

> If he [the Apostle] would remove those things which are only the indica-
> tions of wealth, as gold, and pearls, and costly array; how much more those
> things which imply studied ornament, as painting, coloring the eyes, a
> mincing gait, the affected voice, a languishing and wanton look; the exqui-
> site care in putting on the cloak and bodice, the nicely wrought girdle, and
> the closely-fitted shoes? . . . such things are shameless and indecent. (433)

Reading the text as a pastor concerned about his congregation's visible virtue, about the ways their bodies and dress testify (or not) to their Christian
identity, Chrysostom sees some shortcomings in the scanty Pauline definition of "decent apparel." He accordingly rewrites 1 Timothy 2 to fill in

missing details about makeup, gesture, intonation, and so on. Indeed, his elaboration of sexualized particulars suggests that, despite years of severe ascetic practice, he is still, as he had been in youth, "troubled by the difficulty he had in controlling his burgeoning sexuality."[44] Under his gaze, almost any feminine "ornament"—from makeup to footwear—becomes sexual display. Even virgins are exuberantly sexualized:

> But what virgin, you say, wears gold, or broidered hair? Yet there may be such a studied nicety in a simple dress, as that these are nothing to it.... For when a very dark colored robe is drawn closely round the breast with the girdle (as dancers on the stage are attired), with such nicety that it may neither spread into breadth nor shrink into scantiness, but be between both; and when the bosom is set off with many folds, is not this more alluring than any silken robes?... What can one say to the perpetual rolling of the eyes? to the putting on of the stomacher, so artfully as sometimes to conceal, sometimes to disclose, the fastening?... and we might speak of their walk, and other artifices more alluring than any ornament of gold.... These things and many others, invented only to be seen and to attract beholders, are more alluring than golden ornaments. These are no trifling faults, but displeasing to God, and enough to mar all the self-denial of virginity. (433–34)

Chrysostom notes every detail of women's dress, from the precise folds over a bosom to a hidden fastening. He recalls gestures, a way of walking. From his perspectives, all is "alluring." Clearly, virginity does not ensure virtue. Neither does poverty exempt women from blame: "Say not, 'Alas, I wear a threadbare garment, mean shoes, a worthless veil; what is there of ornament in these?' Do not deceive thyself. It is impossible [*sic*: the context suggests he means "possible"], as I said, to study appearance more by these than by costlier dresses; especially when they are close-fitted to the body, fashioned to an immodest show, and of shining neatness" (434). From Chrysostom's perspective, poverty only enhances women's seductive appearance. He reduces women's subversive potential to the titillations of style, thoroughly detailed for each social group: married women, virgins, the poor. He consistently locates the responsibility for his gaze and his desire in the women, who, he assumes, intend to "attract beholders" like him. Through his exegesis, he transforms men's desire into women's problem; reforming women's dress enables masculine asceticism (at least in theory).[45]

Women's dress signifies more than their religious identity or practice of virtue, however. Chrysostom classifies women according to their sexual activity and relation to men—and seeks to clothe them in visible signs of that patriarchal system.[46] Hence married women should not look like courtesans or actors. He finds contemporary attire troubling precisely because it blurs boundaries between classes of women, obscuring their place in the patriarchal order: "We can no longer distinguish harlots and virgins" (434). From his perspective, women should dress to support masculine interests, either making their sexual availability clear or devising an entirely unalluring presence (a difficult if not impossible task, it seems). Women's failure to advance patriarchal interests becomes in this sermon a spiritual fault, a refusal to accept "Paul's" teaching about their place in the social order. Chrysostom exhorts women to internalize men's needs as their own, to subordinate themselves to patriarchal ideology. In this he exercises a kind of "symbolic violence" that fosters a "subjective experience of relations of domination."[47] Since women can evidently subvert patriarchal order with the smallest gesture or stylish nuance, they must adjust their intentions as well as their behaviors to serve masculine interests. Women must themselves take on the work of symbolic violence and make that violence part of their own subjectivity.

Chrysostom's second sermon concentrates on the injunction that women be silent in church and on the promise they will be saved by childbearing.[48] Like Jerome, he is known to answer feminine interlocutors, though this sermon does not imply respect for women's intellectual capacity or interest in their point of view.[49] As he understands "Paul," worshipful decorum requires women's silence: since "the sex is naturally...talkative," apt to engage in "much clamor and talking" about "unprofitable subjects," women need to be quiet in order to learn (435). "Paul" does not state his motive for prohibiting women's teaching, so Chrysostom supplies one from his own pastoral experiences: women are chatterboxes, unfit to instruct anyone; they can participate only by being quiet.[50] Chrysostom at once reveals and fills a void in the Pauline text, attributing to the apostle a critique of contemporary social norms, and grafting his own irritation onto the biblical text. Although Chrysostom authorizes his interpretation through scripture, he notably revises the sense of 1 Timothy 2: he focuses on women's conversation rather than on their instruction of men.[51] As he has it, the quality of women's speech prevents them from teaching men. Women's only discursive virtue is silence. Chrysostom reaccentuates the biblical text to deliver a cutting pastoral message to the women in his congregation.

Chrysostom continues by developing the, for him, weightier theological mandate of women's subordination to men, a principle that governs his attitudes toward women and sexuality: "For the woman taught the man once, and made him guilty of disobedience, and wrought our ruin. Therefore because she made a bad use of her power over the man, or rather her equality with him, God made her subject to her husband" (435).[52] Chrysostom makes all women—including the pre-lapsarian Eve—innately "weak and fickle" (436), suggesting a flaw in the order of creation. The theology becomes difficult. Adam eats the fruit because persuaded by his wife, but only the woman is guilty: "here the female sex transgressed, and not the male" (436). Because of woman's original sin, women are subjected to men and saved through childbearing. Chrysostom does not touch on the apparent mystery of men's damnation, nor does he answer one of his own questions about how barren women or virgins are to be saved in this patriarchal spiritual economy. By privileging married women over virgins, he implies that the principle of feminine subordination overshadows that of physical integrity.

The sermon coherently legitimates marital sexual intercourse and the patriarchal family, the accepted foundation of social order. Indeed, far from encouraging virginity, Chrysostom counsels early marriage: "Especially let us train them in chastity, for there is the very bane of youth. For this many struggles, much attention will be necessary. Let us take wives for them early, so that their brides may receive their bodies pure and unpolluted, so their loves will be more ardent" (436–37). Chastity is a temporary state that gives way to lay couples' passionate married love, and Chrysostom approves their "ardent" love, procreation, and virtuous (which is to say, male-dominated) family life. He endorses precisely the social structure that Jerome rejects as a relic of "carnal, Jewish" history. Each exegete invents a spiritual hierarchy, but not the same one: Chrysostom insists on men's precedence over women; Jerome, on virgins' precedence over married people.[53] Although both represent their interpretations as repeating what "Paul" has already said, they actually replace the biblical text with their own.

Jerome and Chrysostom help us recognize that a polemical treatise and pastoral sermon can encourage forcefully different interpretations. They demonstrate that 1 Timothy 2 can be read as an argument against marriage or an endorsement of married love, proving, if we need such proof, how easily the Bible can either challenge or endorse traditional social values. What the passage means clearly depends on the exegetes' choice of genre, audience, social concerns, and hermeneutic strategies.[54] For all their differences, however, both men follow what is usually called a "literal" hermeneutics—an uninformative label that tells us little about their actual hermeneutic practices. "Literal" signals a difference from "allegorical," "tropological," "spiritual," "moral," "typological," "anagogical," etcetera hermeneutics. Beyond identifying a category in a conventional fourfold system, "literal" is too nonspecific to be useful. By relying on such a broad label, we obscure a tremendous variety of hermeneutics: atomizing the text (concentrating on just one word, *castitas*); translating it (*castitas* rather than *sobrietas*); supplying an authorial intention ("Paul" intends garrulous women to remain silent so they can learn); expanding the text (adding the details of contemporary style "Paul" neglects to mention); and reaccentuating it (emphasizing feminine sexuality rather than leadership). Grouping these and other strategies under the heading "literal" does not promote critical acuity.[55]

We might realistically expect ascetics to converge on feminine sexuality when they read 1 Timothy 2, and Jerome and Chrysostom do not disappoint. By concentrating on *feminine* sexual excess and its proper Christian regulation, both exegetes expose the libidinal tensions that drive their (s)exegesis. Their attempts to regulate the feminine body mask their attempts to govern the self, to manage an uneasy but ever-present sexual desire. Ascetic exegetes put tremendous pressure on the sexualized body, marginalizing the complex of economic, intellectual, and ecclesiastical concerns that informs 1 Timothy 2. Consequently, they degrade the woman in authority, the speaking and teaching woman of scripture, to a sexually charged body, intellectually unthreatening even if overwhelmingly seductive.[56] From "Paul" to Chrysostom, the feminine figures resistance to masculine regulation, but the form of resistance narrows. For Jerome and Chrysostom, the biblical text speaks primarily to their experience of being tempted by women, and their need to externalize and denigrate the source of that temptation. Even as they claim the spiritual authority of their "manly" self-control, they divulge their constant struggle against the "feminine" vices and voices that threaten to undermine them.

Jerome and Chrysostom transform knowledge of scripture into claims of ecclesiastical and social power. Their exegesis "transmits and produces power; it reinforces it"; but, as we have seen, "also undermines and exposes it, renders it fragile and makes it possible to thwart it."[57] This subversive undertow is obvious in the sexual anxieties that ripple through their commentaries. It is more subtly apparent in the prior feminine speech—women teaching in 1 Timothy 2, or protesting Jerome's ascetic rigor, or talking in Chrysostom's church—that relativizes their assertions of authority. That prior speech reveals that exegetes' claims to knowledge and the power derived from knowledge are contested within their social settings. Jerome and Chrysostom try to control perceptions of that contest by reaccentuating feminine speech as "carnal," irrational, and senseless. Although feminine bodies hinder their self-control, women's speech does not directly threaten their intellectual systems or discourse. Their exegesis thus moderates the broad threat of feminine subversion implicit in the biblical text. In short, they produce a "safer" Bible, one adapted to the needs of masculine ecclesiastics. By studying their scriptural supplements, we gain insight into the historical, discursive labor of adapting scripture to support a gendered ecclesiastical and social hierarchy.

The *Gloss* on Feminine Sexuality

Early exegetes recognize the fact of interpretive diversity and invent strategies for establishing authoritative readings and inventing ecclesiastical coherence. Augustine of Hippo invents a powerful method for restraining profusion into meaningful patterns. A glut of exegetical debates and the difficulty of arriving at definitive interpretations initially encourage Augustine to emphasize the imperfect authority of individual exegetes. Éric Rebillard proposes that his attitude changes during the Pelagian controversy (after c. 418), when Augustine begins to argue from patristic citations and to locate authority in a consensus of reliable commentators.[58] Augustine now posits that agreement among many exegetes compensates for the fallibility of any individual. Shifting his confidence toward a perceived consensus, he subtly transfers authority from the biblical text to the human interpreters (to the extent that they agree with one another). He discounts innovation and diversity. Augustine's strategy remains useful to the church, especially in polemical times, as witnessed by its revival at the Council of Trent against the Protestant Reformation (1545–63).[59] Augustine's strategy can be useful to modern secular critics, in that a long-standing consensus points toward a dominant interpretation and implies its wide diffusion: such a consensus can plausibly illuminate a literary allusion.[60] At the same time, even a durable consensus does not constrain all exegetes, who can and do depart from traditions.[61] Exegesis evidences both coherent interpretive traditions that circulate relatively unchanged from the patristic era into the late fifteenth century and sudden reinventions of even the most established traditions. Discerning which possibility applies to any given context is the interesting challenge of historical criticism.

The most influential twelfth-century commentary, the *Gloss* (compiled c. 1130–60), epitomizes a later development of Augustine's respect for ancient authority and resistance to novelty.[62] The *Gloss* reveals what monks consider authoritative, which interpretations are widely available, and how those interpretations are being shaped, even substantially changed, for new audiences. Perhaps most significantly, the work conveys the ideal of a coherent exegetical community. The *Gloss* stages no exegetical debates or polemical contests; rather, it presents the textual illusion of a harmonious interpretive community, with each exegete entering in turn, decorously, to expand the analysis. Source selection creates a consensus, however much the exegetes selected might disagree on large and small doctrinal, theological, and hermeneutic questions. In the *Gloss,* Jerome and Chrysostom and Augustine et al. agree by editorial diktat, or their minor differences humbly demonstrate that a text's meaning cannot certainly be determined in the present state of knowledge.[63] The purposeful creation of this interpretative community—necessitating the suppression of many polemical and even nasty debates—is perhaps the compilers' greatest literary achievement. For consensus, and the authority arising from consensus, is far more a human invention than an objective fact about exegesis.

The *Gloss* was much copied and survives in more than 2000 manuscripts, making it central to an understanding of contemporary monastic and academic culture. Unfortunately for modern scholars, no reliable edition of the twelfth-century work exists. Though often cited, the *Patrologia Latina* edition is "worthless," a crudely amputated version of the historical work.[64] The more reliable *editio princeps* (Adolph Rusch, 1480/81) captures *a* historical version of the work, but not an original twelfth-century version. Nor is there a single "best text" manuscript to consult in lieu of a modern edition. Manuscripts vary considerably and evidence innumerable revisions. The *Gloss* evolves over time: prologues, prefaces, arguments, and prothemes are added; glosses are added, omitted, and rearranged; and postils and supplements accumulate, designed to bring the text up to date.[65] The material forms of the *Gloss* foreground the fact that it is from first to last the product of many hands, a uniquely collaborative work. Gillian Rosemary Evans cogently wraps up a meticulous study of the *Gloss*'s progress through the thirteenth century by calling attention to its provisional status: "the *Glossa Ordinaria* might be said to fall on the face of it into the categories of compilation or commentary; yet perhaps it is most accurately classified as a working tool, rather than a book in its own right.... It is not for mere quoting but for quoting and wrestling with."[66]

The *Gloss* is a work in progress, continually rewritten for new contexts. Each version potentially gains a new social logic. Mark Zier, for instance, discerns in one group of manuscripts evidence "of how the development of the *Gloss* responded to, and perhaps promoted, the theological currents of the time," and of how new moral interpretations are added in response to the work's increasingly pastoral uses.[67] Suzanne LaVere demonstrates that original twelfth-century glosses significantly revise the emphasis of earlier exegesis by stressing the value of the active life over the contemplative, and by stressing the importance of preaching, probably aimed toward an audience of students preparing to be preachers.[68] Manuscripts evidence specific historical demands on exegesis and compilers' strategies for meeting those demands. The *Gloss* does not just record authoritative interpretations, then; it also displays changes in what precisely it authorizes. The *Gloss* is a complicated series of biblical supplements rather than a single fixed work.

A great deal more manuscript study is needed to clarify the work's historical development, and an authoritative modern edition of an early version would certainly be helpful (a digital edition of important versions would be even better). In the meantime, scholars can use the Rusch *editio princeps* of 1480/81 cautiously, recognizing that it does not exactly represent the original twelfth-century *Gloss*, which would likely be shorter than the Rusch text.[69] Although Rusch stands at some distance from the original *Gloss*, the edition does incorporate twelfth-century exegetical practice, and it can allow for provisional conclusions about the historically various and textually problematic *Gloss*. In the case of 1 Timothy 2, Rusch gives us access more accurately to Peter Lombard's version of the work than to Anselm of Laon's, in whose school the *Gloss* originates.[70]

Rusch centers scripture on the page and surrounds the passage with "marginal" commentary, an inapposite label since the "margins" typically take up most of the page.[71] The marginal commentary begins with a word or brief phrase, the *lemma* or subject of the commentary, purportedly from the biblical passage under discussion.[72] The *lemma* ties the marginal commentary visually to the centered scriptural passage. Brief interlinear glosses provide another layer of commentary. This mise-en-page guides the reader through a meditative rumination on each word, each verse in turn. As Professor Evans insightfully remarks, the *Gloss*'s form mirrors a "slow, reflective reading, an attempt patiently, and over many years of humble acquaintance with the text, to penetrate its depths."[73] Whereas Jerome and Chrysostom plunder scraps, the *Gloss* seeks to meditate on the whole. Each annotated page of the *Gloss* thereby testifies to a monastic method of reading: each word is understood in context; each passage contributes to a sequence. A host of named and unnamed authorities participate in this effort, conducting the reader into a coherent, unified interpretive community.

Although the *Gloss* compilers depart far from Jerome's and Chrysostom's reading strategies, they maintain earlier exegetes' focus on feminine sexuality. The marginal gloss elaborates three main points—the necessity of women's silence, woman's guilt for the Fall, and woman's salvation through childbearing—and each point centers on woman's too-material body. This thematic coherence emerges as the *Gloss* proceeds systematically from one biblical phrase (or *lemma*) to the next (*lemmata* are italicized in the following commentary on "Let the woman learn in silence" and "I suffer not a woman to teach"):

> *In silence...* If she speaks, she excites and is more excited to luxury [*luxuria*]. *To teach, etc.* Behold he not only taught woman to have a humble and respectable manner, but he also denied authority to her teaching, and he warned that she submit herself to man, so that by her manner in submission, she might be under the authority of man, from whom she draws her beginning.[74]

Woman's speech, like her body, becomes another source of sexual temptation, merely exciting herself and others to wantonness, excess, riot (in a word, *luxuria*). The compilers imply "Paul's" intention for the ban on women teachers: he denies women authority in order to prevent sexual temptation (a significant shift from the intent Chrysostom inferred). "If she speaks," she will lead men astray. Woman's distracting body renders her words irrelevant. The *Gloss* thus concisely summarizes women's incapacity for leadership in the church. The compilers hasten to add that women should submit to men; that is, women should take on themselves the labor of maintaining the patriarchal system.

Since woman is primarily a source of sexual temptation, the *Gloss* reduces the virtues of "faith, and love, and sanctification, with sobriety" (I Tim. 2: 15) to sexual temperance (*lemmata* are again italicized):

> *She will be saved.* Notwithstanding woman was made the cause of sin, yet she will be saved, not only a virgin and continent, but also a married woman, so long as, never ceasing from the work of marriage, if, advancing through the generation of sons, she depart from this world. *If she continue in faith and love and sanctification,* namely that she not know another man except her own. *With sobriety.* That is, temperance, even with her own man.[75]

Woman's social duty now consists of laboring at sexual intercourse, giving birth to sons, knowing no man except her husband, and using even that one man in sober temperance. The *Gloss* transforms the banned feminine teachers of 1 Timothy 2 once again into sexualized bodies, now harnessed to serve patriarchal genealogies. In fact, woman has no legitimate social function here aside from breeding. The *Gloss* means to fix the terms of women's self-regulation: one marital and no extramarital partners, moderate demands on him, and an intention of procreative intercourse. The detailed rules imply concern about women expressing independent or excessive desire. Women retain a capacity for resisting clerical mandates, through any nonprocreative or nonmarital sexual act or intention. The *Gloss* thus reaccentuates women's resistance, situating it in the nonverbal realm of sexuality. This interpretation severely contracts women's potential for subversion and contains it within the domestic sphere, making women's anticipated resistance less threatening to social hierarchy—and irrelevant to ecclesiastical hierarchy. The compilers effectively insulate clerics from the feminine challenge embedded in 1 Timothy 2, thereby creating a "safer" Bible for the *literati*. If women disobey these strictures, they only ensure their own damnation. Indeed, the idealized clerical standards implicitly judge women who falter in their conjugal labor, fail to bring forth sons, or want more sex than a monk would approve. Although women must marry, marriage evidently opens many doors to sin. Women seem to have few choices in this prison house of sexuality.

The *Gloss* makes woman's salvation depend on her relationship with a man, not on her individual piety. This focus on married and procreative women is hardly inevitable in a twelfth-century monastic context. We might expect ascetic interpretations—Jerome's argument about chastity, or the traditional hierarchy of virgins, widows, and wives—to get more play here. Yet the commentary turns away from asceticism, even going so far as to make virgins, the continent, and wives essentially equal in spiritual standing, all heirs of Eve, all redeemed through subordination to patriarchal desires: "she will be saved, not only a virgin and continent, but also a married woman, so long as, never ceasing from the work of marriage." Rather than advocating virginity or asceticism, the *Gloss* insists that women conform to "the work of marriage," that they serve, as Jerome would put it, the law of the flesh. The *Gloss*'s allegorical reading of 1 Timothy 2 reinforces this implication: woman is a type of the flesh ("mulier typus est carnis"), properly subordinated to the spirit.[76] The *Gloss* compilers limit woman's role in church and society to physical generation. They could have selected other, more ascetic sources, including Jerome's reading of chastity. They choose, however, to make asceticism the exclusive property of male monastics—themselves. That choice exposes their interest in maintaining the gender and ecclesiastical hierarchies that support their own power. That monastic exegesis should rationalize the power of a clerical elite is unsurprising, even perhaps predictable within this institutional context. More interesting is the compilers' ability to erase almost all traces of their role in creating this particular sense for scripture. As compilers, they invent nothing new, or so it seems.[77] The compilation form implies that this sense has existed from the age of the fathers until the present—even as the compilers drastically revise the usual patristic emphasis on both male and female asceticism.[78] The *Gloss*'s form at once promotes its aura of authority and obscures the compilers' ideologically powerful mediation of scripture.

The text proceeds to reflect at length on the devil's seduction of Eve, importing for the purpose an extended Genesis narrative and commentary. Since Eve caused the Fall and universal damnation, women are henceforth forbidden to teach. The *Gloss* uses the Genesis narrative to redefine woman's speech as inevitably deceptive and dangerous; silence becomes the only conceivable remedy for women's discursive flaw. This interpretation makes Eve the first transgressive teacher, the originary source of women's resistant speech in 1 Timothy 2. The problem with women teachers thus traces back to an immutable created order. Clearly, even before the Fall, even in her most perfect state, woman was inherently unfit to teach men. Of course, this idea of woman's incapacity witnesses less to natural order than to specific social-historical circumstances, and again the compilers' exegetical choices are not inevitable. The *Gloss* is compiled in an age of controversy about women teachers. Women had for centuries been involved in church ministries, including preaching. Abbesses openly teach in this period, often addressing high ecclesiastics, and doing so with considerable authority.[79] Dissent from 1 Timothy 2 is hardly dead, nor restricted to heterodox groups.[80] Perhaps largely in response to the heterodox threat, the *Gloss* takes an unambiguous stand against women teachers. To some extent, this position might be expected in a work created by monastic scholars seeking to establish an authoritative, "safe" interpretation of scripture. In the case of 1 Timothy 2, "safe" equates specifically with male social and ecclesiastical dominance.[81]

This reaccentuation adapts the biblical text to a twelfth-century monastic ideal of a hierarchical, centralized church, in which women are banned from altar ministry and ordination, precluded from service by their guilt for original sin. In fact, Gary Macy persuasively argues that the *Gloss* plays a crucial role in promoting both this idea of the church and this theory of women's incapacity, as against a competing idea of the church as an "extended family," in which women are ordained and serve at the altar. In just a few sentences on woman as the cause of damnation, the *Gloss* provides a definitive theological framework for excluding women from altar ministry. The work's rapid dissemination and unequalled authority quickly establish this interpretation as normative, and earlier traces of women's ordination are quickly reinterpreted or erased.[82] The *Gloss* demonstrates the potentially far-reaching ideological effects of exegesis—and exegetes' power to initiate profound social and ecclesiastical change. Discourses do not by themselves create change, but they can, as here, legitimize the inclinations of a powerful elite.

Thus far, medieval exegesis reveals not a single dominant interpretation of 1 Timothy 2 but a series of interested attempts to fathom scripture and a continual reinscription of the text for particular contexts and audiences. In the course of the twelfth and thirteenth centuries, the proliferation of questions about scripture, and the multiplication of authorities, make exegetical consensus increasingly difficult for any individual exegete to discern. This leads to a gradual centering of authority in the church and to the invention of institutionalized consensus.[83] At the same time, the multiplication of religious vocations in the era of the *Gloss*'s compilation leads to a proliferation of exegetical methods. The mendicants, for example, use scripture to gloss scripture in their sermons, demonstrating not only a different hermeneutic method but also a stunningly different idea of authority than that conveyed by the *Gloss*'s apparent deference to centuries-old sources.[84] In fact, the fraternal preaching mission inspires the creation of new material texts, including handy pocket Bibles stripped of all glosses, and new collections of authorities to be used in the battle against heresy.[85] The *Gloss* has an undeniable cultural impact, but it is only one of many influences on exegesis.

If a single interpretation of 1 Timothy 2 does not emerge from our limited survey, an interpretive bias does: a tendency to reduce women to the sinful flesh and to equate masculinity with control over that wayward flesh. Exegetical investments in a gendered social and ecclesiastical hierarchy remain constant despite massive changes in hermeneutics, ways of reading, and institutions. Exegetes create and recreate the hierarchies of masculine reason, feminine passion; masculine knowledge, feminine ignorance; masculine rule, feminine deviance. Those common threads reveal exegetes' own social and embodied positions. Perhaps most tellingly, exegesis on 1 Timothy 2 enables men to redirect their own struggles with sexuality, the subversions of their "feminine" flesh, into shaping rigorous rules for *women* to follow. Exegetes shift the burden of sexual sin ineluctably onto women's backs and command women to internalize their symbolic violence. In the *Gloss*, men appear unaware of resistance to their scheme.[86]

Alison's Dissent

As we have seen, Jerome stages a contest between his authorial persona and the women who reject his ascetic rigor: "What am I to do when the women of our time press me with apostolic authority, and before the first husband is buried, repeat from morning to night the precepts which allow a second marriage?" (I.47.383). The Wife of Bath's self-interested exegesis recalls the women's position: she too seeks in scripture what will legitimate her desire for remarriage, talking back to the authorities who counsel sexual renunciation.[87] Indeed, Alison goes so far as to deny even apostolic authority. When her husbands preach to her from 1 Timothy 2, Alison rejects both the text and their gloss: "After thy text ne after thy rubryche / I wol nat werke as muche as is a gnat."[88] Chaucer rewrites Jerome's gendered contest over the biblical text, creating for a new audience the possibility that a "carnal" lay woman might pick and choose whom she will consider authoritative—or contradict. Whereas Jerome puts women's exegesis into his voice, Chaucer gives Alison a voice of her own, which she uses to discount her husbands' exegesis. Chaucer reverses the terms of discursive power, denying the masculine exegetical perspective its naturalized dominance. Through Alison, Chaucer gives new life to the feminine resistance implicit in the biblical text, and explicit in Jerome's treatise. By fictionalizing the bourgeois reception of 1 Timothy 2, Chaucer spectacularly reaccentuates both "Paul" and Jerome. In effect, Chaucer puts a lay woman in the discursive place of the church father, privileging "carnal" hermeneutics and elaborating a gendered scriptural argument.[89] Throughout her *Prologue*, Alison appears the sexualized feminine body into which many Greek and Latin exegetes rewrite women teachers. Yet she cannot be reduced to that silenced body, for she forcefully articulates the dissent exegetes variously denounce and repress.

Chaucer crafts the Wife's Prologue in a particularly unsettled religious climate, lending an added transgressive charge to his persona. Vernacular writers of the fourteenth and fifteenth centuries confront inconsistent (explicit and implicit) ecclesiastical positions on the question of women preachers, as well as centuries of exegetical developments around 1 Timothy 2, one of the core texts on this issue.[90] In Chaucer's cultural context, many writers dissent from conservative ecclesiastical positions and advocate for women's capacity to preach or teach. Indeed, women are often seen as standard-bearers for resistance to established systems of religious and social authority. This tendency is obvious in works now labeled Lollard, but it is not restricted to Lollardy. English religious culture evidences a mix of Lollard and orthodox sympathies, rendering distinctions between the two problematic.[91] The Wife of Bath enters history in the midst of unresolved controversies over the relation of the laity, and particularly women, to scripture. As her provocative first act, she delivers a literate antimatrimonial "sermon," replete with scriptural citations and translations, before a mostly male fictional audience. In the course of that sermon, she rejects both spousal and apostolic authority, enacting ecclesiastics' worst-case scenario about what would happen if women gained access to vernacular scripture.

Chaucer certainly makes Alison controversial, yet he does not make her heretical. His portrait ambiguously mixes orthodoxy (most obviously, she goes on pilgrimage) and quasi-Lollard claims on scriptural interpretation (she translates and interprets a good bit of scripture).[92] Although Alison suggestively recalls Jerome's dissident women, moreover, she generally agrees with him about the priority of virgins in the spiritual hierarchy, and she borrows heavily from—and largely agrees with—the antimatrimonial arguments in *Against Jovinian*.[93] She does not adopt Jerome's interpretation of 1 Timothy 2, but that in itself means little: neither does the *Gloss* cite Jerome's philology. Alison's uncertain religious position opens the text to diverse possible readings and to readers at opposite poles in the debate. The chameleonlike persona functions as the poet's protective disguise, allowing him to engage the heated controversies circulating in his culture while distancing himself from "Alison's" subversive challenges to traditional authority.

Rather than commenting independently on 1 Timothy 2, Alison reports her husbands' interpretations, giving Chaucer another layer of fictional distance from the exegesis in question:

> Thow [the husbands] seist also that if we [wives] make vs gay
> With clothyng and with precious array
> That it is peril of oure chastitee
> And yet with sorwe thow most enforce thee
> And seye thise wordes in thapostles name
> In habit maad with chastitee and shame
> Ye wommen shal apparaille yow quod he
> And nat in tressed heer and gay perree
> As perlys ne with gold ne clothes ryche. (337–45)

"Gay" attire endangers "chastitee," and "chastitee" excludes "gay" adornment: the chiasmus turns the husbands and apostle into mirrors of each other, making the domestic and ecclesiastical systems of authority appear a unified whole. These authorities have no voices of their own, however—any more than women do in conventional exegesis on this passage. Chaucer takes from men their discursive hegemony and subjects them to a feminine ventriloquist. In other words, he overturns exegetes' usual strategy of marginalizing women's response. This change in the voicing of scripture signals a change in perspective. Chaucer treats the *masculine* point of view as strange, belonging to someone else, the object of parodic imitation.[94] His voicing of 1 Timothy 2 focuses attention on Alison's skeptical reception ("thow seist"), on the feminine reaccentuation rather than on the original text. He creates a dialogic relationship between the masculine exegetes and their resisting feminine auditor, animating anew the gender tensions of 1 Timothy 2.

As represented, both the husbands and apostle treat the regulation of feminine dress and sexuality as inextricable. From the husbands' perspective, women's implied economic independence (they can "make" themselves "gay") takes on erotic implications. Financial independence equates with autonomous sexual desires, and with separation from patriarchal interests. The husbands apparently lack the power to curb Alison's independence, so they appeal to the higher authority of scripture. They domesticate exegesis, making it a weapon in their campaign to control their wife's spending. Notably, the husbands ignore the ecclesiastical agenda of 1 Timothy 2, forbidding women to teach or preach, as well as the emphasis on good works, and the notion of salvation through childbearing; they focus only on "precious" material goods. By exposing the husbands' bourgeois, money-oriented self-interest, Chaucer desanctifies their preaching.[95] Their materialism calls their "spiritual" guidance into question.

The context for this passage—a long series of misogynous remarks—also renders the husbands' exegetical intent problematic. As Alison reports their arguments, the husbands say that a poor woman costs too much, a rich woman is too proud, and a fair woman unchaste. They say women are desired on every side and no one can keep the castle so long assailed. They say an ugly woman will leap on any man she can. A woman is like the leaky roof or smoking fire that makes a man flee his home. Women hide their vices until they marry; men can try all goods except a wife before buying them; women are unhappy unless they are being praised, and so on. This context puts 1 Timothy 2 on a level with misogynous proverbs (some of them also biblical), makes it similarly expressive of masculine assaults on feminine sexuality, independence, vices, and secrets. The boundary between sacred words and human expressions collapses. The passage displays the husbands' promiscuous mingling of human and divine authority, their appropriation of "wisdom" to their own polemical purposes. Their sermon develops an obsession with misogynistic stereotypes, the basis of their partisan biblical interpretations. By putting this antifeminine tirade into a woman's voice, Chaucer relativizes it: he portrays authoritative utterances that have lost their authority, at least for this auditor. The feminine voicing presents the husbands' perspective and their wisdom as inevitably contested.

These spousal exegetes are, moreover, "dronken as a mous" at the beginning of the sermon, and still "in hir dronkenesse" at its end (246, 381). The simile makes the men irrational rodents, subject to their own sensuality—as unruly as the wife they seek to control. Their disordered sermon raises questions about their fitness to govern themselves, let alone Alison. By the way he frames and voices the husbands' speech, Chaucer constructs them as satiric targets—doubtful exegetes, unpersuasive in their manipulation of scripture, and hardly qualified to act as anyone's spiritual head. By reversing the gendered perspective on 1 Timothy 2, Chaucer undermines the implicit masculine claims to virtue and rationality that typically support exegetical authority. He uses Alison to pose a significant challenge to institutionalized masculine power.

Like the Summoner, Friar, Pardoner, and Monk, the husbands of Bath typify exegetes whose sins discredit their sermons. By what right do they assert power over their wife and scripture? Does their privilege come from divine grace, human law, the superior exercise of masculine reason and virtue? Chaucer denies the men a claim to grace or rational self-governance, thereby raising questions about their dominion that recall (but are not restricted to) contemporary Wycliffite and Lollard arguments.[96] Wyclif argues that dominion properly derives from grace, the exercise of reason, and obedience to divine law. From his perspective, sin should lead to loss of dominion, and the laity can virtuously resist unlawful "superiors."[97] Wyclif and those who share his opinions seriously challenge the status quo; not surprisingly, they stir up a long-lasting controversy. The intoxicated husbands of Bath present domesticated versions of the corrupt clerics denounced by reformers. The collapse of three husbands into one voice in this passage makes their sinful dominion appear a pervasive cultural problem, entirely commonplace and often repeated, rather than restricted to a few clerics or exceptional circumstances.

In their inebriated sermon, the husbands of Bath take on the task of educating their wife in holiness, as ecclesiastics have for centuries argued they should. Jankyn performs a version of the same ideal when he reads to Alison from the Book of Wicked Wives. Chaucer subjects this clerical ideal to "subversive outrage"[98] and implies the naivete of those who assume that men are capable—by virtue of their gender or learning—of governing themselves, let alone instructing their wives to good effect. Readers can easily extend Chaucer's critique to civil and clerical dominion, which are traditionally analogous to and dependent on the domestic hierarchy. Indeed, Chaucer invites that readerly supplement by describing a drunken sermon in an age of Wycliffite controversy. Yet the husbands of Bath embody a problem that, once recognized, cannot be restricted to a Wycliffite frame of reference. The husbands reveal decay in the foundations of social order, the conventional microcosmic hierarchies of husband over wife, reason over sensuality. What happens then to the macrocosm, the supposedly immutable divine order mirrored in the microcosm? Although the scene raises disturbing questions about the symbolic order, Chaucer's text immediately represses them. After relating her husbands' speech in great detail, Alison proclaims the entire performance a lie (379–85), revealing to readers how cleverly they (and the husbands) have been played. The poem thus diverts attention away from the men's inadequacies, away from the insecure basis of the culture's sustaining ideology. Chaucer distracts the reader (and perhaps himself) with Alison's garrulous unruliness, providing an easier explanation for the instability of masculine dominion.

Alison rejects all of her husbands' antifeminine ramblings, and especially the apostle's counsel: "After thy text ne after thy rubryche / I wol nat werke as muche as is a gnat" (346–47). She shrewdly identifies the biblical text as her husbands' possession: "thy text." Their sermons remove scripture from general circulation and make the Word their own property. Alison at once names and denies their act of possession, their claim to such great dominion. The apostle's stricture ("thy text") and husbands' exegesis ("thy rubryche") become one text, and her dismissal of both is shockingly explicit. To be sure, her audacious "I wol nat werke" is buried in a repetitive series of similar rejoinders to her husbands' chronic misogyny. Her riposte is also persuasively motivated, perhaps even justified, by her husbands' drunken provocation. That she dismisses scripture is nonetheless potentially scandalous. But the scandal is deferred: so far as I can discern, no one—either in the fiction or subsequently in the work's reception, including everyone from the poor Parson to D. W. Robertson—interrupts to rebuke her or register dismay.[99] The lines are not edited out of any fifteenth-century manuscript or incunabula, though one scribe alters them substantially, perhaps registering discomfort with the content. Several manuscripts add a Latin source note for the biblical text, rendering it highly visible, but no early reader adds so much as a marginal "nota" to indicate that he or she even notices Alison's dissent.[100]

Judging from the absence of widespread negative reactions to this passage, we may assume that Alison's readers generally find her dissent from canonical as well as spousal authority literally unremarkable. Readers' sensibilities, then as now, allow Chaucer to narrate a blunt feminine dissent from masculine spiritual dominion as domestic comedy, without serious social or theological consequences. In fact, the underwhelming medieval and modern responses to this passage imply that a woman might be expected to oppose a drunken misogynous sermon delivered at her hearth. To be sure, Chaucer limits Alison's rebellion: she elsewhere accepts the authority of scripture, challenges no doctrinal verities, and rejects only a particular misuse of scripture in an ale-inspired sermon. Through Alison's dissent, Chaucer nonetheless stages a rebellion against unfit preachers and their interested uses of scripture, and, as if in play, challenges the authority of such homilists. He nudges the reader to recognize that a compromised preacher lacks even the authority of the Word he recites: outspoken dissent appears a right and proper response to one who preaches while under the influence. Chaucer pictures contemporary ecclesiastics' worst fear. A lay woman, given access to a vernacular Bible, defies both the Word and the "legitimate authority" interpreting it.[101] But Chaucer defuses the threat, transforming clerical anxieties into the comic subversion expected from a disobedient wife. In effect, he dramatizes the feminine dissent implicit in 1 Timothy 2, invents for that dissent a sympathetic motivation, and wins it a congenial reception. He turns exegesis inside out, discrediting "superior" androcentric interpretations, and giving the stage over to the feminine perspective that exegetes typically repress. Through Alison, Chaucer acts out a provocative inversion not only of Jerome's exegesis, but also of the gendered assumptions that shape most exegesis on 1 Timothy 2.

Alison's comic revolt diverts readers from the implicit threat of masculine misrule, replacing that danger with the safer literary code of the unruly woman, which ultimately only affirms the symbolic order.[102] After all, woman epitomizes disorder; this "fact" at once excuses her unruliness and rationalizes her subordination. Although comedic, however, Alison is not simply risible, nor, despite Chaucer's naïve literary pose, can he have been oblivious to the cultural tensions implicit in this passage, or to the likelihood that his portrait of Alison and her husbands might prompt nervousness in some quarters. Alison's husbands potentially make readers aware of masculine misrule, Lollard critiques of corrupt ecclesiastics, and the uncertain basis of symbolic order. For her part, Alison makes it possible to conceive of rebellion against masculine dominion, and of a masculine vice that justifies that rebellion. Insofar as the portrait of Alison and her husbands creates imaginative possibilities for readers, women as well as men, it could promote actual resistance to authority—particularly since authority appears vulnerable.

Chaucer uses the feminine persona both to critique male dominion and to redirect that critique into misogynistic comedy. This persona allows him obliquely to engage contemporary controversies over dominion and to interrogate masculine fitness for spiritual dominance. To this end, he gives Alison considerable subversive power. At the same time, he contains her power within conventional misogynistic limits, allowing readers, perhaps even inviting them, similarly to deflect the critique of men into a negative commentary on women.[103] The poet wavers between an ambivalent respect for Alison's subversive power—at once legitimating and discounting "her" critical perspective on masculine dominion—and his own uneasy deflection of that power.

Troubled Hierarchies

Scripture is nothing if not generative: it invites rereadings and edgy negotiations over meaning, provokes furious controversy, and inspires a vast array of texts, from straightforward biblical commentaries to polemical treatises, sermons, encyclopedic compilations, and poems. Exegesis obviously comes in many guises and can reward literary scholars who take for granted the verbal complexity, ambiguity, and, indeed, poetics of all cultural texts. The selection of texts in this chapter foregrounds the degree to which exegesis can also be performative: an assertion of authority, often against opposition—a bold claim on some fragment of perceived truth.

The nature of that performance changes considerably in the centuries covered here. Jerome and Chrysostom develop interpretive strategies that support their Christian praxis, and they assert their interpretations against acknowledged opposition and resistance. They represent an age of polemical exegetical contests. In their lifetimes, ecclesiastical power is still unsettled and decentralized, in the process of being consolidated; social and governmental institutions are not yet effectively aligned behind a single unified conception of the church. The rules of exegesis are only beginning to be invented. Peter Brown coins the term "Micro-Christendoms" to describe historical diversity in a later era of church history, but the term describes the disunified, local character of patristic Christendom as well.[104] Scripture is both the ground over which competing factions battle and, ultimately, the weapon with which the winners secure power. As we discover with Jerome and Chrysostom, the "winners" articulate social and ecclesiastical hierarchies that appeal to many of their contemporaries, perhaps most significantly because they buttress an unstable class and gender system of domination.[105] Exegesis plays an important role in legitimizing the transformation of ancient male social domination into Christian ecclesiastical authority.

The *Gloss* hides its compilers' exegetical performance and their labor of constructing a "universal" consensus out of just such disparate local interpretations. It presents a unified face of authority to its readers, one that brooks no contradictions or resistant readers. The work all but represses feminine subversion of the clerical agenda, though its rules for women's sexual behavior reveal anxiety about the limits of masculine control. The *Gloss* epitomizes exegesis at the height of its medieval cultural power, when it is used to privilege monastic asceticism and spiritual labor. It makes women irretrievably carnal, limiting them to the physical work of breeding. It stigmatizes women's speech as inherently deceptive and sinful, the source of the Fall; women apparently become incapable of pious speech, let alone authority. The *Gloss* effectively consolidates gendered social and ecclesiastical hierarchies and grants them a compelling theological rationale. In the process, it witnesses to important ecclesiastical innovations: a sanctified ideal of clerical privilege and a centralized organization of ecclesiastical power.

By the late fourteenth century various movements—to democratize learning, challenge clerical privileges, advance vernacular literature, and convey scripture to the laity in the mother tongue—once again destabilize ecclesiastical authority.[106] Composing the Wife's *Prologue* in this energizing context, Chaucer explores what might happen if women read scripture and spoke back to authority. He exposes the problematic arbitrariness of masculine exegetical dominion and overturns conventionally gendered discursive assumptions. By voicing his exegesis through a "carnal," unruly woman, he recreates feminine resistance to the historical construction of gendered power hierarchies. Of course, nothing really changes: a woman presents only a comic threat to male dominion and clerical privilege. Behind this fictional mask, Chaucer nonetheless raises serious questions about the legitimacy of masculine dominion, and about the authority of traditional exegesis.

Exegesis undergoes a series of transformations, as the discourse takes shape in the Micro-Christendoms of the patristic era, develops coherence in the twelfth century, and then fragments under the pressure of social and ecclesiastical changes in the later fourteenth century. These discursive transformations demonstrate that exegetical authority is always contested, always subject to revisionary supplements. Its social logic adapts to each new institutional or historical context, each new reader. As a consequence, exegesis lays bare the historical labor that goes into the formation of power hierarchies and gender roles. A feminist approach to the discourse is promising precisely because it foregrounds the often difficult personal, hermeneutic, and social struggles that pervade this literature, guiding us away from theological conceptions of church unity and toward an awareness of cultural diversity and contestation. In the process, we replace myth with history, sanctified signs with literary texts. We become more able to recognize dissent within the Christian community, from Jerome's explicit critique of patriarchal social order, to the Wife of Bath's dismissal of her husbands' sermons. As we interrogate exegetes' claims to power and authority, we begin to recognize that the ecclesiastical hegemony was always internally contested. The feminine voices through which exegetes reflect on these contests have received little scholarly notice, but even a limited survey demonstrates that these voices—even or perhaps especially when repressed—witness to the strategies by which exegetes invent, consolidate, and challenge ecclesiastical authority.

Feminist theory offers productive approaches to the historical reception of scripture, allowing us insight into the sexual tensions and anxieties that underlie constructions of biblical meaning, the gender performances that so profoundly influence exegetical discourse, and the perceived "feminine" subversions that exegetes attempt to correct through their readings of scripture. A feminist-historical method points up the tremendous disparities in the specific social logic of these four texts and allows us to perceive far-reaching shifts in the contexts and purposes of medieval exegesis, as well as in hermeneutic methods. The nervous repression of feminine authority, sexuality, and economic power that drives 1 Timothy 2 gives way to narrower ascetic and monastic agendas, and, finally, in Chaucer's poem, to a view from below (compromised, to be sure, by the misogyny incorporated into that view). Each work constructs power relations between ecclesiastical men and women tendentiously defined as laity, but each work also reveals the contested nature of those relations.[107] Masculine ecclesiastical power emerges from these works as unsettled. Those who articulate power—"Paul," Jerome, Chrysostom, the *Gloss* compilers, the husbands of Bath—at some level recognize "feminine" resistance to their programs. Each work suggests that such speakers reach for something beyond their grasp, seeking to create a conceptual reality that can never come into being. These influential works of the Western literary canon thus witness to an enduring, dynamic tension between clerical power and lay, feminine resistance. Far from naturalizing men's authority, these works represent it as tenuous, contingent, and anxious, undermined by a keen awareness that women can escape men's control, if only through their sexual desires. In this way, medieval exegetical literature invites a revision of modern theories that assume masculine domination is sustainable only when naturalized.[108] The works examined in this chapter suggest that the work of naturalizing dominance is more an ongoing process—susceptible to disruptions—than a perceived reality.

Dissenting women do not threaten the ideology of masculine power—they are easily contained by misogynistic stereotypes, as Alison is—but their presence in literature can nonetheless trouble the cultural imaginary. Women's fictionalized willingness to contest authority prevents a structure of domination from being naturalized. Exegetical literature therefore serves as a reminder of profound social conflicts: between clergy and laity, men and women, ascetics and the "worldly." Exegetes at times try to resolve such conflicts and pretend that society is unified: the *Gloss* compilers arguably do this; Jerome, Chrysostom, and Chaucer do not. The latter authors reflect cracks in the notional image of hierarchical order and suggest that the body of society—so often in the medieval era figured as an organic unity, each member contributing to the good of the whole—suffers internal struggles, its members clashing with each other, its purported harmony a mystifying fiction.[109] Unruly women expose the insecure basis of clerical authority, and the troubled social and gender hierarchies of medieval culture.

CHAPTER 3

GENDER TROUBLE IN AUGUSTINE'S
CONFESSIONS

[The psalmist] made God father; he made God also mother. God is father because He created, because He calls, because He commands, because He governs. God is mother, because She cherishes, because She nourishes, because She suckles, because She embraces.[1]

Augustine of Hippo has become a patristic myth, a father of the church alternately revered and despised for his influence over the Middle Ages, Reformation, and every age since. He comes to us robed in all the weight of tradition, the quintessential Great Man who exercises writers as diverse as Hannah Arendt and Jacques Derrida. It is hard to remember that he did not enjoy this aura at the start of his ecclesiastical career. Soon after his conversion, he unexpectedly became bishop of a minority church, outnumbered by the dominant Donatists of the region. As we saw in the last chapter, his was a polemical age, filled with vigorous contests over exegetical principles, and, indeed, over the very text of scripture. Augustine's voice was initially one of many, and not the most widely acclaimed among them. The local and divided character of Christianity did not favor exegetical consensus behind the bishop of Hippo—or Rome, for that matter. Augustine's past created additional difficulties for him when he was suddenly entrusted with an ecclesiastical position: he had a reputation as a Manichean to overcome, before he could establish his Christian credentials and authority as a bishop.[2] At this crucial turning point in his life, while preparing to assume episcopal office, he begins writing *Confessions* (c. 395), and in the process invents himself as a Christian bishop.[3]

Augustine rose to authority and power within the church, and achieved exceptional status, in part because he invented a compelling ecclesiastical persona. This literary self-fashioning is nowhere more apparent than in the flawed but insightful persona of *Confessions*.[4] Here he explains himself to his critics and to those skeptics who remember him as a Manichean; authorizes himself as an intellectual by detailing his journey through Neoplatonism to Christianity; and describes his conversion and present spiritual life. He concludes with an extended analysis of the creation account in Genesis, demonstrating his orthodoxy and command of scripture. *Confessions* situates exegesis firmly in the context of an individual confession of faith, particular life experiences, and intellectual vita. Indeed, Augustine makes autobiography and exegesis inextricable from one another in *Confessions*.[5] That choice distinguishes the work from his earlier, nonautobiographical commentaries on Genesis. Such a formal innovation can result only from a thoughtful purpose: Augustine obviously means to attach his exegesis to his life story. Perhaps more than any other work of the time, therefore, *Confessions* promises access to the personal as well as social logic of exegesis and to the strategies by which one exegete authorizes his interpretations in this contentious age. Gender is central to his authorizing strategies, but not in a conventional or predictable way. He accepts the role of man on top in some situations, yet he also challenges the legitimacy of that role. Gender hierarchy emerges from his work as a deeply problematic cultural construction not easily aligned with Christian faith.

Gender Trouble

When fashioning himself as priest and bishop, Augustine necessarily follows Christ, who proves a difficult model for a late antique Roman man: "For us he is victor and victim before you and victor because he is victim. For us before you he is priest and sacrifice, and priest because he is sacrifice. Before you he makes us sons instead of servants by being born of you and being servant to us."[6] Augustine defines Christ's manliness in terms radically different from those of dominant Roman culture, where masculinity is typically shown through the pursuit of power, rank, and precedence. Christ expresses manliness through an abdication of power, through chastity rather than sexual dominance.[7] By humbling himself, he achieves paradoxical reversals: the victim becomes victor; the sacrifice creates a priest. Augustine's Christ subversively rewrites Roman military and religious ideologies. He redefines victory by transferring the battle from a military to a spiritual realm; he reinvents priesthood by becoming the innocent sacrifice.[8] Christ rejects Roman standards of manliness.

To follow this deity is to identify not with power but with powerlessness: "My weakness is known to you," Augustine confesses, "I am a child [*parvulus*]."[9] He denies his adult status and ecclesiastical position, picturing instead his "infant condition" that must "suckle" at the breast of divine "wisdom."[10] Indeed, Augustine portrays himself throughout *Confessions* as a child or infant, his dependence on his deity figured through imagery that fuses maternal and Eucharistic implications: "When all is well with me, what am I but [an infant] sucking your milk and feeding on you."[11] He defines his episcopal role through similar tropes of inversion: "You have commanded me to serve them [fellow believers] if I wish to live with you and in dependence on you."[12] As a bishop, he enacts the roles of dependent servant or infant, wholly dependent on his deity.

Augustine's *imitatio Christi* emphasizes a dependence typically associated, in Roman culture, with women, children, and servants.[13] He treats this not just as an eccentric personal choice, but as essentially Christian. Stories of flawed pagan masculinity weave through the work, exposing cultural norms at odds with Christ's life. Augustine's father is marred by obdurate paganism, violence, lust, pride, and ambition. For the first part of his life, Augustine reenacts many of his father's sins; together, father and son make the man on top appear an exclusively pagan role. As converts, men reject not just pagan practices but also traditional masculinity. Hence the noble Victorinus enacts dependent roles after his conversion: he is "not ashamed to become the servant [*puer*] of your Christ, and an infant [*infans*] born at your font."[14] Modern scholars see this kind of humbling as feminization, and the text supports that analysis. Yet we should not reduce all powerlessness to feminization. Augustine's language at this point emphasizes multiple, related hierarchical inversions—adult male reduced to servant (*puer*), child (*parvulus*), or infant (*infans*)—rather than gender crossing. His strategies for feminizing himself are, as we will see, typically more direct than this.

Augustine and Victorinus are not so much feminized, as spiritualized after the example of Christ; faith reverses power relations (or, more accurately, the representation of power). In each case, the trope of inversion establishes fundamental disparities between the sacred order and the secular empire, between the community of faith and dominant Roman culture. Christ's, Victorinus's, and Augustine's spiritual gender roles implicitly critique Roman ideologies of power and authority. The trope of inversion speaks to Augustine's highest spiritual aspiration: like many medieval men, "he sought reversal because reversal and renunciation were at the heart of a religion whose dominant symbol is the cross—life achieved through death."[15] Augustine portrays himself as a bishop by reversing the terms of social power, by making himself one of the least rather than the greatest. This representation does not reflect reality (that is not the function of representations), but it does reveal Augustine's ideology of episcopal power/lessness.

When Augustine represents himself as a child, he pictures his deity as a mother.[16] The feminine deity is not one of the most widely celebrated aspects of Augustine's theology, but Robert J. O'Connell's close analyses of language and imagery establish her presence in Augustine's writings, including *Confessions*.[17] When the philosophically inclined narrator returns to the source of being, he consistently discovers feminine nurturance. This is not, of course, the only way Augustine describes his deity. He also draws vivid portraits of a divine bridegroom or spouse, a caring or punishing father, a healing physician.[18] Father and mother, bride and bridegroom, son and servant appear diverse aspects of one divine being. Clearly, gender does not apply to an immaterial deity in the way it does to material bodies. Material bodies prove similarly unstable, however, for Augustine appears not only as infant and servant, but also as son and bride.[19] Like the deity, the narrator seems to transcend his gendered body. His and his deity's multiple roles raise philosophical questions about the relationship between being—and being male or female.[20]

Much of *Confessions* depicts a narrator struggling to conform to his spiritual ideals, to be the servant rather than the master, the infant rather than the all-powerful mother or father. He assumes roles that deny power. At the same time, Augustine remains part of his culture and accepts some forms of masculine privilege. His occasional cultural conformism appears vividly toward the end of *Confessions*, when he comments on the Genesis creation narrative. He interprets the *imago dei,* the image of God manifest in humans, as "the power of reason and intelligence" by which humans reign over irrational animals, and men dominate women.[21] He presents himself to the reader (unironically) as the idealized man he writes about: privileged in his closeness to God, capable of subjugating his passions and his woman alike. He enacts a conventional masculine identity at odds with his self-fashioning elsewhere in *Confessions*. Augustine elaborates a similar interpretation in each of his two earlier commentaries on Genesis, and his confidence in repeating the point implies that it carries in his mind the unquestioned authority of bedrock catholic belief.[22]

By integrating exegesis with his life narrative, Augustine exposes contradictions between his faith in paradoxical reversals, and the dominant cultural role his audience expects him to assume, which he in fact needs to assume in order to assert episcopal authority. Far from resolving these contradictions, Augustine foregrounds them by picturing himself on the one hand as an infant nursing helplessly at god's breast, aspiring to Christlike humility, and on the other hand as a magisterial exegete, confidently wielding the authority of his office. When he appears as infant and servant, he implies that the traditional basis of masculine power is unsuitable for the church, which requires its leaders to sacrifice self and power. To become a Christian bishop is necessarily to subvert Roman gender norms. At the same time, the bishop does exercise power and must command the respect due to a man in dominant culture. Augustine's shifting images of himself imply his ambivalence about both Roman and Christian ideals: he cannot exclusively occupy either role. He therefore performs gender as a series of rhetorical masks, provisional literary faces that partially express his episcopal ideals.

By speaking through these several masks, Augustine creates a version of Judith Butler's "gender trouble": he challenges the basis of masculine power, subverts traditional gender norms, and disturbs the naturalness of gender identity.[23] He in fact disrupts precisely the hierarchical gender scheme usually attributed to "the Church Fathers."[24] Butler's theory helps to illuminate the performative and subversive aspects of Augustine's episcopal self-fashioning, but of course Augustine's ideas about gender depend on other, distinctly unmodern cultural and intellectual traditions.[25] This chapter examines two dominant sources for his gender ideology: his study of Neoplatonism and his understanding of scripture.

As he assumes his various masks, Augustine reveals something beyond the merely personal. His shifting roles disclose conflicts not only within himself, but also between an ancient social order and a nascent Christian gender ideology. Subsequent history obscures the dynamic possibilities of this particular moment by burying the "Fathers' " diversity under the sediment of a supposedly uniform orthodoxy and by tempting us to read into their works signs of things to come. When Augustine composes *Confessions,* however, there is no orthodoxy on gender issues, and his early representations of gender do not predict later developments, even in the narrow context of his own writings.[26] Rather, *Confessions* exposes fault lines between antique Roman cultural norms and Augustine's early aspirations for himself as a Christian. Straddling the fault lines in his culture, and in himself, Augustine wrestles with what it means for him to be a bishop. *Confessions* reveals his difficulties in conceptualizing and exercising a manly Christian power, in his life as in his exegesis. He both rejects and accepts the position of the man on top.

Suckling at Wisdom's Breast

Augustine adopts principles of Neoplatonism that lead him to privilege the transcendent word of God over the material text of scripture; and he bases his exegetical authority on his capacity to identify with a transcendent deity rather than on his command of worldly epistemologies or elegant rhetoric. During his years as a Manichean, he looks down on scripture, disgusted by its gross content and overly simple style. When

he first listens to Ambrose preach on the Old Testament, however, he
discovers that the texts that "seemed to contain perverse teaching" can
nonetheless reveal "spiritual" meanings.[27] Augustine does not record
Ambrose's actual interpretations, or tell how offensive narratives are
stripped of their literal veils and reclothed in the spirit, for he is not
concerned to rationalize an exegetical method or preserve specific interpretations.[28] To the contrary, he mystifies the apprehension of biblical
truth, presenting it as the gift of divine grace: "By believing I could
have been healed. My mind's eye thus purified would have been directed
in some degree towards your truth."[29] Knowledge of truth comes from
faith, through a spiritual process that renders scripture and sermon alike
seemingly redundant.[30] Ambrose introduces Augustine to a persuasive
way of reading, but "whether what he said was true" remains a crucial
open question for the skeptical auditor.[31]

At this pivotal moment in his progress toward conversion, Augustine
marginalizes reason: "we were too weak to discover the truth by pure
reasoning and therefore needed the authority of the sacred writings."[32]
In context, "pure reasoning" (*liquida ratione*) is code for Manichean
claims to knowledge, which he now rejects.[33] Since Manicheans mock
the Old Testament, Augustine demonstrates his orthodoxy by accepting
the canon, just as he will by interpreting Genesis in the final books of
Confessions. Notably, he begins the work with a deft allusion to Genesis:
"My faith, Lord, calls upon you. It is your gift to me. You breathed it into
me by the humanity of your Son, by the ministry of your preacher."[34]
Augustine conflates the creation of man in Genesis ("you breathed into
me") with his own recreation as a Christian ("by the humanity of your
Son"), anticipating an autobiography that will mirror the accepted biblical narrative of creation, fall, and redemption. From beginning to end,
he displays his orthodoxy and ability to connect the two testaments, the
first witnessing to creation and the second to recreation. His reverence
for all of canonical scripture, but especially Genesis, signals his departure
from Manicheism.

Although Augustine develops a lucid argument against Manicheans,
he does not detail the hermeneutic method by which he progresses from
"sacred writings" to "the truth." Scripture is given so that people might
"through it believe" in God, "through it seek" Him, and "reflect on" it
in God's presence.[35] Augustine takes his object of knowledge to be the
deity, not scripture; he discovers the deity "through" (*per*) the text. By
designating God the object of knowledge, Augustine renders masculine
privileges (education, study of scripture, ordination) extraneous to the
pursuit of truth. All believers—men and women, priests and laity—are
equally capable of spiritual insight. In other words, Augustine presents

spiritual knowledge as exclusive, but not exclusively clerical; the gift of grace, not of study.[36] Augustine's language suggests a prayerful openness to transcendent truth—a theory of inner illumination—rather than a specific interpretive method.[37] The linguistic details of the text (such as the variants that occupy Jerome as he labors over the Vulgate) appear almost irrelevant, the material body of the text rather than its real being (a point to which I will return in greater depth).[38]

Throughout *Confessions*, the tension between materiality and transcendent being reveals Augustine's debt to Neoplatonism.[39] His philosophical orientation is made explicit in two passages that narrate his ascent to transcendent truth. In the first ascent, at Milan, Augustine is raised into the symbolic light of the divine and discovers "the unchangeable and authentic eternity of truth" that "transcend[s] my mutable mind."[40] Neoplatonism structures the system of polarities evident in this ascent: immutable and mutable, eternal and temporal, being and body.[41] Philosophy gives Augustine an idea of spiritual transcendence and a language in which to describe the (dis)connection between his body and his deity. Guided by philosophy, his power of reasoning can "discover the light by which it was flooded."[42] This illumination enables Augustine's understanding of the God who is: "So in the flash of a trembling glance it [the power of reasoning] attained to that which is [*id quod est*]. At that moment I saw your 'invisible nature understood through the things which are made' (Rom. 1:20)."[43] The ascent climaxes in Augustine's recognition that scripture and creation manifest God's being. The passage advances with stunning economy a claim to divine illumination and presents the bishop as an exegete authorized by his knowledge of transcendent being.

Augustine immediately qualifies his authority by commenting retrospectively on his imperfect insight at the time of the ascent: "I thought of Christ my Lord only as a man of excellent wisdom…the mystery of the Word made flesh I had not begun to guess."[44] He comprehends that God may be understood through the creation and scripture, but he does not recognize Christ as the union of eternal being and mutable form, the visible sign of the invisible God. Only when the narrator discovers that truth, can he at last become one with the deity. He describes this union with mingled maternal and Eucharistic imagery: "The food which I was too weak to accept he mingled with flesh, in that 'The Word was made flesh' (John 1: 14), so that our infant condition [*infantiae nostrae*] might come to suck milk from your wisdom [*sapientia*] by which you created all things."[45] He represents himself as a powerless infant, utterly dependent on sustaining wisdom. What keeps him from knowing God in this way is not a flaw in his philosophy, but rather a lack of humility: "To possess God, the humble

Jesus, I was not yet humble enough. I did not know what his weakness was meant to teach."[46] By recognizing his own weakness, the narrator finally grasps the paradox of incarnation, the truth his philosophy cannot illuminate. The image of the infant at the breast implies Augustine's separation from adult learning, masculine independence, and self-will, and his recreation as an innocent bound closely to God. The narrator traces his progress from the ascent narrative, with its learned metaphysics, to his retrospective viewpoint, which discovers his infantile dependence. He depicts spiritual maturation paradoxically as regression. In this one brief passage, Augustine grounds his exegesis in both philosophical vision and infantile dependence, in effect juxtaposing an ancient system of masculine authority and its Christian inversion. The ascent allows the narrator at once to use a respected worldly epistemology and to reveal its limits.

The ascent narrative serves as a literary vehicle through which Augustine explores the bond between abstract being and bodies. Neoplatonic philosophy guides his approach to understanding his deity, and it provides him with a useful language and conceptual framework, but it can neither reveal the truth that comes through faith nor transform him.[47] Neoplatonism nonetheless continues to offer him a language and conceptual structure by which to narrate his increasing understanding of his deity, and through which to characterize his knowledge of a real but immaterial deity. After his conversion, he details another ascent, this one shared with Monica at Ostia: "Our minds were lifted up by an ardent affection towards eternal being itself...to the region of inexhaustible abundance where you feed Israel eternally with truth for food. There life is the wisdom [sapientia] by which all creatures come into being, both things which were and which will be."[48] The imagery of food and eating once again figures incorporation of the truth that exists beyond the realm of the senses, in the transcendent site of being. Wisdom signifies the life-giving and life-sustaining maternal aspects of Augustine's deity, the feminine power on which he depends.

This ascent elaborates Augustine's theory of scripture and the word, the foundation of his exegesis. He distinguishes between ephemeral words and a transcendent word, that is, between the body of language and its being. To arrive at knowledge of the deity, the soul must transcend both the body and language. Only when "all language and every sign and everything transitory is silent" does God "speak not through them but through himself."[49] Then, the narrative continues:

> We would hear his word, not through the tongue of the flesh, nor through the voice of an angel, nor through the sound of thunder, nor through the obscurity of a symbolic utterance. Him who in these things we love we

would hear in person without their mediation. That is how it was when at that moment we extended our reach and in a flash of mental energy attained the eternal wisdom which abides beyond all things.[50]

Language pertains to the mutable, transitory order of bodies, so language is at best a mediated and obscure expression of the God who is. Since wisdom is beyond words, Augustine reaches God by transcending material scripture. Both ascent narratives identify wisdom, not a text, as the object of knowledge, and divine illumination as the only reliable epistemology. The ascent narratives establish Augustine's knowledge of his deity as independent of scripture. He is like a baby suckling the milk of wisdom, like Israel feeding on the manna of truth. He uses Neoplatonism to subordinate the material text to the truth it imperfectly expresses.

Strikingly, Monica participates equally with her son in this ascent. Since surviving literature rarely pictures a woman engaging in philosophical dialogue, and perhaps never a shared ascent, her presence here demands attention.[51] The shared ascent draws together two narrative threads: Monica's visionary progress toward God and Augustine's inner journey through Neoplatonism to Christianity. From Augustine's childhood, Monica has participated in a mystical religion: a dream reassures her that her son will one day stand with her in her church; a vision promises her safe harbor from a storm at sea. Physical and metaphysical realms are bound closely together in her world, and her deity uses dreams and visions to reveal himself. As a mystic, she is not unique—a vision tells Ambrose where to find holy relics—but she is consistently authoritative: events confirm her visions. The narrative portrays her with one foot on earth, the other in heaven, as if her body, like Christ's, were a living bridge between time and eternity. Yet her fullest previous vision is humble in comparison, centered on homely concrete detail rather than philosophical images: "Her vision was of herself standing on a rule made of wood. A young man came to her, handsome, cheerful, and smiling."[52] Where Augustine ascends to abstractions (*sapientia, id quod est, veritas*), Monica sees a handsome youth. Their shared ascent draws Monica into Augustine's philosophical experience, giving her a part in the wisdom that evidences "no past or future, but only being."[53] The language dignifies Monica's piety by rendering it abstract. The narrative ascent fuses their separate mystical and philosophical experiences into one, uniting mother and son with the divine and with each other. Preceding her death by mere days, her visionary passage into eternity anticipates her imminent transfiguration, giving her life a hopeful narrative closure.

The ascent narrative also brings Monica's motherhood to an apt conclusion. Her maternity consistently embraces both flesh and spirit: she

"brought me to birth [*parturivit*] both in her body so that I was born into
the light of time, and in her heart so that I was born into the light of
eternity."[54] Monica prays for her son as she "births" him "in the spirit
[*parturiabat spiritu*]," much as she "travailed in labour [*parturiebat*]" for his
"eternal salvation."[55] Her spiritual maternity serves as a powerful model
for his writing: he brings her narrative to birth in his soul (*anima parturit*),
becoming his mother's mother.[56] The same verb (*parturire*) expresses their
acts of mutual maternal love before their ascent. The ascent identifies the
source of that love, the "wisdom by which all creatures come into being."
When they birth each other, they mirror the generative work of wisdom.

The narrative similarly pictures Monica's nursing as a reflection of
wisdom. In Augustine's infancy, she feeds him with the name of Christ:
the "name of my Saviour your Son, my infant heart had piously drunk
in with my mother's milk."[57] Augustine's witty play on "Word made
flesh" anticipates the image of suckling at wisdom's breast and associates
Monica with nurturing divine wisdom and spiritual rebirth. She bears
her son first in the flesh and then in the spirit, like the deity who creates materially and recreates spiritually. The imagery connects God and
Monica: God's maternity mirrors Monica's, as her mothering mirrors
God's. Sharing her son's ascent, Monica perfects her spiritual labor and
becomes one with her son; she also becomes one with the deity whose
love she reflects throughout her life. Monica's narrative thus progresses
from her son's fleshly birth to his spiritual rebirth and ascent to wisdom,
a progression that cogently transforms her from maternal body to mirror
image of divine wisdom. Augustine uses the ascent narrative to draw his
mother's spiritual biography to an elevated close.

If Monica's visionary experience becomes more philosophical at this
climactic moment, Augustine's Neoplatonism is, as it were, baptized,
drawn into the realm of her simple piety and faith. Fashioning himself as
an infant, Augustine incorporates his earthly and transcendent mothers'
milk and becomes one with them; he transcends the separation inherent
in bodily existence. Indeed, his spiritual journey culminates in the ascent
that fuses self with nurturing others. The ascent pictures mother and son
as one being: "with the mouth of the heart wide open, we drank in the
waters flowing from your spring on high, 'the spring of life.'"[58] As their
hearts open to take in life, they enjoy a metaphysical union. They think
and act as one: "we attempted in some degree to reflect [*cogitaremus*] on so
great a reality."[59] They know each other through their dialogue, but they
know also what is not expressed verbally: "We ascended even further by
internal reflection [*interius cogitando*] and dialogue and wonder."[60] Their
unity blurs the boundaries of self and other. Their minds move together.
Ascending with Monica to eternity, Augustine returns to the source of

being. In this complex metaphorical realm, that source is both his mother and the generative maternity of divine love, "the wisdom by which all creatures come into being."[61] Their ascent rewrites Augustine's erotic desire for women, turning the feminine into a philosophical source of being and image of wisdom.[62]

This ascent narrative weaves several threads—Augustine's Neoplatonism, Monica's visionary piety, and the maternal deity—into aesthetic and philosophical coherence. In eternity, the narrator is capable at once of childlike faith and manly erudition. His unity with his mother and mother God completes his preparation for exegesis, and he turns in the following books to comment on Genesis. Unlike many readers, I find the autobiographical narrative of the first nine books and the straightforward exegesis of the final four to be closely connected.[63] Taken as a whole, *Confessions* unfolds a carefully wrought structure that makes autobiography and exegesis interdependent: the narrator's long philosophical and spiritual journey prepares him for exegesis, and it explains the source of his insights; his commentary on Genesis, which begins in his first chapter and continues into the last one, elaborates his growing intimacy with his deity and increasing authority over the Word. From the first page to the last, *Confessions* presents exegesis as an intimate dialogue between a man seeking to understand scripture and his deity's ongoing revelation. Their collaboration is perfected in the final books that elaborate the quiet drama of their colloquy over the text of Genesis.

Integral to this collaboration is the union of the exegete and his deity, and maternal imagery continues to inflect that relationship. The fact that the deity also appears as father perplexes gender difference and disrupts traditional gender binaries. Postmodern gender theory offers various explanations for such confusion, but we should recognize that Augustine's principal debt to Neoplatonism—the idea that God is immaterial—virtually mandates gender instability. Gender pertains only to bodies. Just as the Word transcends spoken words, so does the deity transcend the gender attached to mutable bodies. Augustine's deity *is* neither gender and so can be represented figuratively as either or both. Philosophy teaches Augustine to treat gender as a transitory feature of mutable bodies, not as an aspect of being.

Augustine therefore calls on multiple gender codes to signify aspects of his relationship with his deity. When he represents himself an infant, his deity is a mother; when a child, his God acts as a father; when a priest, his salvation appears in his sacrifice; when an ardent bride, his lover responds as a bridegroom. Augustine destabilizes gender to capture the complex relationship between his embodied self and his eternal deity. The multiple roles assumed by narrator and God gradually imply the all-sufficiency of their relationship, which both mirrors and replaces all human relationships.[64] Consequently, the narrator's gender finally appears as unstable and situational—as figurative—as the deity's. The narrator transcends his gendered body; he renders distinctions between "masculine" and "feminine" increasingly uncertain. Gender becomes performative, a matter of roles assumed and set aside, like so many ephemeral costumes—or bodies. From the perspective of eternity, gender, like the body, is mutable.

Although Augustine confesses his intimacy with God on every page, he figures their bond most provocatively in the image of a mother and nursing infant. This image creates the narrator as humble, dependent on God, advancing nothing through his own power, intelligence, learning, or rhetorical skill. Like an infant, he can only incorporate the milk of wisdom the maternal deity provides for him. The infant at wisdom's breast expresses the security of utter trust, the sensual union of suckling lips and nurturing nipple. The images add emotional resonance and depth to the narrator's abstract philosophical representations of his deity and create evocative thematic parallels between his mother and wisdom, between himself and generative femininity. The mother-child union stands out, moreover, as Augustine's brilliantly counterintuitive definition of his own ecclesiastical authority: the motif emphasizes his human weakness and entire reliance on God.[65] Wisdom's babe stands for the obverse of traditional Roman masculinity and expresses the narrator's repudiation of pride and power, his trust in faith and inspiration over learning. As wisdom's child, Augustine claims no authority of his own— but a secure access to the truth he conveys to his readers. The imagery of philosophical ascent allows him to present himself as at once authoritative and self-effacing, commanding and weak.

The Problem of Power

As *Confessions* unfolds, Augustine defines himself as a bishop through the metaphor of philosophical ascent. Hence he figures his episcopal dependence on his deity with an image of maternal nurture: "Lord, we are your little flock ... Stretch out your wings, and let us find refuge under them."[66] Like a broody hen, God gathers her chicks under the protective shelter of her wings, giving safety and comfort to the fearful. Augustine acts only in submission to his deity: "I carry out your command by actions and words; but I discharge it under the protection of your wings (Ps. 16: 8; 35: 8). It would be a far too perilous responsibility unless under your wings my soul were submissive to you."[67] As bishop, Augustine rejects the social role of paterfamilias, and, at least ostensibly, denies the exercise of power: he acts only at God's command, and his agency consists only of submission.[68] In effect, Augustine relocates power to the eternal realm and authorizes himself by renouncing a traditional masculine role.

His renunciation belongs, of course, to the realm of rhetoric; he calls for no social revolution and may, like many of his contemporaries, actually help preserve the status quo of masculine privilege.[69] His symbols for the deity nonetheless make it possible to imagine a less hierarchical social organization, at least within the church, and to counter normalized patriarchal structures. Although Augustine's literary self-fashioning does not directly change the world, moreover, it does expose how the new bishop attempts to work out the implications of a faith that promises the greatest spiritual rewards to the least in society: "But God forbid that in your tabernacle the rich be preferred to the poor or the noble to those of low origin. You have chosen in preference the weak things of the world to confound the powerful, and you have chosen the low of this world and things that are despised."[70] How can a man who has attained high office, be one of the poor, the weak, the despised? Augustine's self-presentation in *Confessions* suggests that he takes the gospel challenge seriously. He critically assesses Roman cultural traditions, finds them inadequate for his spiritual mission, and rejects the role of a powerful Roman official. He aspires to become a servant, one of the least, unmanly by the standards of dominant culture. In this way, he marks his departure from conventional Roman gender roles and manly ambitions. He defines his episcopacy through tropes that destabilize gender and social hierarchies, setting his church apart from Roman power structures.[71] Indeed, the social meaning of his episcopacy is his alterity within dominant culture, the clear difference between this office and others, whether familial or imperial.[72]

Augustine could express his rejection of conventional manly power through a simple narrative *imitatio Christi,* and Christ's life certainly shapes his idea of spiritual manliness. In order to represent the ideal of inversion, however, he invents a more radical narrative model: he makes Monica the originary paradigm for his faith and the prototype for his priesthood. In his earliest experience, Christianity is a matriarchal religion, with Monica mediating between her son and the deity: "She anxiously laboured to convince me that you, my God, were my father rather than he [Patricius], and in this endeavour you helped her to prevail over her husband. His moral superior, she rendered obedient service to him, for in this matter she was being obedient to your authority."[73] Monica's service to her deity exemplifies her son's episcopal ideal: the spiritual power of powerlessness. The woman on top in religion is Augustine's boldest trope of inversion.[74] By adopting the virtues of humility, service, obedience, and subjection, Augustine follows his mother and forsakes his father.[75]

While Monica outwardly obeys her husband, she structures Christianity as a supersession of patriarchal order. Augustine uses her to voice the problem facing the Roman Christian—s/he can follow only one father—and attributes to her the idea that Roman social order does not reflect divine order. He uses her displacement of Patricius to focus his critique of social norms and of the dominant cultural values against which he defines his church. The visible flaws in Roman patriarchy motivate Augustine's trope of hierarchical inversion, and he presents his family as a microcosm of Christian truth: the least is actually the greatest, and the greatest, least. Monica therefore becomes the positive model for her son's life, leading him to present himself self-consciously as another obedient servant of the divine paterfamilias. Her instruction foreshadows Augustine's episcopal self-fashioning and prefigures his rejection of pride and temporal authority as the vestiges of a superceded pagan masculinity.

Augustine pushes Monica's exemplary role further when he describes her as a quasi-priestly figure. She is the first, and most consistently important, mediator between his soul and his deity. God speaks through her, as through an inspired priest: "whose words were they but yours [God's] which you were chanting in my ears through my mother, your faithful servant?"[76] Later, when he realizes that God is speaking through her (*per quam*, as God speaks through scripture), he regrets scorning her "womanish advice" (*monitus muliebres*).[77] Put another way, God assumes a despised "womanish" voice in order to instruct Augustine in his/her ways. The narrator must learn to listen respectfully to "womanish" words, putting aside his prejudices in favor of learning and eloquence. Not coincidentally, he must also learn to value the humble style of scripture, a parallel educational process. Augustine's retrospective account validates "womanish" speech, and it makes Monica's words a model for his own priestly speech. As a servant of God, he too humbles himself and submits to God's ways, becoming an instrument through which the divine voice may speak.

Monica appears more obviously a priest in her sacrifices on behalf of her son: "By my mother's tears night and day sacrifice was being offered to you [*sacrificabatur*] from the blood of her heart [*de sanguine cordis*]."[78] The evocative language of blood sacrifice elevates her sorrow to priestly mediation and creates her as a Christ figure, offering "the blood of her heart" to redeem her son. Like Christ, and like her son, she is both priest and sacrifice. She presents her son as a continual offering to God, and her faith restores him to life: "In her mind she was offering [*offerebat*] me before you on a bier, so that you could say, as you said to the widow's son 'Young man, I say to you, arise.' "[79] Augustine invents Monica as the privileged mediator between his soul and his deity, as the priest on whose faith and sacrifices his own priesthood is founded. Much as Monica mirrors God the mother in her maternity, she mirrors Christ in her priestly function. Augustine conceives of himself as priest by adopting her virtues, role as mediator, and sacrificial love. He feminizes himself in order to display his holy subversion of social order.

Whereas Augustine signifies men's faith by lowering them to the status of children and servants, he figures Monica's holiness by elevating her to the rank of "virile woman," picturing her in "the clothing of a woman but with a virile faith."[80] This compliment, though unfortunate from a modern point of view, is well-conceived to counterbalance Augustine's other gender inversions. Together, mother and son establish complementary tropes of reversal: Christianity turns the least into the greatest, and the greatest into the least. Augustine uses these tropes to articulate Christian humility and difference. As a "virile woman," Monica is set apart from dominant culture, just as Augustine is when he makes himself infant and servant in the faith, and when he makes her the narrative paradigm of his priesthood. Although hierarchical inversions affect the sexes in opposite ways, the narrative consistently turns the least in society into the greatest in faith, and the greatest into the least. The bottom of the social hierarchy becomes the top of the religious hierarchy. Such reversals are not ends in themselves, but part of a cyclical process: "In their weariness they fall prostrate before this divine weakness which rises and lifts them up."[81] The believer falls before the deity in order to be raised up again. The fall into humility prefaces a return to the source of being, in much the way that the soul falls into the body and then returns to eternity. Hierarchical inversions not only realize a gospel ideal, but they also adumbrate a Neoplatonic cycle of being.

A literary trope of inversion is not, of course, the same as a social revolution, nor does the trope argue for a positive attitude toward women other than Monica.[82] Augustine's *imitatio Monicae* is nonetheless significant in that it reveals his attempt to renounce familiar cultural expressions of power and authority and to invent a church consistent with the gospel. By associating himself with the lowly in society—by modeling himself as a bishop after the example of his mother, a married, lay woman who occupies the lowest rung on the ascetic ladder—he marks his fundamental difference from ambitious office holders, proud family men, and soldiers. He signals his difference also from more rigorous ecclesiastics who insist on ascetic hierarchies that denigrate women and the laity. His episcopal ideals poignantly expose his spiritual aspirations: his attempt to become a bishop in terms consistent with his faith, eliminating as well as he can the traces of manly pagan pride that thread through his life story. He makes himself unmanly to show his spiritual regeneration.

In this way, Augustine counters the abiding temptation of his office: "Lord, you alone exercise rule without pride... [another] kind of temptation (1 John 2:16) has not ceased to trouble me, nor during the whole of this life can it cease. The temptation is the wish to be feared or loved by people for no reason other than the joy derived from such power, which is no joy at all."[83] This is one of Augustine's few explicit comments in *Confessions* about the temptations associated with his episcopacy, and it helps us comprehend his purposeful self-abnegation. It is precisely because he recognizes in himself a "wish to be feared or loved" for his own sake—not as a representative of God—that he renounces power. By playing the part of child and servant, by following his mother's humble piety, Augustine repudiates the dangerous joy of pride.

Throughout *Confessions,* therefore, Augustine's self-fashioning represses his actual episcopal status, authority, and precedence. Such a sustained literary denial does not solve the problem of power; it does, however, let slip the bishop's awareness of a problem, and his desire to develop an alternative to traditional Roman dominance. As his literary mask disguises his supremacy, it also divulges his anxiety about wielding power, about being still a proud, ambitious Roman man. Power is the unresolved problem in Augustine's episcopal persona.

Augustine exposes a resistance to power built into the foundations of the church—not, as Michel Foucault would lead us to expect, the struggle of those without power, but the (for Augustine) more fundamental Christian resistance to the sin of wielding power. Augustine attempts to construct a symbolic universe in which a bishop holds no power, is in fact the least of all—like a devout lay woman, like a babe in arms. This construction reveals his desire to enact saintly extremes, to separate from the world and depend wholly on his deity. He presents himself to his imagined reader as if he were a desert saint, another Antony of Egypt, defined by his ascetic difference and repudiation of social norms, by his visible alterity from dominant culture.[84] Of course, Augustine is a bishop, not a desert monk; he cannot pursue the extremes of ascetic powerlessness. His discursive self-fashioning can at best compensate for the constraints of his office. Only in *Confessions* can he perform the role of child and servant, heir to his mother's faith and priestly sacrifices; only in discourse can he renounce the world as if he were a desert saint. Creating himself as child, servant, and womanish priest, he performs his asceticism best before a reading audience. For, as Richard Valantasis perceptively argues, "Every kind of asceticism involves an audience (whether personal, social, or divine), and, therefore, every asceticism becomes a performance."[85]

Confessions reveals a conflict between Augustine's desire for dominion, inherited from his Roman past, and his ascetic self-abnegation, the legacy of his mother, the desert saints, and Christ. His literary self-fashioning reveals a fundamental contradiction between his ascetic ideals and the power he holds as bishop—and his inability, at this point in his episcopacy, to resolve that contradiction. He conceives of his deity in terms of the absolute power a mother has over an infant's life and well-being, but he does not imagine himself exercising a similar power over his children in the faith. This is perhaps hardly surprising, given Augustine's historical circumstances. Twenty-first century women, with a long feminist history behind them, likewise have trouble recognizing or devising nontraditional expressions of power.[86] Augustine later abandons the ideal of inversion and ascribes to a traditional patriarchal order for both church and state.[87] His literary experiment with gender inversions nonetheless reveals his capacity to think beyond the constraints of social norms and to recognize in his mother a challenging model of Christ-likeness, the rock upon which a church could have been built. Similar inversions and uses of maternal imagery recur in the later history of the church and suggest churchmen's persistent awareness of the problem of power, their ambivalence about ecclesiastical authority, and their desire to demonstrate, to themselves and each other, their dependence on God alone.[88]

Manly Exegesis

Developing his exegesis of Genesis in the final books of *Confessions*, Augustine claims a divine inspiration that transcends the separation of self and other, recalling and extending the implications of his narrative ascents to a mother God. Just as Neoplatonism influences his theory of gender, so it shapes his practice of exegesis. In the final, explicitly exegetical books of *Confessions*, however, he complicates his gender ideology. In the context of the present study, his revisions of gender are most provocative for the ways they gradually exchange the garb of humble child for robes of exegetical manliness.

Augustine bases his exegesis in *Confessions* on a Neoplatonic-inspired distinction between the human language of scripture and the divine Word: the former temporal, mere sounds that strike the "external ear"; the latter eternal and uncreated, heard in the "internal ear."[89] The Word is to words as Being is to bodies, or as eternity is to time: as God puts it, "scripture speaks in time-conditioned language, and time does not touch my Word, existing with me in an equal eternity."[90] Since the Word (truth) exists in eternity, the only way to access it is through divine inspiration: Augustine claims that "With you [God] inspiring me I shall be affirming true things, which by your will I draw out of those words."[91] Since the narrator can arrive at truth only through inspiration, he turns, at moments of potential controversy, to the God who speaks with a "loud voice" in his "inner ear."[92] As the inspired auditor of the Word, the narrator bypasses the variable form of scripture's material text and the learned hermeneutics centered on that text.[93] He produces exegesis through prayer, making God both the object of knowledge and its sole source. As he describes his exegesis, the work often has little to do with words per se: "Within me, within the lodging of my thinking, there would speak a truth which is neither Hebrew nor Greek nor Latin nor any barbarian tongue and which uses neither mouth nor tongue as instruments and utters no audible syllables. It would say: 'What he is saying is true.' "[94]

Augustine's philosophy of the transcendent Word supports his representation of himself as inspired; indeed, such a philosophy makes inspiration the only reliable route to knowledge.[95] The inspired persona implies Augustine's humility: he adds nothing to truth, but only inscribes what God speaks in his heart. In short, he devises in *Confessions* a mask of sanctity that presents him to the reader as an absolutely authoritative and virtuously humble exegete. The narrator therefore appears much the same in the narrative ascents that establish his access to transcendent truth, and in the exegetical prayers that enact his continuing illumination. Neoplatonism unifies Augustine's narrative ascents with his exegetical methods.

Augustine most fully develops his inspired persona in the final books of *Confessions,* which become a tour de force performance of sanctified ecclesiastical authority. His earlier attempts at interpreting Genesis, *On Genesis against the Manichees* (c. 388–89) and *On the Literal Interpretation of Genesis: An Unfinished Book* (c. 392–93), bring his invention of this extraordinary persona into sharp relief. Neither of the earlier works presents Augustine as an inspired exegete.[96] In the first commentary, the persona derives his authority from the consensus of "learned men" he represents.[97] He develops a straightforward rational discourse, seeking to establish clear differences between Manichean and catholic interpretations of Genesis: "they [Manicheans] say that there exists an evil nature…we [Christians] say that there is no natural evil."[98] The first person plural constructs a unified church ("we" all believe the same thing); "they" are an equally unified Other. Augustine makes no claim to divine inspiration and records no prayers for divine guidance, let alone answers to such prayers. Arriving at exegetical conclusions is a more mundane business than it becomes in *Confessions*. In the subsequent unfinished literal commentary on Genesis, Augustine appears less confident about drawing conclusions and proposes one interpretation after another, typically without concluding in favor of any. The unfinished commentary has, as Robert J. Teske aptly remarks, a "hesitant and aporetic character."[99] Here Augustine claims neither to be inspired, nor to know God's (or perhaps any) meaning for the scriptural text. The earlier commentaries help us recognize the novelty of Augustine's exegetical persona in *Confessions*, which allows divine illumination to fill the unsatisfying lacunae in human understanding. By means of the inspired persona, Augustine cogently authorizes his exegesis and himself as bishop.[100]

As we have seen, Augustine celebrates in *Confessions* a single, unified Truth. This does not lead to a single interpretation of any part of scripture, for he does not hesitate to develop multiple interpretations of passages that interest him. His exegetical principles in *Confessions* allow for a plenitude of meaning without aporia. Although extraordinarily intimate with his deity, he in fact produces few definitive interpretations in the final books of *Confessions*, and those typically corrections of Manichean error. Augustine focuses on authorizing his process of discovering truth, rather than on advancing decisive conclusions. Since exegesis is an ongoing, developing dialogue with God, the narrator can and perhaps must return many times to a single text. He does so in *Confessions* with one passage that resonates for him: the moment in Genesis when God creates man in his own image. In the course of *Confessions*, Augustine addresses this passage at least four times, and each time discovers anew its potential for meaning. He does not produce a single, exclusively authoritative interpretation; instead, he demonstrates how the verse reveals particular truths, no one of which excludes the others.

Initial Error

Augustine begins his exegetical journey in error: "I was wholly ignorant of what it is in ourselves which gives us being, and how scripture is correct in saying that we are 'in God's image.'"[101] This crystallizes Augustine's Manichean error—his belief that God has the material form of a human body. The retrospective point of view allows him at once to recount his temporary lack of knowledge and show how efficiently Neoplatonism solves the philosophical problem: our being is created from God's image. He uses Genesis to correct Manichean errors about the Old Testament and to demonstrate that sect's philosophical poverty.

Christian Manliness

Augustine next reads the creation as an allegory for Christian conversion, using New Testament promises of renewal to unlock the Christian meaning of Genesis. According to this analysis, the creation prefigures an inner recreation, for the person "whose renewal is in the mind and who contemplates and understands your truth."[102] This soul learns of and from God and grows into the image of God: "So man is 'renewed in the knowledge of God after the image of him who created him' (Col. 3:10)."[103] This renewal depends on God's minister, "who generates sons [*filios*] by the gospel (1 Cor. 4:15) and does not wish to have permanently immature believers [*parvulos:* lit., little ones] fed on milk [*lacte nutriret*] (1 Cor. 3:1–2) and cherished as if by a nurse (1 Thess. 2:7)."[104] God's minister exhibits spiritual manliness: he brings forth sons, weans them from breast milk and nurses, and gives them the knowledge they need to mature. The sons become manly by outgrowing a childlike dependence on nurses and breasts. In other words, manliness, for both the priest and his spiritual sons, depends on separation from a social dependence coded as feminine. Here Augustine defines maturity in the faith as an adult masculinity that excludes the feminine Other. Renewed in the image of God, men become...manly. The commentary reverses the narrative image of Augustine as an infant taking in the milk of wisdom, and replaces dependence on the deity's nurturance with an idealized masculine genealogy and independence. As a minister, Augustine assumes the hitherto problematic role of paterfamilias. The minister's manly potency and a child's trusting passivity are alternating images of Augustine's episcopal authority. Clearly, for him neither image in itself adequately defines his episcopacy. As Augustine vacillates between conventional power roles and Christian inversions, he evidences ambivalence about the roles and images available to him.

In its biblical context, the verse in Genesis literally narrates the creation of the material body, but Augustine here ignores that level of meaning to emphasize the verse's unity with the New Testament. The creation of Genesis transforms into the recreation of Romans and Colossians, and the image of God becomes the Christian knowledge of doctrinal mysteries. Augustine's intertextual method serves a twofold purpose. On the one hand, he translates the creation account into an allegory about believers' recreation, discovering the verse's immediate spiritual relevance for Christians. On the other, he implicitly argues against Manicheans, using the apostolic texts they accept to reveal the meaning of a book they scorn: once again, the former Manichean demonstrates his orthodoxy and hermeneutic agility. In the process, he aligns himself with the consensus of learned men he seeks to represent against the Manicheans. By endorsing the long-established and almost universally accepted role of adult male, he appears an uncontroversial exegete, respectful of catholic tradition and conventionally authoritative.

Augustine's gender performances respond to particular discursive problems. When he seeks to establish his Christian identity against that of his pagan father and dominant culture, he enacts the role of humble dependent. To put distance between himself and Manicheans, he plays the part of traditional catholic man. He adapts his gender role to set himself apart from the Other, be that Other a pagan father, an immature believer, or a Manichean. Augustine's continual refashioning of his persona generates contradictions. Finally, his shifting self-presentation demonstrates a Neoplatonic truth: gender is relational and performative, never an aspect of being.

The Power of Reason

In his continuing argument against Manicheans, Augustine returns again to the creation of man, this time reading it as the originary account of a hierarchical order that unifies microcosm and macrocosm:

> We see [*videmus*] the face of the earth adorned with earthly creatures and humanity, in your image and likeness, put in authority over all irrational animals by your image and likeness, that is by the power of reason and intelligence. And as in his soul there is one element which deliberates and aspires to domination, and another element which is submissive and obedient, so in the bodily realm woman is made for man. In mental power she has an equal capacity of rational intelligence, but by the sex of her body she is submissive to the masculine sex. This is analogous to the way in which the impulse for action is subordinate to the rational mind's prudent concern that the act is right. So we see that each particular point and the whole taken all together are very good.[105]

At each point in the grand cosmic scheme, the power to dominate pairs with the power to submit, so that each pair—the capacities of the soul, man and woman, human and animal—reflects the created order of the whole. This passage forms the crescendo of an extended argument against Manichean dualism, and it seeks to demonstrate the goodness of creation, its intelligibility, and orderliness.[106] Augustine describes created order in the gnomic present tense—*videmus*, we see something at all times true—thereby eliding differences between the garden of Eden and post-lapsarian society. He makes God's original design for his creation survive the Fall unchanged, and he uses the immutable beauty of this order to prove the Manicheans wrong. Manicheans, who scorn the material world, miss the goodness of created order.

Of course, the idea of an immutable order in the human microcosm ignores original sin, which, in Augustine's theology, radically alters the dominance of mind over body, reason over passion. Earlier in the work, Augustine devotes considerable space to proving that reason or intelligence alone cannot dominate passion, and that the fallen will is inherently corrupt and divided.[107] In the post-lapsarian world of Augustine's experience, masculine reason, though designed to govern impulse, fails to do so; the capacity of the soul aligned with beasts and the womanly body, and meant to be submissive, is anything but. The whole of *Confessions* renders the hierarchical order of microcosm and macrocosm a distant, unrealizable ideal and anticipates its failure. No one, after the Fall, can so perfectly subdue the impulsive flesh, to say nothing of animals or women. Augustine's continuing struggles with temptation after his conversion, even in his sleep, make the corruption of the will, the internal rupture caused by the Fall, an inescapable part of daily life.

In context, the idea of an immutable created order, which supports both rational domination of self and masculine dominion over others, presents obvious difficulties.[108] The idea is in itself traditional and familiar to his contemporaries, however, and Augustine probably inserts it here precisely because it is familiar and, from the perspective of dominant culture, incontrovertible. His pressing concern is to refute the Manicheans, and this particular passage borrows the authority of the Aristotelian philosophical tradition in order to refute Manichean error. The urgency of affirming the goodness of created order trumps, for the moment at least, the ideal of the church as different from dominant culture.

Confessions presents contradictory models of the human condition: an immutable created order in which rational self-governance prevails; and a post-lapsarian order in which a divided will is at war with itself.[109] Reason and man are on top—and not. Focused on denying Manichean principles, and seeking the most compelling argument for his purpose, Augustine may be unaware of the fundamental contradictions between these ideas of creation. From a distant historical perspective, however, the divergent threads of his work call attention to a widening gap between ancient social theory and a new theology of sin and grace.

God as Reason

Augustine offers one final allegorical interpretation of the *imago dei,* in which he once again interprets Genesis through New Testament promises of renewal. The creation of matter is now analogous to the formation of the church: the Spirit hovers over the waters to raise the godly out of their sins; the spirits of the godly become lights in the firmament; the sacraments appear as the firmament. Finally, God creates the allegorical Adam, the "living soul" of the believer:

> Then you formed [*formasti*] 'the living soul' of the faithful [*fidelium animam vivam*] with their affections disciplined by a strong continence. Then you

renewed [*renovasti*] the mind (Rom. 12:2) after your image and likeness (Col. 3:10) to be subject to you alone and in need of no human authority as a model to imitate. You subjected [*subdidisti*] its rational action to the superiority of the intellect, as a woman to her husband.[110]

The deity, the grammatical subject of the active verbs in this passage, recreates the mind after his/her image and likeness, subjecting "rational action" to "intellect." Augustine thus emphasizes the deity's creative power and subordinates human agency to divine. The reference to a woman and her husband recalls the conventional Aristotelian order, which we have seen Augustine use against the Manicheans. Here, however, Augustine significantly alters that order. Most obviously, he no longer expects humans to rule themselves by reason. Agency belongs to God, and God alone subjects impulse to reason. The allegory represents God rescuing the godly from sin and bringing them into a new creation, the church. This allegory reconciles the omnipotent deity and the fallen human will in a new (re)created order. In this context, Augustine minimizes woman's subjection to man, presenting it not as part of a detailed microcosmic-macrocosmic scheme that renders woman's body analogous to passion and irrational animals, but merely as an analogy for the order God creates within the faithful soul.

The "living soul of the faithful" and the renewed "mind" in this passage are not gendered male or female. The allegory presents the godly as the stars in the firmament, their gender erased, and the equality of their souls made visible: "you kindled lights in the firmament, your saints 'having the word of life' (Phil. 2:16), shining with a sublime authority made manifest by spiritual gifts."[111] The image reveals the transcendent reality of the church: all the saints share in divine illumination and authority. The allegory extends the authority of Augustine's own illumination to all the saints, making the bishop one of the flock. Despite the equality of the faithful, however, a subtle hierarchy reenters the church.[112] The lower rank of the faithful possess the authority of their spiritual gifts and are "subject" to the "authority of [the] book"; while the upper rank have a "higher authority" and are subject directly to God.[113] The transcendent church affirms both the equality of the faithful, and the need for priestly mediators between the deity, signified through book and sacraments, and the faithful. All are alike in their submission to God and to each other, as all are alike in their capacity for spiritual gifts; yet traces of Roman cultural order persist in the structure of the eternal church.

Augustine variously subverts traditional hierarchical order, endorses it, and rewrites it. Gender reversals and inversions disclose differences between the church and dominant Roman culture; ancient gender hierarchy enables a persuasive rebuttal of Manicheism; the equality of believers witnesses to the recreation that is the church. In the course of *Confessions,* Augustine's shifting gender schemes reveal conflicts between dominant social order and his Christian ideology. Despite (or perhaps because of) his occasional attraction to hierarchical order, gender is an unsettled, conflicted issue in *Confessions.* Although his occasional assertions of gender hierarchy imply the compelling power of that scheme in some contexts, and perhaps his own covert longing for masculine dominance, *Confessions* vividly illustrates how remote the ideal is from his own experience and highest spiritual aspirations. Versions of the ancient hierarchical ideal, though several times reiterated in these final books, must finally be interpreted within the larger context, where reason appears a seriously compromised guide, and where, from the bishop's retrospective viewpoint, the desire to dominate is only pagan pride.

Exegesis in History

By putting on and taking off his variously gendered masks, Augustine fashions for himself an unstable gender identity. When he comments on Genesis toward the end of *Confessions,* he nonetheless affirms traditional hierarchies of male and female, reason and sensuality, reinstating the cultural model he has so thoroughly challenged. He enacts a Christian gender identity at once radically different from and continuous with that of pagan Romans. Christian gender becomes a paradoxical construction, a union of opposites, neither of which can be fully occupied. Like all paradoxes, this one is inherently equivocal. Once "masculine" and "feminine" become sites of contested meaning, subject to redefinition, they no longer present as authoritative truths. Throughout *Confessions,* Augustine creates the "subversive confusion" that, in Judith Butler's theory, destabilizes "naturalized and reified notions of gender that support masculine hegemony and heterosexist power."[114] In short, he troubles the notion of a gendered being, and thus of an innate gender hierarchy.

Augustine's *Confessions* expresses ambivalence about Christian gender identity: he alternately celebrates and denies masculine privilege, asserts and eschews manly poses. His narrative persona is composed of diverse pieces, drawn from ancient philosophy, contemporary social norms, textual exempla (Victorinus, Christ), gospel ideals, and human models, both masculine and feminine. In part because created from so many puzzle pieces, each offering a glimpse of Augustine's world, *Confessions* develops a complex portrait of religious identity, perhaps most satisfying because the narrator refuses to succumb to one-dimensional stereotypes or a binary notion of gender. The work reminds its readers that the bishop occupies multiple positions in the social and symbolic orders, some of which conflict with each other. Because Augustine self-consciously explores gender in his study of scripture, he reveals how existing social norms are both projected onto scripture and undermined by biblical models. In short, he demonstrates a potentially dynamic interplay between culture and scripture, which, for him at least, sometimes challenges social norms.

Adrienne Rich exhaustively defines patriarchy as "the power of the fathers: a familial-social, ideological, political system in which men—by force, direct pressure, or through ritual, tradition, law, and language, customs, etiquette, education, and the division of labor, determine what part women shall or shall not play, and in which the female is everywhere subsumed under the male."[115] (Only a poet could get so much into one sentence.) The early Christian foundations of this system are obviously far from monolithic, whatever we might believe about later developments. For Augustine, masculinity is both inescapable and suspect precisely because it is bound up with a "familial-social, ideological, political system." From his perspective as a new bishop, the church is not supposed merely to perpetuate that system, but to redefine it. As he invents his episcopal persona, he envisions an ideology of power/lessness that conforms to the example of Christ and his own mother. This does not mean he escapes complicity with patriarchal "ritual, tradition, customs" and the rest; yet he adds to the historical record a serious critique of conventional masculine power, and an invitation to rethink the relationship between social hierarchy and religious community. His philosophically informed inquiry into the nature of being offers a provocative alternative to the modern conceptual foundations of gender theory, an alternative worth studying if only to recover the astonishing complexity of gender discourses in the early church, which are later repressed, and finally lost to history. Certainly, his work counters any tendency we might have to universalize the idea of God the father in the early church. *Confessions* invites us to rediscover and perhaps reclaim the still invigorating implications of Augustine's early meditations on gender and religion, in which the "church father" repudiates that title.

Confessions insists that we understand exegesis in relation to complex personal, historical, and philosophical contexts.[116] It does not pretend biblical interpretation is an objective, rational discourse, but rather makes exegesis an act of self-exposure. The work details close connections between particular life experiences and hermeneutic agendas. Difficult struggles with sexual impulses gradually develop into interpretations of Paul's internal warfare, Eve's creation, and Adam's temptation—allowing us to trace the transformation of desire into discourse, experience into (s)exegesis.[117] Augustine's autobiography foregrounds the subjective pressures on biblical interpretation, articulating at every moment the presence of the unique individual at the center of the exegetical project. Although Augustine closely integrates autobiography and exegesis, his readers often separate the two. For centuries, scholars have sought to understand his exegesis by plucking discrete interpretations out of context, and reading them as if they were self-contained, unconnected to the life experiences and web of thought in which he embeds them. Scholars even now select, for instance, the passage that grants man the power of reason, and treat that passage as complete in itself, almost self-explanatory. Medieval exegetes gathered this passage together with other similar works and presented the collection as a coherent interpretive tradition. In this way, texts like the *Gloss* create a conservative, authoritative consensus about what any passage of scripture means.[118] This selectively encyclopedic method invents exegesis as a transcendent and unified discourse, exhibiting at every moment the Spirit that inspires it. Taken out of context, this one analysis of Genesis presents a seemingly coherent and, for later Catholics, authoritative teaching about gender hierarchy. Theology may be served by this method; historical scholarship is not. Augustine's teaching about the *imago dei,* much less about gender, does not reside in any single passage, but in his long process of discovering the truths of creation and recreation, by listening to his deity teach him, often in a womanish voice, about his dependence on another. No particular analysis of the *imago dei* presumes to state the definitive truth, or presents Augustine's last word on the subject. Each interpretation supplements preceding analyses and expands scripture's potential meaning. Augustine treats gender hierarchy as just one of several strategies for disputing Manichean claims, compelling in that limited context, but useless for defining the bishop's relationship to his deity or his flock. What he actually endorses in *Confessions* is not gender hierarchy but gender trouble.

CHAPTER 4

AFFECTIVE EXEGESIS IN THE FLEURY
SLAUGHTER OF INNOCENTS

In order to make up our minds we must know how we feel about things; and to know how we feel about things we need the public images of sentiment that only ritual, myth, and art can provide.[1]

Augustine is not alone in conceiving of God as mother. Similar images of the deity reappear in many twelfth-century Cistercian texts, when, as Caroline Walker Bynum demonstrates, writers wish to express their pious withdrawal from "the world" and dependence on God alone.[2] In Professor Bynum's analysis, maternal imagery articulates "a new sense of God, which stresses his [*sic*] creative power, his love, and his presence in the physical body of Christ and in the flesh and blood of the eucharist."[3] Gazing on the body of Christ, twelfth-century Cistercians see his likeness to humans—his vulnerable infancy, his capacity to bleed and feel pain. Their focus on Christ's human body creates positive possibilities for real and imagined women, not only stigmatized as the flesh, but also redeemed through the flesh. Professor Bynum accordingly associates affective Cistercian devotion with a "feminization of religious language," apparent not only in images of God as nurturing mother, but also in increased devotion to feminine figures (saints, the Virgin), and in praise for stereotypically feminine characteristics (weakness, humility, tears).[4] The focus on affect encourages representations of the feminine in religion—mother deity, mother church, mother saint, mother abbot— and enhances the value of "feminine" virtues such as mercy, tenderness, and love.

Affective religion is of course not limited to the Cistercians, nor does it live only in the monastic writings Bynum examines (chiefly letters and sermons). Of all the genres in this highly literate age, liturgical drama most blatantly stimulates affective responses to scripture, which is doubt-less why poignant scenes of the nativity and resurrection are regularly performed in the cathedrals, churches, and monasteries of twelfth- and thirteenth-century Europe. Liturgical biblical plays act out what Clifford Geertz calls "public images of sentiment": the Magi rejoice at the nativ-ity, the Marys grieve at the sepulcher. The plays show the faithful not only what they should know about scripture, but as significantly what they should feel and how they should express their sentiments. Liturgical drama functions as an authoritative guide to affective devotion. To the extent that the plays selectively reproduce scripture (expanding here, condensing there), they also, inevitably, comment on it. Indeed, the plays develop an innovative form of exegesis, at times dependent on academic exegesis, at other times independent of it. As significantly, they achieve what academic exegesis does not attempt: they kindle emotional responses to scriptural narratives.[5] Liturgical drama is consequently among the most compelling "affective technologies" of the Middle Ages.[6]

The Fleury *Slaughter of Innocents* (*Interfectio puerorum*) exemplifies both the affective power of liturgical drama and its innovative contributions to exegesis. The play enlarges on an emotionally charged (apocryphal) narrative in the gospel of Matthew: Herod orders the death of the infant Christ, who escapes into Egypt while the Innocents die in his place; Rachel laments the infants' deaths, fulfilling an Old Testament prophecy; finally, Herod dies, Christ returns to Galilee, and the Innocents enact the resurrection of the saints.[7] Literally, the Innocents are Jewish boys, and the story is about Jewish suffering during an oppressive Roman occu-pation. Academic exegetes rewrite the narrative, turning the Innocents into Christian children, and the murderers into Jews. Hence the pre-eminent contemporary authority, the *Gloss* (*Glossa Ordinaria*), identifies the Innocents as the first Christian saints martyred by Jews.[8] A com-mentary on Matthew formerly attributed to Bede (ca. eighth century), and Thomas Aquinas's *Catena Aurea* (compiled ca. 1261–64) offer similar interpretations and witness to an exegetical tradition extending from the eighth century to the thirteenth.[9] These interpretations advance the idea that Jews are (in the present, as in the past) actively antagonistic toward all things Christian—a stereotype evident in many discourses throughout the twelfth and thirteenth centuries.[10]

The *Gloss*, Pseudo-Bede, and Aquinas present their authorities as if they formed an essentially unchanging hermeneutic community—as if the church spoke in one incontrovertible voice. Although points of agreement certainly exist, the impression of a unified interpretive com-munity derives more from literary art than from an objective transhistor-ical consensus. As we have seen, exegesis is not monolithic. Interpretive emphases vary from work to work, and, from a historical perspective, these variations are at least as important as areas of consensus. This chapter therefore examines the Slaughter narrative in academic exegesis and liturgical drama, seeking to establish dominant interpretive traditions as well as differences among exegetes' representational strategies and thematic emphases. Academic exegesis and liturgical drama are arguably best understood as complementary intertexts. Only by grasping the methods of academic exegesis can we recognize a playwright's innovations; only by comprehending a playwright's strategies can we appreciate academic exegetes' silences and tendency to rely on abstraction. In short, this chapter examines academic exegesis and the Fleury play together in order to discern how each establishes the meanings and affective implications of the biblical Slaughter of Innocents and how each presents Rachel's authority as an exegete.

The anonymous author of the Fleury *Slaughter* is certainly familiar with and influenced by academic exegesis, but he does not merely repeat existing interpretations. Just as exegetes revise earlier texts, so the playwright rewrites academic exegesis. Whereas academic exegetes comment rationally on Herod, the children, and Rachel, the playwright mobilizes them in space, gives them voices, and through them advances affective devotion to the body of Christ. The play thus expands on exegetes' learned demonstrations of Jewish guilt and calls attention to Christ's and Christians' human vulnerability. In the play, Herod realistically performs the guilt and violence attributed to him, the first Jew who tries to kill Christ, the Jew who actually kills Christian children. He is a concrete form of exegetes' featureless "hermeneutical Jew."[11] Silent in academic exegesis, the Innocents are similarly fleshed out in the play, where they explicitly identify with Christ and proceed willingly to martyrdom. Their deaths turn exegetes' abstract conflict between Jew and Christian into a scene of heartbreaking pathos. Rachel, who appears fleetingly in the book of Matthew, becomes the affective center of the play after the Innocents fall. As we will see, academic exegetes have difficulty deciding on Rachel's significance; ignoring interpretive issues, the playwright simply exploits her affective potential. He uses her to voice a mother's inconsolable grief in emotionally powerful phrases of great lyrical beauty. Through these dramatic characters, the playwright reaccentuates both scripture and exegesis, recreating the ancient narrative through the voices and actions of violent Jews, heroic children, and a loving mother. The audience learns what happens in the Slaughter; more significantly, they learn how they should *feel* about the ancient scene. In short, the Fleury *Slaughter* uses the unlearned dramatic perspectives of children and a woman, the perspectives excluded from academic exegesis, in order to convey the emotional meaning of scripture. The play treats the least in the ecclesiastical hierarchy, as greatest in affective power.

Unfortunately, this particular "feminization of religious language" has disastrous implications in the immediate cultural context. In the late twelfth and thirteenth centuries, the play's image of infanticidal Jews is all too pertinent, for it evokes the contemporary myth of ritual murder: the relatively new but widespread belief that Jews ritually commemorate Christ's death by crucifying Christian children.[12] Sparked by a few putative cases in the 1140s and 1150s, this myth spreads rapidly through Europe. Several children allegedly murdered by Jews are venerated as Christian martyrs, among them William of Norwich, Hugh of Lincoln, Harold of Gloucester, and Richard of Paris (originally Richard of Pontoise). The sites of their deaths become cult and pilgrimage centers. By supporting these cults, the institutional church authorizes the myth (though popes steadily deny its truth).[13] The cults of the child saints unite affective piety and hatred of Jews; they disseminate the belief that Jews still murder innocents. The written and homiletic lives of these saints lend powerful literary expression to the myth. Legal authorities legitimate the myth by charging Jews with ritual murder and by executing them. Arguably most infamous is a case in Blois, where thirty-two Jews are condemned to death in 1171. (If the Fleury play was composed at Blois, its central action is particularly loaded.) The charge continues to be compelling in northern France during the reign of Philip II Augustus (1179–1223), who, according to his biographer Rigord, believes that the Jews of his kingdom really do crucify Christian children, and who in his youth is devoted to the cult of Richard of Paris.[14] He is not alone in his credulity. Henry III of England has nineteen Jews executed in 1255 on the charge of murdering Hugh of Lincoln.[15] Such royal actions substantiate the myth and enhance its contemporary credibility.

These events form a sensational context for the Fleury *Slaughter of Innocents*. Exegesis, liturgical drama, saints' lives, and royal policies collectively advance the myth of ritual murder. Exegesis creates the image of a deicidal, infanticidal Jew, and generalizes Jewish antipathy, making the Slaughter of Innocents a story about perpetual conflict between hostile Jews and martyred Christians. The Fleury *Slaughter* (along with many similar plays) dramatizes these images, revealing one of the cultural mechanisms by which academic concepts become communal beliefs. Saints' lives and homilies likewise popularize the myth. Twelfth- and thirteenth-century history witnesses the tragic enactment of a widely shared belief in Jewish hostility, rooted in the variously popular and learned discourses that give the myth of ritual murder prestigious cultural authority. Medieval texts therefore remind us that "discourses are also events, and they make both acts and the acceptance of acts possible."[16] Although exegesis and drama are not alone in shaping the myth of ritual murder, they play active roles in rationalizing the myth and lending it affective force.

By studying the *Slaughter* and its exegetical intertexts in detail, we will be able more fully to comprehend the myth of ritual murder as the product of a dynamic interchange between ecclesiastical discourses and political history.[17] When it enacts this myth, the Fleury play heightens affective devotion to the bodies of Christ and the saints; it also fosters profoundly destructive attitudes toward the religious Other. The play suggests that the "feminization" of religion had cultural consequences that we may not as yet fully appreciate. Many scholars have demonstrated that the increased focus on religious affect in and after the twelfth century promotes among the faithful an increased emphasis on humility and a tendency toward lachrymose prayers. Affective religion is not, however, limited to expressions of the gentler, supposedly feminine virtues. Human affect, and consequently affective religion, also encompasses rage, ferocity, pride, and intolerance. We should not be surprised that devotional texts sometimes connect tenderness for the savior with hatred of those who kill him, or that some works appeal to visceral anger and fear as well as nobler aspirations. Affective religion creates complex entanglements of emotion, reason, and faith, with sometimes tragic cultural consequences.

The Murder of Christian Innocents

> While Herod was planning murder for the infants, Joseph was advised by an angel to take Christ the Lord into Egypt, a land full of idols. After the persecution by the Jews and the intent on the part of a wicked people to kill Christ, Christ Himself deigns to cross over to the gentiles, who were given over to idols. Leaving Judea, He is carried to a world which did not know Him, to be worshiped.[18]

The first and longest part of the *Slaughter* presents three simultaneous actions in the church nave: the Innocents process to their martyrdom, while Herod determines to slaughter them, and an angel warns Joseph to flee with Mary and the Christ child to Egypt.[19] The play begins with the Innocents processing joyously through the nave, singing in praise of Christ's glorious kingdom.[20] Their first text ("O how glorious is the kingdom") is borrowed from All Saints' Day, when the church prays for those who die in persecutions.[21] Much of the play is similarly created from preexisting texts, each of which adds layers of meaning to the dramatic exegesis. From the Innocents' initial procession to their death and resurrection, the play borrows texts from All Saints' Day, Innocents' Day, the Advent and Christmas season, Epiphany, the Purification, Good Friday, and the Assumption. The extensive borrowings recall Dom Jean Leclercq's description of monastic attitudes toward the liturgy: the monks delight in treating the liturgy as a living commentary on scripture and the church fathers; accordingly, they adapt existing texts to new contexts to rediscover fresh meanings in the familiar words.[22]

Dying With Christ

So too does the play bring existing liturgical texts into contexts that enlarge their meanings. By giving the Innocents a text from All Saints' Day, the playwright presents them as members of the Christian community, united with all those who have been and will be victims of persecution, and united too with the monks who pray for and with the saints. The boys' physical presence in the nave signifies the continuing presence of the saints, living and dead, in the community of the faithful. As they proceed, the Lamb appears to lead them. Their next text ("Send forth the Lamb") recalls one of the Epistle verses for Holy Innocents' Day (Apocalypse 14:1), in which Christ appears as the Lamb of Sion, attended by 144,000 martyrs bearing His name on their foreheads.[23] Through his choice of preexisting texts, the playwright depicts the Innocents as the first martyrs of the church, trusting in Christ's eternal victory over death and joyously anticipating the kingdom of God.

This representation coheres with exegetical tradition. Pseudo-Bede succinctly expresses the basic idea: "the slaughter of the little ones signifies the destruction of Christ's martyrs."[24] We might note that scripture recounts a single event; exegetes turn it into a recurring history of martyrdom. The *Gloss* elaborates the idea, focusing on the martyrs' role in creating the church:

> As soon as Christ appeared to the world persecution began in it, which figured the persecution of the saints; and while the infant was sought, infants were slain, in whom the pattern of martyrdom is born, wherein the infancy of the Church is proclaimed.[25]

The Innocents (*infantes*) mirror Christ (*infans*); their death constitutes the infancy (*infantia*) of the church. Dying, the Innocents give birth (*nascitur*) to a new form: martyrdom.[26] Life and death, martyrdom and generation, and human and divine infants are all paradoxically connected. Aquinas as clearly (though less poetically) associates the children with Christ: "while he [Herod] thus persecutes Christ, he furnished an army (of martyrs) clothed in white robes of the same age as the Lord."[27] As Aquinas reads it, the Innocents' "passion" both anticipates and follows Christ's (exegetes delight in paradoxes).[28] This line of interpretation derives Christian identity from a literal *imitatio Christi*, as if the church were founded on the rock of suffering. The *Gloss* presents the Innocents as the first in a line of martyrs, and Aquinas too discovers in the narrative not only the beginning of martyrdom but also its persistence throughout history. He notes, moreover, that their youth signifies the humility by which the faithful proceed to glory, a familiar inversion that privileges the childlike over the manly.[29] The Innocents' deaths foreshadow not only the Crucifixion but also the continuing persecution of the saints. This approach to the Gospel makes the church seem internally unified throughout all time, always identified with the suffering Savior, always beset by persecutors. As they process through the nave, the Fleury Innocents turn exegetical themes into accessible public images: they represent a church united against its enemies and committed to an ideal of humble suffering with Christ.

Before the Innocents die, they sing a Christmas Eve antiphon taken from John the Baptist's greeting to Christ at the Jordan: "Hail, Lamb of God! Hail, you who take away the sins of the world."[30] The boys walk to their deaths trusting in their redemption, in the baptism of blood that identifies them with the savior. After the slaughter, an angel bids the boys to cry out. Responding with a text from the liturgy for Epiphany, they align themselves with believers, and more specifically with the Magi, the first Gentile believers.[31] By adapting texts from All Saints' Day, Innocents' Day, and Epiphany to the new context of the *Slaughter,* the playwright transforms a biblical story about the slaughter of Jewish children into an allegory about Gentile martyrs who die with and for Christ.

Thus far, the allegory is implicit. The Innocents make it explicit when they express their faith in the Lamb:

> To the sacred Lamb slain for us,
> To Christ, we consecrate, under this banner of light,
> The splendor of the Father, the splendor of virginity.
> As those whom the anger of Herod seeks out in many ways,
> We will be saved by the Lamb;
> We will die with Christ.[32]

The Innocents express a serene eternal perspective on the action: the Lamb's sacrifice is as salvific to the Innocents who die in his place as to those who live and die centuries later. As the Innocents die "with Christ," they evoke the image of themselves on the cross. In medieval literature and art, the Christ child often appears as eucharistic sacrifice, expressed in images of a broken and bloodied baby in the chalice. Leah Sinanoglou astutely proposes that plays about the Innocents could have recalled these devotional images.[33] Her study illuminates the Fleury play's fusion of infancy and Crucifixion, sacrificial death and redemptive blood, infant and infants. The Fleury imagery adds fresh devotional depth to the familiar narrative. The play thus opens with a complex affective nexus: it balances the horror of infanticide against the serenity of the child martyrs; and it invites something like relief that Christ escapes death, even as it foreshadows his Crucifixion.

The Fleury Innocents enact the central image in the myth of ritual murder: they present themselves as children crucified in place of and with Christ, like the children supposedly crucified by Jews in contemporary Europe. The play is clearly both influenced by and independent from exegesis; or, more accurately, the play is itself a commentary that, like the *Gloss* or Aquinas's *Catena Aurea,* like the liturgy itself, creates new emphases from preexisting texts. The play guides its audience to feel tenderness toward the vulnerable Christ child, but that feeling is inextricably connected with a foreboding awareness that the church community is also exposed, its innocents subject to sudden, violent death. The play offers the Slaughter as a challenging test of faith.

Myths of Jewish Violence

As the Innocents process through the nave, a man-at-arms offers Herod a scepter, presenting him to the audience as a Jewish king whose reign is eternal: "Upon the throne of David, and over his kingdom, he will sit for ever."[34] Mistaking Herod for the Messiah, the man-at-arms expresses a "carnal," "Jewish" understanding of prophecy.[35] A literate monastic audience would recognize that the man-at-arms fails to comprehend the "spiritual" (that is, Christological) meaning of David's throne. The play at once reveals and denigrates his incomprehension, setting his address to Herod, "King, live forever!," against the Innocents' celebration of Christ's "glorious kingdom."[36] The Innocents and man-at-arms embody a binary opposition of Christian truth and Jewish error. The man-at-arms locates Herod in the lineage of David, presenting him as a Jewish king expected to defend his kingdom against the Christ child. This identification is crucial to Herod's import in the play.

It is not a foregone conclusion in this time that Herod would be Jewish, or that the Jews (collectively) would be vicious murderers. Other choices are possible, though negative commentaries tend to predominate in the high Middle Ages. Pseudo-Bede delivers what will become a stereotype. His Herod witnesses unambiguously to Jewish hatred toward

Christ and Christians: "Truly, Herod signifies the hatred of the Jews, who were wishing to wipe out the name of Christ and to kill those believing in him."[37] Jeremy Cohen argues that this generalized conception of Jewish guilt becomes popular in the twelfth century and dominant in the thirteenth, replacing Augustine's more benign hypothesis that Jews killed Christ because they were ignorant of his divine nature.[38] We might note that canon law witnesses to a similar notion of Jewish guilt for the Crucifixion.[39] Yet exegesis is not entirely coherent on this issue. The *Gloss* at one point reads Herod as the "faithlessness of the Jews," but the work presents contradictory ideas about Jewish guilt, suggesting interpretive uncertainty.[40] Aquinas makes determined, if "strikingly tendentious," attempts to resolve the contradictions.[41] He argues in the *Summa Theologiae* that Jews are both ignorant and hostile: their "affected ignorance does not excuse guilt, but actually exacerbates it, for it shows that a man is so strongly attracted to sin that he wishes to remain ignorant so as not to avoid it."[42] Consistent with this logic, Aquinas's commentary on the Slaughter depicts Jews as willfully ignorant and therefore condemned. Aquinas nonetheless explicates Herod as a polysemous figure: historically a foreign (Idumaean) ruler threatened by a Jewish king; morally, the devil, grieved by the call to the Gentiles and opposed to God's grace; and allegorically, Jewish envy.[43] Clearly, Herod's import varies in exegesis.

The Fleury play cuts through academic subtleties in order, quite bluntly, to demonize Herod. He appears in the play as a violent Jewish king, a brash character who, on hearing that the Magi have departed, rushes to the very brink of suicide. A rubric describes the action: "Then let Herod, as if demented, having seized a sword, prepare to kill himself; but let him be finally prevented and pacified by his followers, as he is saying: 'Let me quench my burning vehemence by destroying myself.'"[44] Herod's attempted suicide at this moment is, to say the least, unusual, and probably, as Miriam Anne Skey argues, unique in liturgical drama. Other plays have him order the massacre at this point and turn to suicide only later, in his old age. Skey concludes that the Fleury innovations serve to characterize Herod as angry and disturbed.[45] Herod's demented sword play certainly gives concrete form to the Jewish wrath that seeks out the Innocents and Christ in this play.

The playwright's timing of the near-suicide directly connects Herod's attempt to destroy himself with his success in butchering his subjects, his kingdom's future. In this, his actions foreshadow the end of the Jewish kingdom. This implication is consistent with the theory of supersessionism, which holds that Jews lose their chosen status because they fail to understand the Messianic promises contained in their scripture.[46] The armiger exemplifies this error, and he foreshadows the Jews who later reject and kill Christ (as Herod tries to do), the act that, according to Christian theory, finally provokes God to punish them with the loss of Israel. By engineering their Messiah's death, Jews precipitate their own destruction. The theory of supersessionism is refined in the works of the church fathers and persists through the Middle Ages in *Adversus Judaeos* polemics, becoming a commonplace by the twelfth century (the theory officially prevails until rejected by the Second Vatican Council in the 1960s). The Fleury Herod and his man-at-arms represent the guilty Jewish nation, and Herod's self-destructive actions foretell their doom.

For all Herod's violence, his man-at-arms actually incites the massacre: "Determine, my lord, to vindicate your wrath, and, with sword's point unsheathed, order that the boys be slain; and perchance among the slain will Christ be killed."[47] Conforming to the harshest exegetical traditions, the man-at-arms identifies wrath as the motive for this first attempt on Christ's life. The armiger's part has the effect of generalizing guilt for the crime, making a Jewish conspiracy rather than a single individual responsible for the attack. Thus the play popularizes the exegetical notion that the Innocents are martyred because Jews hate Christ and his followers; it elaborates the idea of brutal Jews who are willing to kill many children on the off chance that they will also destroy Christ.

Both the *Slaughter* and exegesis reveal in seminal form the myth of ritual murder: the association of wrathful Jewish murderers, child saints, and the Crucifixion. Indeed, the Fleury play develops an explicit biblical foundation for events supposedly taking place in twelfth- and thirteenth-century Europe. For a contemporary audience, Herod and his man-at-arms are anything but remote historical figures or exegetical abstractions: they are the first Jewish murderers of Christian children, and their progeny presumably continue in their ways. The Fleury play not only illuminates the exegetical contexts behind the myth of ritual murder, but it also demonstrates how the myth is conveyed through the affective performance of scripture.

Exegetes sometimes draw more general spiritual meanings from the Slaughter, which can grant us further insight into the play's contemporary import. The *Gloss* frames the broader meaning of the episode: "The death of the little babes represents the passion of all martyrs, who are slain small, humble, and innocent, not in Judea alone but everywhere they suffered from the impious, whom Herod signifies."[48] Martyrs exemplify a childlike innocence and humility, demonstrating the commonplace religious inversion by which those who make themselves least, become greatest. According to the exegetes, the Slaughter is both originary and recurrent. The Innocents continue to suffer; Herod continues as their enemy. The reader is called upon to identify with the children, to discover simple black-and-white distinctions between pious martyrs and impious murderers, between Christians and their enemies, in the past as well as in the present.

Like the exegetes, the Fleury playwright portrays the Christian community as small, humble innocents. When the play is performed, the bodies of real children represent the body of the church, a community made up of both the living and the dead, both the faithful in the choir and nave, and the saints who precede them. The Innocents dramatize the virtues Christians need to be included in this community: the faith in Christ's salvific blood, the figurative smallness of humility, and the willing submission to a divine plan. They also call attention to the perils such a virtuous community faces in the real world, where the fate of the powerless is to be overpowered. While symbolizing the transcendent church, the children's bodies are subject to the forces that seek to destroy the community of the faithful on earth. We have seen Augustine use the image of childlike dependence and trust to define his relationship with a loving deity (chapter 3). The Fleury playwright employs the image to describe the church's relationship with its enemies. As the child-body of the church undergoes martyrdom (and, later, redemption), the play affirms the beauty of obedience and humility—and recognizes the self-sacrifice involved in pursuing those virtues in a hostile world.

This image of the church must have resonated with the Benedictine monks at Fleury. The Rule of Benedict represents monks as perpetual "beginners": children in faith, bound in obedience to their father abbot. The rule exhorts Benedictines to perfect the virtue of humility and teaches them gladly to receive any suffering that attends their spiritual exercises.[49] Benedictines would find poignant personal meaning in the Innocents who sacrifice themselves for Christ: the children express their own spiritual aspirations. In this performative mirror, the monks could see their own daily attempts at virtue reflected back at them, their sufferings vicariously glorified, and their ultimate reward assured.

Although doubtless inspiring at the time, this representation of the church is built on the unstable sands of a fiction. In reality, Christians are not helpless victims but the dominant majority, while Jews are in most places a persecuted minority. By representing the church in the bodies of powerless children, the playwright turns contemporary sociopolitical order upside down. He does the same with the church: the helpless children who embody the church can only enact martyrdom; they cannot rule or represent the church on earth. In other words, the playwright ignores existing social, political, and ecclesiastical hierarchies in order to construct the church as a passive victim, and Jews as active rulers. Finally, the play makes Christian kingship a logical impossibility: the Christ who must be imitated is king of a transcendent realm and offers no pattern for worldly power. The play denies the quotidian exercise of both ecclesiastical and state power: only enemies of the faith can wield the sword of temporal rule. Whether idealizing the saints or demonizing the Jews, the Fleury *Slaughter* appeals to emotion rather than reason, and its performance is more likely to provoke visceral than analytical responses. An audience could plausibly infer from this work that the dangerously deicidal minority should be contained (their legal rights abridged, their activities monitored), lest they decimate the faithful. The play prompts, at the very least, a felt need for defensive Christian action. Dramatic exegesis thus contributes to the culture of persecution that develops in the twelfth and thirteenth centuries.[50]

Calling all Gentiles

While Herod rages and the Innocents process toward martyrdom, an angel warns Joseph, the real "son of David" (a pointed comparison with Herod on the "throne of David"), about the threat on Christ's life and advises him to flee into Egypt.[51] Heeding the command, Joseph and Mary carry the child to the lay congregation in the church nave. The action recalls the practices of locating the Easter sepulcher and saints' relics in the nave, which similarly bring the religious ceremony close to the laity to heighten devotional fervor. (We might note in passing that the play would likely have been performed at matins, and feast day matins at Fleury were well attended by the laity.[52]) As Joseph proceeds, he bids Egypt not to weep, for the Lord comes to free his people. The words and action present Christ as Moses, delivering a new Israel.[53]

Exegesis can help us to appreciate the specific implications of this action. Pseudo-Bede understands the flight into Egypt as a sign that God has turned away from Israel and toward the church: "Joseph signifies the doctors, Mary, the Church; Egypt, which is interpreted as darkness, truly signifies the people of that land; and this figure of Christ in Egypt signifies his going with his Church from the Israelite people to all nations by means of the ministers."[54] In this analysis, the flight into Egypt marks the birth of the church among the gentiles, the moment at which Christians supersede Jews as God's chosen people. Pseudo-Bede focuses on the Jewish "error" revealed by the action: "night truly signifies ignorance, through which the Jews were left in their error when the apostles made all peoples familiar with the light of faith."[55] While the Gospel brings light, Jews remain in the night of ignorance. Pseudo-Bede takes advantage of the image to charge Jews with failing to comprehend their own scripture and history. The *Gloss* similarly reads the flight into Egypt as an allegory for the Gospel going to the gentiles, leaving the "faithless" Jewish people behind in darkness.[56] In his turn, Aquinas critiques Jewish "ignorance," and he too presents the flight as Christ's departure from the Jews and call to the gentiles.[57] On this point, exegetes discover a consensus about the scene's allegorical meaning: the flight signifies the passing of divine favor from the Jews to the gentiles. In developing that interpretation, exegetes blame Jews for "faithlessness," "ignorance," "error," or "jealousy." These characteristics, seemingly inherent in the Jewish character, serve to explain Jews' rejection of Christ and their consequent loss of divine favor.

This conventional allegory about the founding of the church informs the dramatic action. When the monks carry the Christ child to the lay congregation in the nave, they enact the extension of the Gospel to the gentiles. The lay congregation now embodies the communal church, the local form of a spiritual body. The holy family's journey into the nave celebrates at once the historical beginning of the church and its self-proclaimed triumph over the Jews left behind.

While the action condemns Israel, it exalts Egypt, the figurative home of the church. Aquinas elaborates this implication, comparing Christ with Moses, and reading the Old Testament as anticipating the New. According to this analysis, God sends Christ into Egypt as a sign that his old anger at the Egyptians, a lingering relic of Israel's captivity, has finally passed:

> And therefore sent His Son thither, and gives it this sign of great reconciliation, that with this one remedy He might heal the ten plagues of Egypt, and the nation that had been the persecutor of this first-born people, might be the guardian of His first-born Son. As formerly they had cruelly tyrannized, now they might devoutly serve; nor go to the Red Sea to be drowned, but be called to the waters of baptism to receive life.[58]

Israel's persecutors are redeemed, their plagues healed with a single remedy, their watery grave turned into a baptismal font. Aquinas unifies the Gospel account with Hebrew scripture, turning the ancient narrative about an exclusive chosen people into a myth about a universal, all-inclusive elect. In the *Slaughter,* the procession of Joseph, Mary, and Christ child into the nave likewise celebrates the church as the new Israel, inheriting the life rejected by the first-born people. As they go, Joseph makes this import explicit by consoling the audience with the promise of redemption: "Egypt, weep not, for your Lord will come to you."[59] With this antiphon, Joseph expresses the conventional analysis of the flight into Egypt as God's departure from Israel and call to the gentiles.

The Birth of a Church

At the most abstract, symbolic level, the opening scene of the *Slaughter* establishes martyrdom and the extension of the Gospel to gentiles as the foundation of the church that supersedes Israel. The action defines Christian virtue as humble imitation of Christ's suffering. The play achieves this abstraction through memorable concrete actions: military violence, the children's deaths, and their mothers falling in prayer over them. Although a performance of the play would doubtless strive to be decorous, it would inevitably (and purposefully) convey the horror of children dying for their faith. The devotional emphasis on Christ's tender humanity, on his and his followers' suffering, heightens the perceived savagery of the attack. Affective devotion is further intensified by a dramatic doubling. While the Christ child is carried to the nave, the "lamb" in the midst of the children is rescued.[60] As the sacrificial child/lamb doubles, the pathos deepens. The play creates complex affective associations, mingling reverence for the humanity of Christ and the saints, with profound fear of the demented Jews, who appear irrationally hostile toward all things Christian, including, or perhaps especially, helpless children. In short, the first part of the *Slaughter* dramatizes the myth of ritual murder and bestows on that myth both emotional immediacy and compelling biblical authority.

The Innocents and the Cult of Mary

> The Evangelist by this history of so bloody a massacre, having filled the reader with horror, now again sooths his feelings, shewing that these things were not done because God could not hinder, or knew not of them; but as the Prophet had foretold.[61]

Forcefully contrasting with the triple simultaneous action of the play's opening, the lyrical middle section of the *Slaughter* develops Rachel's static emotional lament. She appears here, as she does in the Gospel of Matthew, in part to affirm the unity of Old and New Testaments. C. Clifford Flanigan cogently summarizes the Gospel strategy: "Matthew's primary interest in this account of the Innocents was to draw parallels between the life of Jesus and events in Israel's national history, thus demonstrating that Jesus fulfills Israel's hopes and traditions, that Israel's history finds its inevitable culmination in the events described in the Gospel."[62] In the

Gospel, Rachel functions to bind the New Testament closely to the Old. The prophet Jeremiah speaks of Rachel in Rama, mourning her children and refusing consolation. Matthew treats her as a prophet who anticipates the Slaughter of Innocents; her Gospel lament fulfills Jeremiah's "prophecy."

Exegetes recognize the problematic ambiguities that arise from Rachel's double role in the Old and New Testaments. Rachel's grief, for instance, is enigmatic and can signify radically different propositions: perhaps she mourns the children as Christian martyrs, trusting in their redemption; on the other hand, perhaps she cannot be consoled because they are Jews and subject to eternal damnation.[63] Despite the interpretive difficulties, Rachel is generally understood as a figure for the church. As the *Gloss* puts it, "Rachel. That is, the Church, laments her tender slain lambs," which is to say, the martyrs.[64] Aquinas develops the analysis more fully: "Rachel affords a type of the Church long barren now at length fruitful. She is heard weeping for her children, not because she mourned them dead, but because they were slaughtered by those whom she would have retained as her first-born sons."[65] This analysis ingeniously produces Rachel as the mother first of Jews and then of Christians; in this double role, she signifies the unity of Old and New Testaments. Her grief for her first-born sons, lost to her, alludes to the theory of supersessionism.

In the play as in the Gospel, Rachel refuses consolation. While exegetes struggle to reconcile her emotion with her allegorical meaning, the playwright alters the allegory to justify her grief. She begins by mourning for the Innocents. Her first words establish her as the affective heart of the play: "Alas, tender babes, what torn limbs we see! / Alas, sweet sons, your throats cut by rage alone!"[66] Expressing a mother's grief, Rachel lingers over the Innocents' bodies, forcefully contrasting their tender vulnerability ("tender babes," "sweet sons") with the savage swords that ended their lives ("torn limbs," "throats cut by rage"). She laments the Innocents' vulnerable humanity and voices the unspeakable shock of infanticide. Her language reinforces the play's affective associations between reverence for the Innocents, fear of the raging Jews, and trepidation for the Christ child, hidden in the nave that symbolizes Egypt.

The Gospel mentions Rachel's inconsolable grief; the play has her articulate her grief at anguished length, has her persist despite others' attempts to comfort her. In fact, the only action in this scene is the lyrical voicing of emotion. The play functions as affective supplement to both the Gospel and academic exegesis, filling their silences with words that give her grief meaning and render it sympathetic. The playwright uses the scene to draw out the expression of both grief and consolation and to sustain those emotions in dynamic tension. When Rachel dwells on her sons' torn limbs, the comforters remind her of their exaltation: "Although you grieve, rejoice that you weep. / For, truly, your sons live blessed above the stars."[67] The comforters expect Rachel to mourn as a mother, but they also assume that she should rejoice, as the church, over the translation of the martyrs. Rachel does not respond as the church. Indeed, she continues to play the mother who looks only for tears: "pour forth weepings of tears, / Weeping for the flower of Judaea, the grief of the nation!"[68] Thus far, she inhabits a historical literal role as the Old Testament mother of Judaea. Rachel and the comforters begin by articulating distinct hermeneutics; they advance conflicting literal and allegorical interpretations of the scene they inhabit.

Committed to their hermeneutic, the comforters persist in reminding Rachel that she should embody the church. They recall her to her precedence over her sister:

> Why do you, young woman,
> Mother Rachel, so beautiful, weep,
> In whose visage Jacob takes delight?
> As if the tender and bleary [literally: inflamed] eyes
> Of your babyish sister pleased him!
> Mother, dry your weeping eyes.
> How are these streams of tears on your cheeks becoming to you?[69]

The comforters can be taken literally as exhorting Rachel to consider how grief affects her beauty, but this seems a frivolous argument for a monastic context. It is more likely that the contrast between the sisters recalls allegorical interpretations of Genesis, where Rachel signifies the church, and Leah, the synagogue. As the *Gloss* puts it:

> The martyr Victorinus explained Rachel and Leah in the likeness of Church and Synagogue. He supposes that Leah, the elder by birth, signifies the Synagogue, because she first brought forth the people of God: she is called blear eyed because the law was covered and sealed through Moses. Rachel, younger and beautiful, at first sterile, afterward fecund, signifies the Church, which was later in time but holy in body and spirit. Her eyes were comely because they have obtained to see the Gospel. But for a long time she was sterile while Synagogue brought forth people. Jacob served for Rachel, and Leah is substituted for her: because Christ, in order that he might take the Church to himself, first joined the Synagogue to himself in marriage.[70]

Rachel, Gospel enlightenment, and the church, supersede Leah, the law, and the synagogue. The play conveys this allegory through the comforters' reference to Rachel's clear and Leah's bleary eyes. This is not, at the time, an arcane reference. Margaret Schlauch establishes the impact of this allegory on a large body of church literature and surveys images of blind synagogue that flourish in thirteenth-century plastic arts.[71] Both exegesis and visual arts treat synagogue's bleary eyes as a condemnation of Judaism, the rejected elder sibling, bound to a legalism emptied of spiritual purpose. When the Fleury comforters tell Rachel to dry her weeping eyes, they seek to recall her to her allegorical role as the church, superior to the synagogue. Rachel, they insist, should rejoice in what cannot be seen and take comfort in the promise of resurrection.

Rachel defends her grief and remains inconsolable. She shifts, however, to mourning for one son who, had he lived, would have defended her and helped his deceased brothers.[72] Her focus on one son implies that her role is shifting. This implication becomes definite in her final utterance, a Good Friday antiphon. As she voices the words, she identifies with the Virgin Mary at the foot of the cross: "My soul is troubled within me; my heart is agitated within me."[73] Rachel is now the *mater dolorosa,* and her son, the dying Christ. The liturgical occasion justifies her grief, presenting it as a sanctified response to Christ's redemptive suffering. Her sorrow, a flaw in exegesis, here becomes an exemplary response to the Lord's death. Indeed, the point of the scene is to demonstrate her laudable emotion. She models what the audience should feel—personal sorrow before the cross, and sympathy for those who grieve at its foot. With this antiphon, the comforters are silenced, their arguments rendered moot, and their interpretation of Rachel set aside. Rachel never accepts the role they keep offering her, any more than she becomes a figure for the contemplative life, a symbolism common in Benedictine circles.[74] Instead of drawing on those established traditions, the playwright uses preexisting liturgical texts to create an innovative fusion of Old and New Testaments matriarchs: mother of Judaea, mother of Christ, mother of sorrows. The playwright turns Rachel into an authoritative image of affective piety.

Rachel's Good Friday antiphon reinforces the connection between the child martyrs and the Crucifixion, a key element in the myth of ritual murder, and one that gains a plausible biblical origin in this play. Instead of following academic exegetes, the playwright develops an original performative commentary on scripture, indebted less to academics than to popular devotion to the Virgin. The mother of sorrows allusion witnesses to this influence, but of course that is only one of Mary's roles. Miracle stories depict her also as a powerful mediator, who, not incidentally, often rescues children from murderous Jews. One popular tale tells how a Jewish couple shut their son in a burning furnace to punish him for taking Easter communion. The infanticide is thwarted, for Mary and Jesus protect the

child even in the midst of the fire.[75] Although Rachel-Mary does not
adopt an intercessory role in the Fleury play, such legends disclose important aspects of her contemporary meaning. Like many other discourses,
miracles of the Virgin advance belief in Jewish violence against children
affiliated (however tenuously) with Christ. Consequently, Mary is often
identified with children purportedly crucified by Jews, and some of the
child saints' feast days recognize this connection: for instance, Richard of
Paris's feast day was the Annunciation of the Virgin.

More telling for our immediate purposes is the fact that Richard's
body was translated to Paris, where he lay in the church of the Holy
Innocents.[76] Ecclesiastical authorities, royal functionaries, a king devoted
to Richard, and the populace all identified the child supposedly crucified
by Jews with the biblical Innocents. As we have seen, many discourses
besides the Fleury play advance this reading of scripture and history;
by the late twelfth century, the Innocents are widely recognized as the
original victims of ritual murder. To read the Fleury *Slaughter* in relation
to historical events, material culture, and other discourses is to become
aware of the many learned and popular threads woven into the playwright's treatment of Rachel as Mary, who mourns at once the Innocents,
the crucified God, and the new child martyrs.

Rachel appears in the *Slaughter* as an Old Testament mother, a representative of the New Testament mothers, a figure for the church, and a
type of Mary, the *mater dolorosa*.[77] This symbolic fusion of Old and New
Testaments implies a further argument against Judaism. Contemporary
Jews were outspoken in their rejection of the Virgin Birth and Incarnation,
and Christians repeatedly try to answer their objections, proving, at least
to their own satisfaction, that all rational beings must assent to doctrine.[78] The figure of Rachel suggests that dramatic art has its own ways
of resolving controversy. The playwright answers Jewish arguments by
fashioning a public image of approved sentiment: a Jewish woman who
adores the incarnate crucified God, born of a virgin. Presented as one,
Rachel and Mary affirm the truth of the contested doctrines. The playwright surpasses Matthew and the exegetes in appropriating Rachel to
validate Christian truth.

In performance, the truth is nonetheless threatened. The work's extensive rubrics do not indicate that Herod should retreat from view after order-
ing the Slaughter; he apparently keeps his position throughout Rachel's
lament, the sign of continuous Jewish power. He and Rachel-Mary
represent two sides of a supposedly ancient religious conflict, and their
simultaneous presence complicates the affective implications of the scene.
While she expresses sorrow and models affective devotion, he reminds
the audience that hostile Jews destroyed the Innocents, the martyrs, and

Christ. Represented in the bodies of the children and women, the church appears utterly powerless, helpless before the threat confronting it, wholly dependent on the deity for life itself. A familiar inversion places women and children on top of the spiritual hierarchy and fosters an impression of the church's humility and affective devotion to the bodies of Christ and the martyrs. Where the church enacts a "feminine" weakness and passivity, power transfers to the "masculine" Other, onto whom the playwright projects all that must be excluded from the "feminine language of religion"—rage, dominance, and pride. Fear of that potent Other is an important part of the nexus called affective piety.

Christ's Army and the Conversion of the Jews

> The return of Jesus to the land of Israel on the death of Herod shews, that, at the preaching of Enoch and Elijah, the Jews, when the fire of modern jealousy shall be extinguished, shall receive the true faith.[79]

The brief final section of the play returns to simultaneous triple action. The Innocents process to heaven; Herod's son Archelaus succeeds him on the throne; and the holy family returns from Egypt to Galilee. As each plot draws swiftly to its close, the play moves toward a disturbingly inconclusive conclusion.

Child Soldiers

The sequence begins with an angel calling the Innocents to enter heaven: "Suffer the little ones to come unto me, for of such is the kingdom of heaven."[80] As the Innocents rise and enter the choir, they dramatize the resurrection of saints, at once providing "ocular proof" of doctrine and claiming the reward of their faith in the lamb. From their first appearance to their elevation, the "little ones" embody the humility by which humans rise to glory. As they proceed, they identify with a heroic and caring Christ: "O Christ, O youth skilled in the greatest wars, how great an army do you gather for the Father...drawing to you the souls of the departed, since you have so much compassion."[81] The Innocents present themselves as warriors, exercising with Christ the paradoxical power of self-sacrifice, and with him achieving victory by becoming victims. The scene brings to life an exegetical image of the Innocents as an army arrayed in victorious white.[82]

The Innocents' description of Christ's army can be read figuratively as a reference to spiritual battle, a metaphor common in monastic literature and certainly appropriate for the Benedictines at Fleury. But the military language also invites the audience to identify Christ's army with the human warriors who vow to defend the church on earth. Read this way, the Innocents evoke the dominant contemporary expression of the church militant: the Crusades. More specifically, by the mid-thirteenth century, the Innocents recall legends about the so-called Children's Crusade. Modern scholars have sometimes traced the impetus for this Crusade to veneration of the Innocents, the church's pattern for child martyrs.[83] Northern France witnessed one vivid scene in this Crusade, when thousands followed a shepherd named Stephen to Saint-Denis in 1212. Alberic of Troisfontaines, the classic source for this Crusade, relates that the crusaders proceeded from Paris to Marseilles, and there embarked for the Holy Land. Two of their ships sank; the remainder landed in Africa. After the long journey, the surviving children were sold to Muslims in the slave markets; eighteen children were martyred for their faith in Baghdad.[84]

The child crusaders, like the Fleury Innocents, exemplify both the vulnerability of children and the stoical, fervent faith of martyrs. The crusading legend reinforces the cult of the Innocents by demonstrating the continuing presence of child martyrs in the medieval world. For a contemporary audience, Fleury's army of victorious boys symbolically encompasses all child martyrs—the Innocents, the victims of ritual murder, and the child crusaders. This army of saints assures the audience of their ultimate victory over enemies of the faith, be they Jew or Muslim. From this perspective, the glorified Innocents affirm the righteousness of the Crusades—contests in which even children can triumph, at least from the perspective of eternity. The Innocents' militant zeal could be understood not just as a call to spiritual battle, but more concretely as a call for vengeance against enemies of the faith, the Jews and the Muslims who kill children. Since vengeance is a widely accepted motive for holy war in this time,[85] it is likely that many in the Fleury audience would see Christ's army as the instrument of an avenging God.

The Innocents' procession into the choir could thus provoke a range of affective responses from the audience, including renewed commitment to cenobitic self-sacrifice, serenity in the face of spiritual martyrdom, devotion to the saints and martyrs, compassion for those who suffer, hatred of those who destroy the little ones, and thirst for vengeance against enemies of the faith. In this play, affect is far from simple. Devotion to the bodies of Christ and the saints gets entangled with fear of the Other, a feeling of victimization (subtly different from self-sacrifice), and a belief that this world is hostile to people of faith. In the course of the play, affective devotion develops complex emotional resonance. The spiritual and material realms get confused with each other, as they do in the Crusades. It is not difficult to imagine the cultural effects of dozens of similar plays being read and performed throughout Europe, for century after century, all of them, like this play, advancing authoritative and deeply moving images of devotion to the bodies of Christ and the saints, together with potent images of the destructive religious Other.

An Ominous Conclusion

While the Innocents proceed to the glory promised the "little ones," Herod dies and is replaced by his son. Academic exegetes witness to a firm consensus about Herod's death: from Jerome to Aquinas, it signifies the end of Jewish hard-heartedness and the beginning of Jews' participation in the one true faith—that is, their conversion.[86] As Aquinas puts it, "by Herod's death the extinction of jealousy in the hearts of the Jews is indicated"; and "the Jews, when the fire of modern jealousy shall be extinguished, shall receive the true faith."[87] In other words, Jews will stop denying the truth and convert. While promising a future reconciliation, exegetes take the opportunity to stigmatize Jewish "error" and the faults that keep Jews from acknowledging manifest truth: hatred, envy, and treachery. These traits appear innate, the apparently ontological inadequacy of an entire people. Herod's death may signify the end of Jewish antipathy, but it brings forth only the rhetoric of Christian antipathy. The exegetes' desire for the conversion of Jews is entangled with their frustration over difference. In this, exegetes both reflect and shape dominant cultural attitudes, and the period of the Crusades offers many opportunities for violence against those Jews who refuse to convert.

The exegetes are not alone in their eagerness to inveigh against Jews.[88] Many learned discourses swell the tide of medieval anti-Judaism, and these discourses—exegesis, liturgical drama, canon law, saints' lives, polemics—collectively demonstrate prevailing attitudes among intellectuals. The more we study these discourses, the more we realize that violence against Jews is deeply rooted in the many and widely disseminated discourses, officially sanctioned by the institutional church, that define Jews as perpetual enemies of God and all believers.

If the Fleury play followed academic exegesis, Herod's death would represent the end of Jewish anger, but the playwright advances a more ominous conclusion. A rubric indicates that Herod is succeeded by this son: "let Herod be removed and let his son Archelaus be substituted in his place, and be raised up as king."[89] Elsewhere in the Playbook, this son passionately advises his father to destroy Christ: "Against that little kingling, against that tiny baby, command, o Father, your son to enter into this battle."[90] The contrast between the vulnerable baby and the vicious warrior could not be clearer. When Archelaus becomes king, he anticipates a continuing Jewish effort to kill Christ, foreshadowing the Crucifixion as well as a long history of Christian martyrs dying at the hands of religious enemies. With Archelaus's accession to the throne, the playwright stages a generalized Jewish antipathy that survives the demise of individuals, to be passed from one generation to the next, as if hatred constituted a genealogy. This plotline ends ominously with the image of a king perpetually armed against the throne of heaven, the embodiment of persistent Jewish rage and envy.[91]

In the Shadow of Judaism

Under this menacing sign, Christ returns from Egypt. An angel initiates the holy family's final procession by announcing that those who sought to kill the boy are dead: "Joseph, Joseph, Joseph, son of David! Return to the land of Judaea, for they are dead who sought the life of the boy."[92] This would seem to ignore the presence of Archelaus and to follow conventional exegesis in making Herod's death mark the end of Jewish hatred. The discrepancy follows from the playwright's use of preexisting liturgical music. He borrows the angel's announcement from the Purification, the first occasion on which Jews (Simeon and Anna) express belief in Christ. The Purification antiphon anticipates the conversion of the Jews, though not in the way Herod's allegorical death does: the play does not stage the final apocalyptic conversion of the Jewish people, but rather the first Jewish witnesses to Christ's standing as Messiah.[93] The Purification antiphon offsets the image of Archelaus: while some Jews convert and affirm the truth of Christianity; others remain implacable enemies.

Christ does not just return to the place of his birth. In the play's rubric as in scripture, he goes to Galilee.[94] Herein we discover the play's final symbolic action, for Galilee is not merely a geographical place but also a figure for the church, or for the small fraction of Jews who convert.[95] At the close of the *Slaughter*, as the holy family proceeds to the part of the church (probably the nave or transept) that stands for the universal church, Joseph sings an antiphon for the Assumption, calling on Mary to rejoice that she has defeated all heresies.[96] The heresy defeated here is, of course, Judaism, but the staging of the play defers Mary's victory to some indefinite future date. The play ends with the cantor leading the congregation to express its communal faith by singing the "Te Deum," the "chant that ritually commemorates the resurrection of Jesus."[97] The closing ritual anticipates the church's ultimate spiritual victory over the Jews, as does the Innocents' procession into the choir. Yet Archelaus continues on the throne, casting the long shadow of Jewish hatred over the prospect of victory. The *Slaughter* finally demonstrates an irresolvable ambivalence toward Jews: on the one hand, a hope for Jewish conversion, on the other, an expectation of Jewish violence. Although the martyrs achieve spiritual triumph, their persecutors remain in power. The play's final actions evince a deep-seated anxiety about the disruptive power of Jews, who occupy the lowest rung in the social and political orders, but whose very existence challenges dominant truths.

From Exegetical Reason to Affective Exegesis

The myth of ritual murder begins, I propose, early in the Middle Ages, when exegetes decide to read the Slaughter as a narrative about Jews who sacrifice Christian children in place of Christ. The idea is repeated for centuries, translated into liturgical plays about the Slaughter, elaborated in legends of child saints, and turned into history through royal and popular actions against Jews. Apprehending the complex genesis of this myth, rooted in the official discourses and acts of both church and state, allows us to recognize its irrefutable contemporary authority. Literature—whether exegetical, liturgical, or legendary—does not cause violence against Jews in the twelfth and thirteenth centuries, but neither are writers exempt from culpability. The textual foundations of the myth in fact discover a cautionary tale for our own time: artists and intellectuals still have the power to shape communal reality by creating the "public images of sentiment" that teach us, for good and ill, exemplary responses to perceived realities.

Modern scholars have for some time followed Gavin Langmuir in assuming that the idea of ritual murder derives from the first recorded account of it, Thomas of Monmouth's life of William of Norwich, composed in the third quarter of the twelfth century.[98] Yet Thomas did not draw the connection between Jewish infanticide and the Crucifixion entirely from his own imagination. John M. McCulloh advances a hypothesis that complements the evidence surveyed in this chapter. After examining Thomas's legend and its dissemination, McCulloh concludes that Thomas did not invent the elements of ritual murder, nor did his text significantly influence the dissemination of the libel. Instead, "it seems likely that Thomas and other early writers on this topic represented views that circulated in the communities where putative ritual murders took place and that these views in turn were themselves based on a widespread popular belief that Jews sacrificed Christian children."[99] The present chapter supports McCulloh's hypothesis: exegetes invented the link between the Innocents' deaths and Christ's crucifixion, between child martyrs and Jewish murderers, centuries before Thomas of Monmouth happened on the scene. The authority of academic exegesis helps to standardize these links, establishes a definitive model for interpreting contemporary events in relation to scripture, and ensures the broad dissemination of the core myth.[100] Liturgical plays such as the Fleury *Slaughter of Innocents* further advance the myth and heighten its affective power. The dynamic interchange between discourses and historical events turns early medieval exegesis into high medieval cultural truth.

The Fleury playbook is often admired for its literary sophistication and musical beauty, and the *Slaughter of Innocents* reveals the book's most powerful aesthetic, intellectual, and emotional appeal. Only by studying the play in relation to academic exegesis and historical events, however, can we comprehend the complexity of its meanings for a contemporary audience, or the affective responses it encourages. In the play as in exegesis, the point is not that a king in a remote time and place ordered (Jewish) infants executed, but that his actions foreshadow a continuous history of Jews murdering Christian children. The play represents the Innocents as first in a long line of martyred children: victims, with Christ, of Jewish rage, and objects of Mary's tender love. Liturgical drama proves a powerful tool for advancing affective devotion to the bodies of Christ and the saints who die for and with him, and for modeling "correct" emotional responses to the Jews who bring on those deaths.

Exegesis and its most brilliantly problematic "affective technology," liturgical drama, evidence the ambivalences and contrary emotions embedded in medieval religiosity: the love of God conjoined with hatred of Jews, the desire for Jewish conversion entangled with frustration over Jewish dissent, the ideal of an all-inclusive universal church compromised by the witness of the Other. The historical significance of academic exegesis lies partly in these messages, just as that of liturgical drama lies in its affective aesthetics. Neither form of exegesis is entirely comprehensible without the other—at least, not at this historical remove. Liturgical drama reveals the affective implications buried in academic exegesis, just as academic exegesis throws into relief the innovations enacted through drama. By studying these forms of exegesis together, we can recognize their interdependence—and the potent ways they collaborate to create the local cultural meanings of biblical texts.

Rachel and the Innocents enact exemplary responses to Christ and the martyrs, modeling the humility and affective responses (love of God and self-sacrifice) valued in their immediate cultural setting. Yet the cultural consequences of their performance are not unmixed, nor do they teach only goodness. They perform an ideal of the faithful called to victimization, expected to endure the violence of the Other. They are wholly dependent on a deity who seems, in this play, emotionally remote and willing to defer justice to the end of time. Their very virtues intensify the impression that the feminized church they represent is threatened, and for all practical purposes unprotected. Worldly power belongs wholly to the masculine Other; in the representational terms the play establishes, power is un-Christian. This dramatic image of the church heightens both affective devotion and the perceived dangers of Judaism. The Fleury playwright's gendered drama of Christian-Jewish relations can therefore only deepen anxieties about religious difference, as it confirms the belief that Jews murder Christian children, in the present as in the past.

CHAPTER 5

THE WIFE OF BATH'S MARGINAL AUTHORITY

C haucer's *Wife of Bath's Prologue* is in part a subversive supplement to
Jerome's *Against Jovinian,* a comic elaboration of the barely sup-
pressed women's voices that attend the history of academic exegesis, mur-
muring a perennial challenge to masculine authority. Read against
exegesis on 1 Timothy 2, the *Prologue* reveals Chaucer's inversion of traditions: he estranges the reader from the traditional masculine perspective,
replacing it with a "feminine" point of view; and he focuses on the vices
that call men's dominion into question. Chaucer neatly turns the tables
on Jerome and his fellow Latin exegetes.[1] Of course, the *Prologue* does not
inevitably call up that intertext for all readers. Just as Chaucer supplements Jerome's work, so do the fifteenth-century scribes who copy the
work recreate it for their own cultural contexts. By adding marginal
glosses to the poem, the scribes shape its meaning for their contemporaries, increasingly removed not only from Jerome but also from the
immediate contexts of Chaucer's composition. The glossing programs of
fifteenth-century manuscripts yield valuable historical evidence of how
Alison's exegesis was presented, though this evidence is far from transparent. Like all paratexts, the glosses are inevitably interested, hinting at the
embodied positions of their authors, and subject to interpretation. In
short, the glosses are also a supplement and can potentially displace the
poetic text.

To read *The Wife of Bath's Prologue* in glossed manuscripts is to become
keenly aware of how much scripture Chaucer translates and comments on
through this unlikely woman preacher. Throughout the fifteenth century,
scribes regularly call attention to Alison's many biblical sources, usually by
copying into the margin some part of the original Latin, creating a mise-
en-page that highlights her acts of vernacular translation. The simplest
glossing programs scatter several Latin notes through the work, while the
most extensive crowd glosses into barely adequate margins.[2] Each glossed

manuscript selectively emphasizes Alison's scriptural borrowings (as well as other features); a number of works reveal how closely her English follows the biblical Latin. When Alison argues that "god bad vs *wexe and multiple*," for instance, the scribe of Oxford, New College 314 links her words to Latin scripture: "*Crescite et multiplicamini*" (Increase and multiply, Gen. 1:28).[3] Scribes continue to draw attention to scriptural translations in the *Prologue* long after Thomas Arundel's 1407/9 *Constitutiones* declare the possession of vernacular scripture potentially heretical. Despite the prohibitions, Alison's vernacular project was apparently not censored, and biblical glosses survive in 19 of the 58 extant manuscripts and incunabula.[4] Some scribes also identify Alison's biblical sources (not always correctly), further highlighting her translations of the Word.[5]

At the time of Chaucer's composition, and throughout the work's early reception, this treatment of scripture is unusual. Vernacular literature typically develops narratives drawn from scripture, usually with considerable elaboration of noncanonical detail, as famously occurs in the Corpus Christi plays.[6] Such "popular Bibles" are not considered threatening to orthodoxy. In fact, verse translations and adaptations of the Word are exempt from ecclesiastical strictures on vernacular theology, even at the height of Lollard persecutions.[7] By contrast, *The Wife of Bath's Prologue* recites few biblical stories, and even those are condensed versions, notably lacking in colorful narrative detail: "Crist ne wente neuere but ones / To weddyng in the Cane of Galilee" (10–11). Nor does Alison draw on a psalter or Book of Hours, detail the Ten Commandments, recite the Creed, or list the seven deadly sins, all of which would be entirely acceptable for the laity of her class.[8] Instead, Alison focuses on vernacular translation and literal interpretation of canonical scripture, detached from conventional Latin glosses.

Although vernacular translation is controversial at the time, most ecclesiastics would theoretically consider Alison's literal hermeneutics suitable to her class and gender, and appropriate for a lay audience.[9] Literal interpretation finds contemporary support among lowly preachers, influential exegetes, and controversial theologians alike, though what writers mean by "literal" varies greatly.[10] While the "letter of the text" is a fluid concept, Alcuin Blamires and Lawrence Besserman astutely propose that the nuances of Alison's literal hermeneutic align her with Lollardy, and this implication is only strengthened by her tendency to translate scripture into the vernacular.[11] Clearly, Chaucer designs his feminine persona to engage unsettled contemporary debates about vernacular scripture and lay hermeneutics. The persona allows Chaucer to enter the debates behind a mask, safely distanced from the "Alison's" subversive scriptural expertise.

Speaking through the Wife of Bath, Chaucer reaccentuates scripture in the most controversial possible voice, that of a lay woman from the artisan class. Alison's class and gender mark her as one of the unlearned people ("Lollards") whose exegesis, officials fear, could dangerously unsettle society. Although Alison is a provocative exegete in an age filled with controversies over lay access to vernacular scripture, a significant number of scribes throughout the fifteenth century appear undaunted by her exegetical daring. Instead of deleting or minimizing potentially heretical material, many scribes highlight the passages most vulnerable to heresy charges: her scriptural references.

If the Wife of Bath figures, in Chaucer's age, the perceived threat of lay access to scripture, the circulation of the glossed *Prologue* throughout the fifteenth century demonstrates both readers' interest in its biblical teachings and their apparent immunity from heresy prosecution. These characteristics apply to the fifteenth-century gentry, who are an important market for *Canterbury Tales* manuscripts, and who, by virtue of their social status, can explore vernacular theology with relative safety.[12] In fact, members of the gentry possess and presumably read vernacular scripture—including the Wycliffite Bible—throughout this period.[13] This fact implies their serious commitment to religious education of the sort Wyclif advocated, though it would be a mistake to label them Lollards on that account. Many members of the gentry practice orthodox customs (such as devotion to saints), while investing in vernacular scripture and "dabbling in theology"—much as Alison herself does.[14] Gentry religion blurs distinctions between the "orthodox" and "heterodox": the gentry, like Alison, can be both. It is not a stretch to hypothesize that these adventurous lay readers would be intrigued by the *Wife of Bath's Prologue*. Alison's focus on the bare biblical text, her expertise in vernacular translation, and her moderate teachings in the interesting realm of marital relations mirror gentry readers' own interests.

By recognizing the possibility of readers sympathetic to some aspects of Lollardy, we gain an initial purchase on the biblical glosses that frame the *Wife of Bath's Prologue* in many manuscripts. Addressed to this audience, the glosses likely encode respect for Alison's vernacular scripture and literal lay exegesis. Analogies support this hypothesis. Comparable glossing programs appear in other works designed for the laity and imply positive attitudes toward at least some aspects of Lollardy, including vernacular biblical translation.[15] The many biblical glosses on the Wife's *Prologue* certainly speak to readers' interest in religious education and probably address readers influenced by some aspects of Lollardy. Almost all the biblical glosses call attention to the Wife's sources, allowing a close comparison of her vernacular translations with the original biblical language, and mapping her exegetical arguments. The glosses illuminate ways of reading the poem in relation to scripture and can substantially enhance our understanding of historical attitudes toward Chaucer's "feminine" exegesis. I will argue that almost all of the glosses endorse the Wife's authority as an exegete; most exhibit respect (serious, if not always earnest) for her treatment of scripture. Through their glosses on Alison's biblical references, the scribes reconstruct Chaucer's subversive persona as a plausible authority figure.

Reception study must steer a course somewhere between the Scylla of the individual, possibly eccentric work, and the Charybdis of unmanageable detail. Each glossed manuscript holds a particular reading of the work, but leads to only limited and tentative conclusions about reception. To comprehend a more general historical reception of Chaucer's most unlikely exegete, we must compare manuscripts, seeking to discern how scribes usually highlight Alison's teaching, what they typically gloss, and which glosses they tend to repeat. Only then can we draw conclusions about broad historical attitudes toward Alison's exegesis.

I employ the New College manuscript (dated to the third quarter of the fifteenth century) to center this inquiry. Professionally and carefully copied, the work allows for plausible inferences about historical reception.[16] It has five short glosses, all but one biblical, and thus invites close textual analysis. All but one of the New College glosses concerns the Wife's teaching about marriage, potentially the most provocative aspect of the work, and the aspect that receives the most marginal comments in other manuscripts as well. By comparing the New College glosses with those of other manuscripts, we may comprehend both its unique glossing program and areas of agreement across manuscript groups.[17] As it happens, the New College manuscript establishes the Wife's biblical authority in ways characteristic of almost all other substantively glossed manuscripts. It therefore leads both to credible conclusions about how one scribe frames the text for anticipated readers and to supportable conclusions about historical reception.[18]

Reading like a Scribe

Early in her marriage sermon, the Wife alludes to the traditional procreative rationale for marriage:

Men mowe deme & glose vp & doun
Wel I wot expresse withoutyn lie
That god bad vs wexe and multiple
That gentil text can I vnderstonde. (26–29, Ne)

In New College, the lines are glossed:

> Crescite et multiplicamini et cetera (28, Ne).
> [Increase and multiply, Gen. 1:28]

The Wife distinguishes between what "men deme" and what "god bad," between men's glosses and the "gentil text," locating authority in the Bible rather than in scholastic commentaries such as the *Gloss*.[19] From her perspective, men's busy glossing up and down produces more smoke than light. Brushing these glosses aside, she emphasizes literal interpretation. The Latin gloss provides a conventional source citation for her text, confirming her point and, not incidentally, her ability to translate Latin ("crescite et multiplicamini") into English ("wexe and multiple"). This source citation appears in eight other manuscripts, spread across several manuscript groups.[20] The gloss validates the Wife's understanding of scripture and demonstrates scribes' willingness to authorize her teaching about procreative intercourse. In fact, this treatment denies her teaching any subversive edge, and it presents her quite simply as an expert on the biblical rationale for marriage. What is not glossed is also important to the Wife's reception: no manuscript supplies even a brief tag from the many men who "glose vp & doun." That is, the scribes do not cite Scholastic or other exegetes who might oppose Alison's take on scripture. The margins represent her as a competent and uncontested exegete and concur with her in preferring the divine commandment to men's glosses.

New College further authorizes the Wife's teaching about marriage:

> For wel y woot that myn husbonde
> Sholde leve fader and moder & take to me. (30–31, Ne)
>
> [Glossed:] Propter hoc relinquet homo patrem et matrem ei et cetera (31, Ne).
> [For this cause shall a man leave his father and mother, Eph. 5:31]

The Latin source displays her adherence to biblical language ("leve fader and moder"; "relinquet patrem et matrem") and again confirms her teaching. The choice of gloss is intriguing, if only as an example of arcane subtlety. Ephesians quotes Genesis, and the difference between the verses is just one word ("propter," for this cause, replaces "quamobrem," wherefore). By citing Genesis, which context suggests is the Wife's obvious source, the scribe would simply support her point. Most scribes do just that.[21] The New College scribe selects the more complicated Ephesians citation, which imposes a specific Christian meaning on the union of man and woman: a man leaves his parents in order ("propter") to love his wife as Christ loves the church. In this reading, the "cause" of marriage is self-sacrificial love. By choosing Ephesians for the gloss, the scribe recalls this implication. At the same time, on a literal level, the gloss emphatically supports the Wife's procreative rationale for marriage: "for this cause"—procreation—a man shall leave his father and mother. The gloss turns the elevated metaphor of Christ marrying the church into a defense of sexual generation. The gloss adds a mischievous (ironic?) note to the Wife's argument.

The New College scribe continues selectively to highlight the subject of marriage. Where the Wife makes a potentially arcane reference to a minor biblical figure, Lameth,

> What Reckith me though men say welaway
> Of shrewd lameth and of his bigamey. (53–54, Ne)

New College provides a marginal explanation:

> Lameth primo induxit bigamiam (54, Ne).
> [Lameth married bigamously first.]

The reader is here expected to be less a biblical expert than the Wife, in need of a Latin gloss to comprehend her learned aside. Similar informative glosses appear in six other manuscripts, some of which link Lameth not only to bigamy but also to homicide.[22] The introduction of homicide implies diverse possible interpretations for Alison's "welaway": do men decry him for bigamy, homicide, or both? Are the two sins related? In these cases, glosses open the text to multiple interpretations.

Lameth gains a diverse reception across the manuscript groups, and the New College scribe does not in this instance represent a clear consensus. Most scribes (fourteen, to be precise) are more interested in the proverbial verse immediately before the Wife mentions Lameth: "Bet is to be wedded than to brynne" (52). Scribes typically highlight the proverb by translating it back into Latin: "Melius est nubere quam vri" (54, El).[23] The marginal Latin once again supports the Wife's biblical teaching. This particular gloss testifies to scribes' interest in proverbial expressions: in fact, proverbs get more attention than scripture in most manuscripts, whether that interest is signaled by a Latin translation or a "Nota." (Chaunticleer was obviously not alone in valuing Latin proverbs.) Hence the Wife's misogynistic confession, "Deceite wepyng spynnyng god hath yeue / To wommen kyndely whil they may lyue" (401–2), is popular with scribes, many of whom mark it with a "Nota" or Latin translation.[24]

Serenely distinct from the masses, the New College scribe ignores this and all other proverbs. Even if he were marking proverbs, he would miss

"Bet is to be wedded than to *brynne*," for the New College text reads "Bettir it is to be weddid than to *wynne*" (52, Ne, emphasis added)—a misprision that may make sense but lacks either apostolic authority or proverbial cogency. The misprision would not actually prevent a Latin gloss, if one were in the exemplar; other manuscripts with similar variations include a mismatched Latin gloss.[25] We may safely conclude that the New College scribe is simply not interested in proverbs.

As New College continues, Alison again cites the Apostle Paul, who counsels virginity but permits marriage:

The Apostil whenne he spak of Maidenhede
He saide that ther of precept had he noon
Men may counsel awomman to be oon
But counsel is no maner comaundement. (64–67, Ne)

Paul testifies from the margin:

De virginibus preceptum domini non habeo (63, Ne).
[Concerning virgins, I have no commandment of the Lord, I Cor. 7:25]

As we by now expect in this manuscript, her "precept" and "comaundement" accurately translate "preceptum," and the gloss substantially affirms her interpretation. The source citation is entirely proper and seemingly sober-minded, though we might pause over the fact that the scribe chooses to authorize yet another of the Wife's scriptural precedents for a nonvirginal lifestyle. The selection of glosses certainly enhances the Wife's biblical argument about marital sexuality. Eight other manuscripts exhibit similar citations, so the affirmation of marital sexuality appears a commonplace, at least among scribes.[26] The scribes' focus on conjugal sexuality would be inapt for a clerical or monastic audience, but well-suited to the married gentry, who constitute an important market for manuscripts, and who would doubtless appreciate the validation of their life choices.

The next New College gloss, the only nonbiblical marginal note, credits Alison with an exemplum:

Ful wel y knowe a lord in his houshold
Hath meny a vessel of siluer & of gold. (99–100, Ne).
[Glossed:] Exemplum (99, Ne)

As the passage continues, the Wife distinguishes between the perfection of virginity and the (lesser) good of marriage, a consistent theme in her biblical teaching. "Exemplum" marks this passage as having moral, didactic value. The implication is unique to this manuscript. Only two manuscripts identify her biblical source for the exemplum.[27] Most scribes pass over this point and concentrate instead on a reference to Jesus' advice about financial management, clearly a point of interest to the expected readers:

> But Crist that of parfeccioun is welle
> Bad nat euery wight he sholde go selle
> Al that he hadde and yeue it to the poore
> And in swich wise folwe hym and his fore
> But swynke with his hondis and labore
> He spak to hem that wol lyue parfitly
> And lordynges by youre leue that am nat I. (107–12)

The direct citation of Christ garners considerable scribal attention, and some version of the source appears in thirteen manuscripts: "Dixit dominus vende omnia que habes et da pauperibus" (108, Mc; The Lord said, sell all you have and give to the poor, Matt. 19:21).[28] We should note that the gloss quotes scripture in a way that turns the passage into an apparently universal command to "sell all." A correct understanding of Christ's teaching (*if you would be perfect,* sell all) becomes dependent on the Wife's exegesis, and the reader is here expected to privilege her interpretation over the biblical source. By putting the reader in this subordinate position, the gloss heightens Alison's authority. The New College manuscript is therefore relatively conservative in its construction of her exegetical expertise; other manuscripts not only document her biblical citations more fully but also script readers' deference to her in more complex ways.

The next New College gloss calls attention to Wife's announcement that men are sexually subject to their wives:

> The power wol I haue during al my lif
> Both of his propir body and nat he
> Right thus the Apostil tolde it me. (158–60, Ne)

With another nod to Latin authority:

> Vir non habet potestatem sui corporis set mulier. (158, Ne)
> [The man does not have power over his own body, but the wife (does), I Cor. 7:4]

As usual, the Wife competently translates scripture ("power" for "potestatem," "body" for "corporis"), and the gloss confirms her teaching.

The New College scribe thus consistently presents the Wife as a dependable biblical authority. At the same time, his careful attention to her biblical support for sexual intercourse suggests a sense of humor akin to Chaucer's—and encourages sly pleasure in the Wife's (s)exegesis, so different from Jerome's.

In contrast to the New College scribe, modern scholars interpret this citation as evidence of the Wife's so-called exegetical failing. They point out that whereas she emphasizes her power over her spouse, scripture gives the same power to both partners. Modern readers regularly conclude that her "partial" citation establishes her self-interested reading practices.[29] This conclusion is based entirely on modern standards of citation and hermeneutic expectations, which have no relevance to the Middle Ages. The New College scribe in fact represents a medieval consensus. This passage gathers considerable attention in manuscripts, and the most often-repeated gloss agrees with New College in affirming that a married man does not have power over his own body, but the wife does.[30] If medieval scribes conformed to modern expectations, at least one would correct the Wife's gendered reading of scripture; none does. Indeed, medieval readers could not possibly perceive her citation as "partial": scripture is not yet divided into verses (that will happen in the sixteenth century), so she simply begins, as medieval exegetes do, with the part of the text that pertains to her argument. Far from countering her gendered exegesis, a number of scribes enhance her position by adding one or more glosses depicting husbands as their wives' sexual debtors, without noting that wives are also their husbands' debtors.[31] In short, most scribes unambiguously support Alison's point about a husband's sexual subjection to his wife. Lopsided scriptural arguments are evidently acceptable, even normative.

Alison continues to interpret apostolic teachings about marriage, with her New College scribe accompanying her:

Right thus the Apostil tolde it me
And bad our husbondis for to love vs weel. (160–61, Ne)

[Glossed:] Viri diligite vxores vestras et cetera. (160, Ne)
[Men, love your wives, Eph. 5: 25 or Col. 3:10]

Although "love" in the Wife's mouth carries an unavoidable sexual innuendo, the gloss affirms that scripture commands just that ("diligite"). Here as elsewhere in New College, both Alison and the scribe argue that the Bible legitimates sexual love in marriage, a message well suited to the manuscript's probably devout but not ascetic gentry readers. By calling attention to these biblical injunctions, the New College scribe implies his appreciation of the argument.[32] The Wife's emphasis on men's roles and responsibilities in marriage, highlighted by these glosses, reverses clerics' characteristic attention to women's duties. Scriptural hermeneutics are obviously gendered, but that does not invalidate Alison's focus. The New College manuscript, along with many others, uses Latin glosses to display her scriptural foundations, in the process cloaking her in the aura of authority. These manuscripts contribute coherently to Alison's undermining of asceticism and clerical authority. Indeed, the manuscripts establish her bourgeois, lay status as an alternate site of cultural power.

The New College margins trace the main points in the Wife's teaching about marriage. Some of these points are gendered: men should leave father and mother, give power over their bodies to their wives, and love their wives. Other points apply equally to men and women: God commands procreation; bigamy is reprehensible; Paul permits marriage. The gendered aspect of her exegesis would be remarkable for her earliest audiences, yet I find no resistance to it in these manuscripts, no pattern of marginal contestation with the text.[33] Notably, the glosses evidence partial and simplified readings of the poem; like all supplements, they displace the original work. As glossed, Alison argues that scripture commands a man to be sexually indebted and subject to his wife. (The manuscripts are not concerned about the wife's subjection to her husband; perhaps they take that for granted.)

In these manuscripts, Alison clearly interprets the "wo that is in mariage" as the strain arising from a man's sexual debt to his wife, his so-called tribulation in the flesh. The glosses lend intellectual authority to Alison's antimatrimonial argument. These glosses also call attention to Chaucer's witty and highly original deviation from earlier arguments. Antimatrimonial literature typically points out the domestic distractions of crying babies, difficult servants, and a complaining wife; a wife's unending material desires; and the continual threat of cuckoldry, poisoning, and lesser betrayals. These domestic trials are memorably detailed in Jerome's polemic against Jovinian and would have been prominent in Jankyn's Book of Wicked Wives.[34] In a striking reversal of Jerome and subsequent antimatrimonial literature, Alison makes sexual intercourse the sole—and surely comical—trial of married life. The many glosses that call attention to this argument can hardly be coincidental. The scribes presumably recognized and appreciated Chaucer's ludic revision of the discourse, as they flagged it for devout readers. According to the glossed manuscripts, scripture unambiguously commands conjugal sex.

In the New College manuscript, the poetic text and marginal glosses reinforce each other, creating the *Prologue* as a sermon aimed at men. Many manuscripts obviously agree. Indeed, on the topic of marital sexuality, most scribes treat the Wife as a persuasive exegete delivering authoritative Scriptural lessons. We must be clear about the character of her exegesis: she is not a Scholastic, nor, judging from their glosses, are her scribes. The manuscript margins nowhere disclose the kind of commentary developed in a contemporary monastery or university context. Alison's authority, like that of her scribes, is limited. Near the beginning of the Prologue, for instance, she recalls Jesus' words to the Samaritan woman at the well, but forestalls interpretation: "What he mente therby I can not sayn" (20, Ne). Although this line appears in almost all manuscripts, it gathers no gloss: apparently, Alison's scribes cannot or will not say "what he mente" either. In fact, she and her scribes typically respect a clear division of labor. The Wife elucidates the meaning of scripture; the scribes selectively copy her sources. The scribes certainly shape meaning, but their glosses do not contest her authority.

The scribes' respect for the Wife's biblical learning could be a reaction to intratextual hints from Chaucer. Within the *Prologue*, the Pardoner dramatically declares himself convinced by Alison's teaching, modeling a semiserious response to the argument:

> Vp stert the pardoner & that anon
> Now dame quod he be god & be saint Iohn
> Ye be an nobil prechour in this caas
> I was aboute to wedde awif alas
> What sholde I bye it my self so dere
> Yit hadde y lever wedde no wif tw yere. (163–68, Ne)

The Pardoner heeds the "nobil prechour" and decides against marriage: the threat of sex puts him right off. His conversion establishes Alison's effectiveness in advancing traditional asceticism. This is a remarkable moment in the history of antimatrimonial literature. Arguments against marriage are almost always, as Jill Mann notes, a "purely male affair...addressed to a man by another man." Such arguments are also consistently "ineffectual," "redundant," and "ignored." Thus in the *Merchant's Tale*, Justinus tries half-heartedly to dissuade January from marriage, but the marriage proceeds apace.[35] Similarly, Alison's fifth husband, Jankyn, reads to her from a book intended to dissuade Oxford clerks from marriage—an obviously ineffectual book, to be sure. When Alison takes the reins, however, the argument against marriage proves remarkably persuasive. Indeed, one historical reader echoes the Pardoner's distaste for the marriage debt: "Nota seruitutem in matrimonio" (155, Ra3). For those readers averse to sex, Alison successfully advances asceticism. This is a *tour de force* supplement to Jerome: whereas *Against Jovinian* obviously does not enable Jankyn to avoid marriage, Alison's performative exegesis induces the Pardoner to do just that. Of course, the ambiguously sexual Pardoner is hardly an exemplary figure, with or without his newly found commitment to asceticism. Still, Alison's rhetorical effectiveness once again subjects Jerome's treatise to "subversive outrage."[36]

Chaucer develops another antimatrimonial argument in "Lenvoy de Chaucer a Bukton," which anticipates having as little impact on the reader as Jankyn's book does. "Lenvoy" continues the Wife's development as an exegete and could further inspire some of the scribes' biblical glosses. The poem quotes Alison twice: first in Chaucer's promise to speak of the "sorwe and wo that is in mariage," and later in his recollection of a proverb she recites ("Bet ys to wedde than brenne").[37] These quotations, together with a reference to the *Prologue*, treat the Wife as an established authority worthy of citation. Like the *Prologue*, "Lenvoy" follows scripture in representing marriage as masculine subjection to women. In marriage, a man:

> shal have sorwe on thy flessh, thy lyf,
> And ben thy wives thral, as seyn these wise;
> And yf that hooly writ may nat suffyse,
> Experience shal the teche. (19–22)

Jill Mann calls attention to the comedy of this poem, implicit in its assumption that the advice will not be heeded: "experience shal the teche."[38] The poem nonetheless concludes by directing Bukton to read the Wife of Bath so as to escape imminent sexual thralldom. The Wife appears a trustworthy exegete, using "hooly writ" to teach the "wo that is in mariage" for men; and her *Prologue* remains Chaucer's best hope (tongue in cheek) for male freedom from the "sorwe" of sex. By discrediting the Wife's exegesis, modern critics have missed the point. The force as well as the comedy of Alison's antimatrimonial argument lies precisely in its valid scriptural authority. The joke is not on the Wife, but on men like Jankyn and Bukton who, refusing to be dissuaded by scriptural warnings, run headlong into the bondage of conjugal sex.

Both the Wife's *Prologue* and "Lenvoy a Bukton" grant a lay woman the capacity to cite scripture persuasively, at least in an argument about marital sexuality. Chaucer's own reception of Alison's exegesis establishes a coherent foundation for the New College and other scribes' biblical glosses. Hiding behind the *Prologue*, Chaucer slyly winks at readers capable of appreciating the humor in Alison's scriptural lesson. The New College scribe gets the joke and in his turn uses biblical glosses to point out the comic implication of Alison's sermon: marriage means sex, so men had

better run the other way! Only an earnestly ascetic (impotent, ambiva-
lently sexual) reader would be turned from marriage by this argument,
while most of the laity would probably be glad to discover in the glossed
sermon an acceptable biblical rationale for the exercise of conjugal piety.

A Historical Consensus

The vast majority of biblical glosses, similar to those of New College,
never question or undermine the Wife's exegetical authority. On the contrary, most manuscripts that supply source notes support her biblical references at every turn, and most call attention to her accuracy of citation.
This is obviously true of twelve manuscripts ranging from the first to the
last quarter of the fifteenth century, all of which reinforce the impression
created by the New College glosses.[39] In fact, these manuscripts allow
us to extend our conclusions about biblical citations to other kinds of
glosses. Each of these manuscripts includes several glosses on the Wife's
biblical teachings, confirming that Jesus went to a wedding in Galilee,[40]
that the Bible commands men and women to increase and multiply,[41] that
a man should leave his father and mother when he marries,[42] that it is better to marry than burn,[43] that Paul had no precept about marriage,[44] that
a man has no power over his own flesh,[45] that the married man owes his
wife a debt,[46] and that Jesus spoke about selling all you have and giving
to the poor.[47] Although the twelve manuscripts differ in their selection
of biblical glosses, each affirms the Wife's treatment of scripture in much
the way New College does. This set of manuscripts points toward a clear
historical consensus: these fifteenth-century scribes present the Wife of
Bath as an authoritative exegete, and not just in the delicate area of marriage relations.

Unlike New College, some of these manuscripts also briefly gloss
other of the Wife's learned remarks. When the Wife claims that even
Argus, with his hundred eyes, could not keep track of her, several scribes
mark the passage, albeit with some uncertainty about just how many
eyes Argus is supposed to have.[48] A mention of Pasiphae, queen of Crete,
prompts marginal notations specifying that Crete is an island.[49] And,
like most manuscripts other than New College, all of these works make
note of proverbs, probably regarding them as serious wisdom literature.[50]
One manuscript pays attention as well to the Wife's scientific learning,
noting her reference to "Protholome" (182, Se) and commenting on an
astrological passage: "Nota the diuersite bitwex Mercurie and Venus"
(675, Se). Taken together, these manuscripts establish a clear pattern of
reception. In these dozen manuscripts, as in New College, the Wife is
represented as a learned authority over several discourses. The margins

of these pages evidence no hint of anxiety about how she uses sources, biblical or other. To the contrary, the margins present her as authoritative across traditionally masculine fields of learning, including but not restricted to the biblical.

In short, a significant number of medieval scribes represent Alison of Bath as a dependable (and sometimes amusing) biblical authority: the majority of scribes who include biblical glosses foster a positive reception of the Wife's exegesis.[51] Hence manuscript study requires us to recognize that this particular lay woman was represented as authoritative over scripture and other learned discourses throughout the fifteenth century. This does not mean that the scribes would regard actual lay women as persuasive exegetes. The scribes who write and select glosses are aware of Chaucer's authorial status, and deferential toward the arcane learning so prominently displayed in this text. Whether they are authorizing the Wife or Chaucer is an open question (they may, like modern readers, occasionally confuse the two). They nonetheless inscribe material pages that support the Wife's claims to knowledge of scripture. In the realm of fiction, at least, a woman preaches to men and does so with authority and persuasive force. Fifteenth-century Chaucer manuscripts serve as midwives to the idea of an authoritative woman exegete—perhaps because she advocates for marital sex.

Peter Shillingsburg cogently remarks that "a literary work is only partially represented in each of its physical manifestations."[52] The New College manuscript witnesses to one scribe's partial reading of the text and discloses his appreciation for the Wife's lessons about men's sexual bondage. Other manuscripts (also partially) concentrate on other discourses, from the biblical to the patristic, proverbial, astrological, and mythological. Collectively, the margins of these glossed manuscripts call attention to the work's astonishing erudition, emphasize the Wife's wide-ranging intellectual authority, and evidence a consistently positive reception of her gendered exegesis. By studying these many partial representations, we may appreciate anew Chaucer's unusual reaccentuation of scripture, and more fully apprehend the work's historical potential for meaning. The Wife's exegetical authority is literally marginal: that is, constructed in and through the Latin margins of material works.

Manuscript margins witness to scribes' interest in Alison's exegesis, and to the authority they grant her vernacular translations. By choosing to highlight these particular features of the text, scribes lead us to infer the presence of buyers who seek precisely these treatments of vernacular scripture. In other words, most manuscripts of the *Prologue* address readers who accept, as Alison herself does, a mix of Lollardy and orthodoxy, and who more than likely mirror her in their questioning of conventional clerical authority and in their desire for lucid (and perhaps also ludic) biblical hermeneutics. The glosses at once reveal and direct the interests of their intended readers.

Marginal Authority

All the manuscripts studied here reveal a close relationship between glossing programs and anticipated readers. New College and the group of twelve manuscripts address readers, most likely among the gentry, who are expected to be deferential toward Alison's (Chaucer's) learning, and to take it at face value. Although each material work is unique, some general patterns emerge from most of the glossed manuscripts: the Wife of Bath appears bold in her translation of extensive scriptural passages, reliable in her biblical references, sure-footed in her understanding of fine distinctions (as between counsel and commandment), and persuasive in her account of men's marital obligations. So far as I can discern, none of these manuscripts challenges Alison's readings of biblical texts, supplements her literal hermeneutic with allegoresis, or imports moralizing comments from Scholastic glosses. This does not mean that medieval readers never supplemented her interpretations with spiritual, typological, anagogical, or tropological analyses; but no manuscript evidence of such a practice survives. Instead, manuscripts that include biblical glosses typically do nothing more than identify selected sources, often focusing on those passages that instruct men about the "woes" of marriage: the obligation to procreate, pay the marriage debt, and be submissive to a wife's sexual desires. On these points, the Wife appears an entirely capable exegete, who drolly redefines the "woe" and "tribulation" of marriage as sexual intercourse. Chaucer's antimatrimonial argument depends on his persona's persuasive treatment of scripture, and scribes' glosses support the improbable authority he fashions for her.

For that matter, the marginal notes lend credibility to the work's playful engagement with scriptural teachings about marriage. Chaucer gives us an ambivalent, comic portrait of a matrimonial specialist, and the New College and other scribes often echo him from the margins, selecting biblical sources so as to emphasize the Wife's risible exegetical competence. At other times, scribes seriously gloss her biblical sources, proverbs, astrological or mythological references, in effect reinventing her as a more or less straightforward authority figure. Manuscripts can thus heighten or mute the notorious Chaucerian irony (and sometimes do both in the same work). For all the variety of these glosses, however, none of them supports the oft-repeated modern idea that Alison is an inadequate or heterodox exegete.

The Wife of Bath's Prologue nonetheless does dramatize the potential threat of a lay woman exegete, and Chaucer uses the *Prologue* to reflect on contemporary ecclesiastical apprehensions that lay women, if given access to scripture, would become irreverent and unruly. Alison affirms these fears, proving concerned officials right. At the same time, Chaucer defuses the danger, for he makes this lay woman entirely orthodox in her exegesis. She agrees, for instance, with Jerome's main argument in *Against Jovinian*: virginity is better than marriage.[53] She avoids a (Lollard) condemnation of clerical celibacy or rejection of virginity.[54] Her exegesis is not eccentric by the standards of the time, nor do her human foibles jeopardize the received truths of religion. To the extent that she represents feminine exegetical authority, she makes that prospect unfrightening, even entertaining. Chaucer turns the threat of feminine exegesis into broad comedy, and many of his scribes seem to appreciate his humor and lend their quills to the cause. Ultimately, however, the *Prologue* confirms the strength of orthodoxy by suggesting that if women took over exegesis, nothing much would change. Chaucer crafts a remarkably double-edged representation of a feminine exegete: at once authoritative and marginal, credible and risible. That representation is further complicated by each scribe who comments on it from the margins. For the most part, though, scribes grant her grounding in canonical scripture and call attention to her lessons on marital sexuality. Scribes translate Chaucer's persona into various representations of "auctoritee," creating new implications for the work through their choice of glosses.

Scribal biblical glosses give us access to the Wife of Bath's marginal and marginalized potential for meaning. In the fifteenth-century glossed manuscripts, Alison represents not just a supposedly feminine "experience" but also the masculine authority of Chaucer and his scribes. She promotes the subversive literary and intellectual pleasures of a gendered exegesis, and it appears her biblical lessons about conjugal piety were appreciated by her early readers. Among those readers, Alison convincingly claims both biblical knowledge and the cultural power derived from that knowledge. Whereas Chaucer develops the Wife of Bath as a contained subversion of *Against Jovinian,* many of his scribes present her as a credible lay preacher of marital rights and responsibilities, suggesting approval of her challenge to clerical asceticism. Fifteenth-century Chaucer manuscripts thus disclose yet another version of the woman on top in medieval exegesis, granted authority to interpret the Word for the laity—and for those readers who, together with many of her scribes, appreciate her orthodox but nonetheless subversive exegesis.

AFTERWORD

Ideology creates, by virtue of its exclusionary nature, social locations outside of itself and therefore capable of making epistemological claims about it. . . . oppressed social locations create identities and perspectives, embodiments and feelings, histories and experiences that stand outside of and offer valuable knowledge about the powerful ideologies that seem to enclose us.[1]

Masculine power is both attractive and problematic in early Christianity. Christ's renunciation of wealth, power, and status makes him an uneasy role model for late Roman and medieval men of faith. His teachings about the value of humility over pride, poverty over wealth, and submission over dominance collide with antique Roman culture and continue to jar against the social norms of medieval Europe. Suspended on thousands of crucifixes throughout Europe, Christ at once enacts a self-sacrificial divine love and watches over the rise of a hierarchical church, the consolidation of a militant papacy, and the amassing of ecclesiastical wealth. The image of the crucified Lord creates the possibility of a counterhistory within the institutional church: a subversive narrative in which the most perfect man eschews conventional social power, and calls upon his followers to do likewise. Medieval men can find easier role models in scripture (Moses, Paul), and the majority clearly do just that. Yet the example of Christ persistently challenges those who aspire to imitate him, confronting them with difficult questions about the relationship between the church and dominant culture, about the basis of their own social authority and institutional power. In response, some exegetes fashion for themselves childlike or feminine personae that express a spiritual authority distinct from traditional modes of social power.

In part, then, Augustine fashions himself after Christ and emphasizes the virtues of humility, patience, and powerlessness. He represents his mother as a priest-figure, his primary intercessor with the deity, and himself as an infant suckling at God's breast. Assuming the role of a child, he comes before the reader as powerless, the antithesis of a proud Roman man. In other words, his inversion of gender hierarchy serves to disavow the corruptions of power and worldliness. In *Confessions,* he treats gender inversion as an expression of Christian virtue, a rhetorical strategy by means of which he and others distinguish themselves from pagans. Although this narrative self-fashioning advances Augustine's *imitatio Christi,* it does not help him conceptualize a legitimate ecclesiastical power. As a child at God's breast, he can claim intimacy with and a privileged knowledge of his deity. For all its rhetorical merits, however, this persona is ill-suited to represent a bishop's authority over his flock, or to rationalize his office of correcting error and heresy. The powerless child does not invoke ecclesiastical authority. When Augustine needs to establish a more muscular faith—as, for instance, when he judges between truth and error in scriptural interpretations—he resorts to a conventional patriarchal gender role: the man on top. Alternating between the performance of spiritual powerlessness and the assertion of episcopal power, Augustine implies the difficulty, perhaps the impossibility, of inventing a model for his office in keeping with Christ's paradoxical powerlessness. His conflicting modes of self-fashioning reveal a gap between ancient cultural norms and the challenging, often socially subversive, teachings of Christ.

Over time, Augustine's legacy has been oversimplified. The Catholic church has declared Augustine one of its fathers and emphasized patristic writings about a father God. Although this patriarchal language has been normalized through centuries of use, it is, from a historicist point of view, distinctly unhelpful. The language serves to project backward in time an idealized androcentric myth of church origins: the "patristic age" evokes a unified hierarchical ideal, at the cost of repressing the reality of diverse and contentious micro-Christendoms. Put bluntly, "the patristic age" is a theological fiction that serves the purposes of a masculine clerical hierarchy but does not help us understand our complex cultural history, which underlies present institutions and widely shared assumptions about religious and social authority. If we think about it, "patristic" is an inapposite label for the likes of Augustine, Jerome, and Chrysostom, who are at best ambivalent about patriarchal social conventions. They do not uniformly describe God as father, let alone accept that role themselves. They consistently advance an ascetic ideology that makes fathering itself suspect, unless transformed into a metaphor about spiritual genealogy. "Patristic" is a misleading label to attach to writers who repeatedly contest patriarchal norms.

Augustine's *Confessions* can productively estrange us from the assumptions about masculine origins coded into the Catholic church's interested creation of its fathers. To the extent that he develops an unstable gender ideology, he subverts masculine dominance and troubles the status quo.

His autobiographical exegesis reveals some of the pressures on gender in the early church, and it allows us access to a historical juncture at which gender norms are in flux and open to revision. Although Augustine's gender innovations are dead ends, they are nonetheless invaluable to modern historicist scholarship, for it is precisely such false starts that illuminate the complex and continually changing relationship between gender and religion. Some of those false starts may help us—*mutatis mutandis*—to reimagine the possibilities for a future in which gender is not considered a significant aspect of being, not fixed by the accidents of embodiment.

Some exegetes, Jerome and Chrysostom among them, exhibit more subtle ambivalence about gender and power hierarchies. Although radical in their ascetic demands, Jerome in *Against Jovinian* and Chrysostom in his sermons on Timothy do not seem to question their own masculine privilege, as Augustine does in *Confessions*. Like "Paul" in 1 Timothy 2, Jerome and Chrysostom distinguish between their own normative discourse and women's illegitimate speech; they discount women's words by picturing woman as the antiascetic Other. From their perspective, the woman on top indicates a departure from divine order. While advocating for gender hierarchy, however, both Jerome and Chrysostom recognize that women are capable of independently assessing and even rejecting their teachings. Both men assert an authority that is not universally accepted within their communities. Knowing their teachings are contested, they seek to persuade their audiences, including women, rather than to impose on them through the power of their position, as will happen in later works such as the *Gloss*. Gender is not the only hierarchical order they seek to advance, moreover. They also elaborate an ascetic hierarchy—virgins over wives and widows—that complicates gender asymmetry. For Jerome in particular, the ascetic life disrupts traditional patriarchal order.

The trope of the woman on top conveys men's struggles for power and authority in the early church. In the case of Augustine, the trope functions to repress the reality of power struggles among men and allows him to assert a humble authority derived from his bond with a maternal God. For Jerome, the trope describes those who disagree with him. Although men in fact dissent from *Against Jovinian,* Jerome relegates dissent to a "feminine" sphere that lacks cultural authority. He at once anticipates dissent and stigmatizes it as feminine error. Chrysostom takes the trope further in his two sermons on 1 Timothy 2. Suggesting that women are all body, he subtly denies them the capacity to assert an alternative exegesis. Feminine dissent reduces to the wearing of fashions "intended" to arouse men. Both Jerome and Chrysostom espouse symbolic violence against women, perhaps most obviously in their efforts to convince women to internalize a masochistic responsibility for men's desire.

The trope of the woman on top reveals exegetes' attempts to (de)naturalize their claims to power and demonstrates men's awareness that questions are circulating about the religious authority they seek to exercise. Each of these exegetes bases his authority on his knowledge of scripture; each creates through the discourse of exegesis an implicit hierarchy of the clerical over the lay reader. This hierarchy appears inadequate to their purposes, however, for each of these writers shores up his position by appealing to time-honored traditions of masculine privilege. They make the emerging discourse of exegesis dependent on the status quo of social power. Despite the range of attitudes they express toward gender and power, all of them contribute significantly to the development of a hierarchical church, constructed according to an ancient social blueprint. Their exegesis both explicitly and implicitly advances masculine clerical power and authority. In other words, all three of these exegetes invent structures of power that authorize their biblical interpretations and legitimize their knowledge of scripture, and all three at some point claim a "natural," inherent authority by conforming to (pagan) gender norms. While recognizing this, we should not oversimplify their reliance on gender normativity or see them as merely conformist. They clearly resist some aspects of dominant culture: Augustine attempts to ground his spiritual authority in the visionary intimacy of the maternal sphere; Jerome renounces patriarchy; and Chrysostom teaches Christian women—whether or not married, whether or not virgins—to dress modestly, revealing bodies set apart for God. Strategic gender normativity most likely enables radicalism on these points.

Augustine enacts the most unstable and subtly subversive gender roles in *Confessions*. Although few of his innovations in this work are accepted into dominant exegetical traditions, he exposes some of the problematic issues that can arise from the gendering of Christian power. Those issues continue to plague exegetes into and beyond the age of Chaucer. Many exegetes after Augustine try, as he does, both to follow Christ and to assert the power of the institutional church. The dissonance between these roles potentially intensifies as the church grows ever more centralized, wealthy, and militant—in a word, powerful. Although the image of a powerless Christ is far from universal in medieval culture, it remains compelling as a symbol of Christian virtue, despite or perhaps because ecclesiastical power is continually expanding. Christ is not, of course, the only sign of this ideology: the woman on top can also signify a humble Christianity, a self-sacrificial virtue associated primarily with women and children. The danger of this trope is that it can create for its audience an appealing false reality, a seductively virtuous self-image that bears little if any resemblance to the real.

The Fleury *Slaughter of Innocents* witnesses to the potentially tragic cultural consequences of this representational strategy. The play carries the trope of woman on top to an extreme: Christians appear in the guise of slaughtered Innocents and Rachel, weak and vulnerable victims. Christendom has no manly defenders in this play, for virility and aggression belong wholly to Jews, the violent Other. The Fleury playwright describes a power vacuum within Christianity. Since manly power cannot attach to those who follow the crucified lord, it becomes the irredeemable attribute of the Other, impossible to reconcile with Christian ideology. Christ inspires a lacuna within the church: his example generates a lack, a persistent absence of power in representations of the ideal church (sadly, reality does not correspond to this ideal). Where Augustine alternates between conventional masculinity and holy inversions, attempting to have the best of both worlds, the Fleury playwright discovers only a choice between passive (Christian) victimization and worldly (Jewish) rule. In short, the play creates a false reality in which Christians are victims, and Jews persecutors. Those who imagine themselves victims of religious hatred can the more easily justify persecuting Jews, their supposedly self-declared enemy.

The Fleury play represents women and children as undeniable authority figures, within certain limits. While the children perform the *imitatio Christi* of martyrdom, Rachel-Mary articulates the proper affective response to his and their deaths. Like dozens, if not hundreds, of liturgical plays, the Fleury *Slaughter of Innocents* elaborates moving images of Christian powerlessness and self-sacrifice. The representation feminizes Christendom and treats all believers as participants in a sacred inversion of social order. Notably, the era of the play also witnesses to a renaissance of God as mother. Gender inversion, expressed through the trope of woman on top, obviously has a continuing dynamic potentiality in religious culture, readily eliding with a devotional *imitatio Christi*.

The Fleury play is roughly contemporary with the *Gloss*, and the two works disclose the contradictory attitudes toward the feminine that circulate in ecclesiastical culture. While the feminine is the site of affective authority in the play, which attributes its most innovative exegesis to a feminine voice, women have no spiritual authority in the *Gloss* on 1 Timothy 2. Indeed, the *Gloss* makes women incapable of exegesis, affective or otherwise. Clearly, neither work alone adequately represents the religious culture of the time. When juxtaposed, though, they suggest a powerful synergy: while the *Gloss* compilers consider women incompetent for sacred clerical functions, the playwright enables the return of repressed feminine authority, gives it a fictional voice and a real audience, and thus allows the feminine a vital subversive presence at the heart of monastic culture. The drama brings what is excluded in academic exegesis back into devotional culture.

The growth of the institutional church creates other possibilities for the woman on top. When, in the late fourteenth century, the church comes under attack for corruption, when schism prompts critiques of the papacy, when monks and friars seem (at least to many antifraternal writers) to have wandered from their missions, conventional religious authority is nothing if not contested. This is the broader context for Chaucer's use of the trope in his *Wife of Bath's Prologue:* calls for reformation of the church open anew the possibility of a woman speaking with authority against a compromised masculine hierarchy. As in Augustine's *Confessions,* as in the Fleury *Slaughter of Innocents,* here the woman on top evokes the principle of inversion that transforms the least into the greatest. Alison of Bath is, of course, an ironic victim, who playfully turns her powerless status into a form of power. Yet Chaucer's comedy depends on Alison being a credible exegete within her cultural context. That she displaces Jerome implies Chaucer's trenchant analysis of a weakness in Jerome's treatise and in fourteenth-century English culture: the absence of an authoritative nonascetic hermeneutic for the laity. Alison can supplant exegetes like Jerome because her biblical supplement responds—as Jerome's does not—to the laity's need for teachings about marriage that do not denigrate it as a social institution. Both the Pardoner within the fiction and a consensus of fifteenth-century scribes receive Alison as a competent exegete because her exegesis fills this need. Indeed, the scribes typically endorse her scriptural proof of married men's sexual duties, calling attention to the biblical texts that make sexual intercourse the "woe" of marriage. Alison's immediate fictional and historical reception thus creates her as an authoritative biblical exegete.

Studying these particular moments in the development of exegesis from the fourth to the fifteenth century exposes historical movements toward and away from supportive institutions (monasteries, universities), as well as changes in writers' methods of authorizing their biblical knowledge. The sites of exegesis clearly influence the messages found in scripture and their declared relevance to expected audiences. This implication emerges most obviously from the survey of exegesis on 1 Timothy 2. While Jerome twists "Paul" to discover an ascetic renunciation of sex, Chrysostom assumes in his homilies that women will marry and enjoy sex but wants every detail of their dress to reflect their Christian chastity. Working in the twelfth-century schools, the *Gloss* compilers concern themselves with restraining women's sexuality within marital and procreative boundaries, and with delegitimizing feminine speech. A few centuries later, looking at the schools from the outside, the Wife of Bath rejects her husbands' narrowly interested exegesis. In the process, she reveals a failure of masculine governance, a core weakness in the symbolic order of church and society. As we progress from Jerome to the Wife of Bath, we move into and away from academic and monastic contexts, toward and away from a centralized church.

Each exegetical text supplements scripture in a new way; each comments on urgent but ephemeral cultural issues. A bourgeois husband addressing his wife tries to hold on to economic power, while she remarks on the flaws his self-governance. An ascetic preacher facing a congregation focuses on the communal moral implications of women's fashion. A liturgical play explains recent reported cases of ritual murder in light of scriptural narratives and traditions of interpretation, thereby creating a biblical context for current beliefs. Taken together, these works demonstrate the vitality of exegesis, its broad cultural and generic diffusion, and its perpetual reinvention. By focusing on ruptures in the developing discourse, we discover that interpretations of biblical meaning are always local, always specific to a particular setting. Exegesis is a sequence of disparate works, supplements that fill perceived gaps—rarely the same gaps—both in scripture and in earlier exegesis. The discourse can be invented as a universal or coherent tradition only by the retrospective intervention of theology, only by substituting an ideology of transcendent meaning for the particularities of each social and embodied position embedded in the texts.

Each of these exegetical works emerges at a moment of change that encourages writers to seek new ways to authorize their exegesis. Augustine, the Fleury playwright, and Chaucer assume their authority behind the fiction of a supposedly inferior child or woman, and in the process encode alternate sites of knowledge and authority, centered respectively on humility, affective piety, and lay literalism. These fictional voices are valuable to exegetes precisely because they signify a humble, apparently powerless social position. Speaking through fictional masks, these exegetes claim authority while seeming to disclaim power. Their complex rhetorical strategies for voicing exegesis hint at their uneasiness with the gendered power structure and tip us off to their ambivalence about exercising power directly. By assuming feminine and childlike personae, these writers destabilize hierarchical gender norms; they simultaneously strengthen those norms by developing a discourse of knowledge and power that excludes actual women (and, of course, children). In the process, these exegetes reveal that their faith is not easily reconciled with the gender hierarchy on which they depend for social authority.

In each of these case studies, voicing emerges as a crucial aspect of exegesis: voicing signals at once how knowledge about God and scripture is being defined, how the authority to interpret the Bible is being grounded, in short, how power is being constituted. Augustine's image of suckling at God's breast mystifies his knowledge about scripture and derives his interpretive authority from his relationship with his maternal deity. He incorporates the Word with his mother's milk, and he conveys to his reader the Word he hears in his inner ear. In this way, he removes himself from polemical interpretive contests over the text of scripture. The voicing of *Confessions* is integral to Augustine's exegetical strategy: he presents the work as a prayer to and dialogue with God, expressing in every phrase the closeness with his deity that authorizes his commentary on Genesis.

Liturgical drama is likewise performative and attributes to specific characters—often women—a similarly mystified knowledge of God. The Fleury Innocents and Rachel have no realistic sources for their knowledge, but their affective exegesis nonetheless discovers vivid parallels between Christ's crucifixion, the Slaughter of Innocents, all Christian martyrs, and the supposed victims of ritual murder. Affect becomes a form of knowledge in this play, and it seems that all humble believers may likewise achieve the Innocents' and Rachel's knowledge of divine history. The affective force of the play contrasts strikingly with the more rational, academic tone of the *Gloss,* and the two works obviously develop dissimilar exegetical methods aimed at promoting different kinds of knowledge. The works nonetheless participate in the same culture of devotional reading. The *Gloss* is organized to prompt a deliberate rumination over each word of scripture; the Fleury play displays the affective force that could develop out of that reading practice.

Chaucer voices his marriage sermon through a middle-class lay woman, which gives him distance from "her" lay hermeneutics, forceful critique of masculine governance, and ludic assessment of men's marital woes. Here too, the sources of "her" knowledge are obscured and can be read as deriving from her clerical husband or from her experience. Chaucer claims no power to interpret scripture: he is, like the *Gloss* compilers or, for that matter, like Augustine, merely conveying the words of another. Chaucer's method is, of course, far more openly transgressive than theirs, but each of these cases demonstrates that voicing can be a vital part of how exegesis means.

The woman on top is an unpredictable trope. Medieval writers often equate women with the body and irrationality, which allows them to associate men with the spirit and reason. Exegetes regularly rewrite the lowly woman as a site of legitimate spiritual authority, and their discursive acts challenge the traditional gender hierarchy. Consequently, the woman on top trope discloses profound conflicts between religion and social norms. Precisely because gender hierarchy is an unsettled issue in medieval culture, the trope has no settled meaning. A feminine persona can be used to voice "gentle" emotions—nurturing love, compassion, self-sacrifice—and a great deal of existing scholarship dwells on these facets of affective piety. We should not, however, romanticize feminine affect. While exemplifying passionate devotion to the body of Christ, women speakers may also promote intolerance toward Jews, as Rachel does in the Fleury play. Feminine speakers may represent serious cultural authority and privileged ways of knowing God, as Monica does in *Confessions;* or they may express illegitimate opinions or supposedly irrational perspectives, as they often do in Jerome's *Against Jovinian.* The woman on top cannot be reduced either to a stigmatized body or to a simplistic affective piety, nor is her wisdom necessarily to be discounted merely because she is a lay member of the church. The discursive value of the trope is its flexibility. Feminine impersonations allow writers to explore the difficult paradoxes of Christian ecclesiastical power, not the least of which is the problem of imitating a savior who refused conventional power. The trope of the woman on top helps writers invent their ecclesiastical power and discursive authority without seeming to overreach.

How writers voice their texts rewards close attention because it brings pertinent discursive and historical issues to light. Each exegetical work makes voicing integral to the invention of specific kinds of authority—visionary, pastoral, affective, scholarly, lay. Most simply, voicing helps to elucidate how exegetes reaccentuate scripture for particular audiences and purposes. This is true even when nothing overtly calls attention to writers' strategies, as when the *Gloss* compilers convey their own interpretive authority through the voices of the "fathers." Voicing gives us a useful purchase on exegetes' conceptions of power relations and gender asymmetry, and on their sometimes anxious invention of their own authority to say what God means. Indeed, exegetes' repeated strategy of misdirection—their hiding behind women—is perhaps the clearest sign that authority over scripture is not easily asserted in any of these contexts.

Literary exegesis does not emerge from this study as subordinate to academic exegesis, though that case has been made in the past, and though some studies of academic works and traditions seem to imply their cultural priority. Academic exegesis has received more study in recent years than belletristic exegesis has, which leads to the unintended impression that academic works carry greater cultural weight. When, a half century ago, Beryl Smalley established the value of studying academic traditions, a shift toward those traditions made complete sense. Smalley's magisterial stature in medieval exegetical studies means that her historicist model continues even now to dominate the field. Although it is entirely right that such a brilliant and tireless scholar should influence the shape of subsequent studies, a certain narrowing of approach can at present be detected in many books and articles about medieval exegesis, a sign of encroaching ossification. Greater theoretical, philosophical, and methodological diversity can only benefit the field. Post-structuralist, Foucauldian, and feminist approaches to exegesis should be encouraged so that we may arrive at a broader conception of exegesis, and so that we may comprehend how the discourse is used to invent power relations, ecclesiastical authority, gender asymmetry, and Christian identity. There is as well good reason to expand the canon so as to enable a more complete understanding of the multiple paths by which scripture is appropriated into culture, its specific meanings invented and reinvented by specific individuals in particular contexts. The discourse of exegesis is not written by academics alone, and the contributions of poets, playwrights, and others may usefully expand our insights into the nuances and complexities of medieval religion.

Exegesis is one of the discourses that constitutes power and gender relations in the Middle Ages as in modern fundamentalisms. No one reading exegesis in its specific historical context can doubt its cultural impact, or wonder whether scriptural interpretations really matter. Both academic and literary exegesis has cultural consequences, and biblical hermeneutics change history. Nor is the influence of medieval exegesis wholly dead even now, though most people remain unaware that their myths about God ordaining feminine subordination, or Jews killing Christian babies, derive from biblical supplements written in ages far removed from our own, in response to perceived threats that no longer exist. It is therefore important for scholars to demystify the authority of exegesis, to reveal how exegetes' teachings respond to particular local pressures and personal inclinations, and to emphasize the fact that their interpretations rarely meet with universal approval, even in their own times. In our time, secular and academic forms of counterexegesis are a potentially a valuable cultural defense against the rise of fundamentalisms, one of the conspicuous dangers we live with, and one that scholars of religious literature might reasonably be expected to address. Medieval exegesis proves that biblical hermeneutics matter culturally. There is reason to hope that sustained feminist approaches to exegesis might foster clearer understandings of the interested personal agendas that shape interpretations of sacred texts in both past and present. This might in turn lessen the power of outmoded beliefs.

Feminists have for decades reiterated the simple fact that all knowledge derives from social and embodied positions. This is no such thing as a universal, disinterested, objective perspective, though rhetoricians on occasion pretend otherwise. Sensitivity to the connections between epistemology and embodiment can only enrich medieval exegetical studies. Exegetes do not respond to scripture in a cultural or personal vacuum. Their interpretations integrate individual experiences, cultural pressures, generic constraints, self-doubts, sexual tensions, and ongoing polemical controversies. They write in particular historical moments, often to persuade audiences to believe or feel as they do, to act (or not) in a specific way. Exegesis, like politics, is always local. Concentrating our scholarship on the historical and personal dimensions of exegesis can help both to recover the logic of the discourse within its original cultural contexts and to map the contours of the discourse as it moves through time and various institutional contexts. In short, post-structuralist feminism offers leverage on how the discourse of exegesis constitutes gender and power in historical time.

Like all discourses, medieval exegesis at once includes some readers and excludes others. Those who are excluded—atheists, Jews, pagans, Muslims, women, readers with little Latin and less Greek—can best recognize how the exclusion operates. By not sharing the exegetes' intellectual and cultural perspectives, we gain a valuable capacity to perceive what they do not: their ideological contradictions, which imply personal or cultural conflicts; the strangeness of their interpretive focus, which is most apparent when least self-conscious; the lack of obviousness in their most forcefully asserted conclusions; the rational implausibility of their claims to know what God means. A feminist distance from the discourse of medieval exegesis enables a historicism that interrogates writers' epistemological claims, challenges their presuppositions, and glances skeptically at their performance of authority. Like poets, feminists can estrange us from oft-repeated "truths" about religion and gender difference. A situated, feminist knowledge of the complex and ambivalent inventions of religious authority in the past may finally generate new possibilities for both men and women in the future.

NOTES

1 Women on Top in Medieval Exegesis

1. Michel Foucault, *The Archaeology of Knowledge and the Discourse on Language,* trans. A. M. Sheridan Smith (New York: Pantheon, 1972), 183.
2. See Elaine Pagels, *Adam, Eve, and the Serpent* (New York: Random House, 1988), 32–97; the essays collected in Lisa M. Bitel and Felice Lifshitz, ed., *Gender and Christianity in Medieval Europe: New Perspectives* (Philadelphia: University of Pennsylvania Press, 2008); and Richard Valantasis, "Constructions of Power in Asceticism," *Journal of the American Academy of Religion* 63 (1995): 775–821. Persistent medieval challenges to gender dichotomy have led scholars to conceptualize a "third gender," for which see Jacqueline Murray, "One Flesh, Two Sexes, Three Genders?" in *Gender and Christianity,* ed. Bitel and Lifshitz, 34–51.
3. Caroline Walker Bynum argues that Christian men tend to reverse gender roles: "'...And Woman His Humanity': Female Imagery in the Religious Writing of the Later Middle Ages," in *Gender and Religion: On the Complexity of Symbols,* ed. Bynum, Stevan Harrell, and Paula Richman (Boston: Beacon Press, 1986), 257–88.
4. "Women on Top," in *Society and Culture in Early Modern France: Eight Essays* (Stanford: Stanford University Press, 1975), 124–51.
5. I refer to Foucault's theory that discourses are "the practices that systematically form the objects of which they speak" (*Archaeology of Knowledge,* 49), which come into being and fade away under specific historical conditions (109), and which accordingly reveal how institutional, economic, and social relations function to form the object of knowledge (164–65, 183).
6. I am indebted to Thomas McCarthy's conclusions about discourse and power: "The Critique of Impure Reason: Foucault and the Frankfurt School," in *Rethinking Power,* ed. Thomas E. Wartenberg (Albany: State University of New York Press, 1992), 124–127; and to Thomas E. Wartenburg, "Situated Social Power," 79–101 in the same volume.
7. See, e.g., E. Ann Matter, *The Voice of My Beloved: The Song of Songs in Western Medieval Christianity* (Philadelphia: University of Pennsylvania Press, 1990); F. M. Young, *Biblical Exegesis and the Formation of Christian Culture* (Cambridge: Cambridge University Press, 1997); Jeremy Cohen,

Living Letters of the Law: Ideas of the Jew in Medieval Christianity (Berkeley: University of California Press, 1999); Elizabeth A. Clark, *Reading Renunciation: Asceticism and Scripture in Early Christianity* (Princeton, NJ: Princeton University Press, 1999); Lisa Lampert, *Gender and Jewish Difference from Paul to Shakespeare* (Philadelphia: University of Pennsylvania Press, 2004).

8. E.g., Elisabeth Schüssler Fiorenza, *In Memory of Her: A Feminist Theological Reconstruction of Christian Origins* (1983; New York: Crossroad, 1987); Schüssler Fiorenza, *Bread Not Stone: The Challenge of Feminist Biblical Interpretation* (Boston: Beacon Press, 1984); Phyllis Trible, *Texts of Terror: Literary-Feminist Readings of Biblical Narratives* (Philadelphia: Fortress Press, 1984); Luise Schottroff, Silvia Schroer, and Marie-Theres Wacker, *Feminist Interpretation: The Bible in Women's Perspective,* trans. Martin and Barbara Rumscheidt (Minneapolis: Fortress Press, 1998); Elaine Pagels and Karen L. King, *Reading Judas: The Gospel of Judas and the Shaping of Christianity* (New York: Viking, 2007). Substantively similar conclusions are of course not exclusive to feminists: see, e.g., Henry Ansgar Kelly, *Satan: A Biography* (Cambridge: Cambridge University Press, 2006).

9. For a challenging development of this idea, see Caroline Vander Stichele and Todd Penner, "Mastering the Tools or Retooling the Masters? The Legacy of Historical-Critical Discourse," in *Her Master's Tools? Feminist and Postcolonial Engagements of Historical-Critical Discourse,* ed. Vander Stichele and Penner (Leiden: Brill, 2005), 1–29.

10. See Gabriel A. Almond, R. Scott Appleby, and Emmanuel Sivan, *Strong Religion: The Rise of Fundamentalisms around the World* (Chicago: University of Chicago Press, 2003), 9–14.

11. Jacques Berlinerblau's expression, which I appropriate for my own purposes, *The Secular Bible: Why Nonbelievers Must Take Religion Seriously* (New York: Cambridge University Press, 2005), 102.

12. Judith Butler's post–9/11 essays on feminist ethics underlie my position: *Precarious Life: The Powers of Mourning and Violence* (London and New York: Verso, 2004).

13. See the seminal work of Beryl Smalley, *The Study of the Bible in the Middle Ages,* 3rd ed. (Oxford: Basil Blackwell, 1983); and her *The Gospels in the Schools, c. 1100–c. 1280* (London and Ronceverte: Hambledon, 1985). For an excellent survey of her influence, see R. W. Southern, "Beryl Smalley and the Place of the Bible in Medieval Studies, 1927–84," in *The Bible in the Medieval World: Essays in Memory of Beryl Smalley,* ed. Katherine Walsh and Diana Wood (Oxford: Blackwell, for the Ecclesiastical Historical Society, 1985), 1–16.

14. D. W. Robertson, Jr., is usually credited with founding "exegetical criticism." His work is not, in my reading of it, a study of exegesis per se, but rather a totalizing aesthetic theory to which exegesis contributes: see his *A Preface to Chaucer: Studies in Medieval Perspectives* (Princeton, NJ: Princeton University Press, 1962), 52–137, 286–317.

15. See, e.g., Ann W. Astell, *The Song of Sons in the Middle Ages* (Ithaca, NY: Cornell University Press, 1990), 25–72; Philip D. W. Krey and Lesley Smith, eds., *Nicholas of Lyra: The Senses of Scripture* (Leiden: Brill, 2000); Lampert, *Gender and Jewish Difference*, 21–57; Deeana Copeland Klepper, *The Insight of Unbelievers: Nicholas of Lyra and Christian Reading of Jewish Text in the Later Middle Ages* (Philadelphia: University of Pennsylvania Press, 2007).

16. A mischievous revision of Bernard Cerquiglini, "meaning was to be found everywhere, and its origin was nowhere": *In Praise of the Variant: A Critical History of Philology*, trans. Betsy Wing (Baltimore and London: Johns Hopkins University Press, 1999), 33. Cerquiglini exempts scripture from the "joyful excess" he finds in medieval variants.

17. For a theological view of the subject, see Henri de Lubac, *Medieval Exegesis, Volume 1: The Four Senses of Scripture*, trans. Mark Sebanc (Grand Rapids: William B. Eerdmans; Edinburgh: T and T Clark, 1998); *Medieval Exegesis, Volume 2: The Four Senses of Scripture*, trans. E. M. Macierowski (Grand Rapids: William B. Eerdmans; Edinburgh: T and T Clark, 2000).

18. I adopt M. M. Bakhtin's theory of "re-accentuation": *The Dialogic Imagination: Four Essays*, ed. Michael Holquist, trans. Caryl Emerson and Holquist (Austin: University of Texas Press, 1981), 419–22. Tamara Warhol's use of Bakhtin for gendering exegesis informs my methodology: "Gender Constructions and Biblical Exegesis: Lessons from a Divinity School Seminar," in *Language and Religious Identity: Women in Discourse,* ed. Allyson Jule (New York: Palgrave Macmillan, 2007), 50–72.

19. Brian Murdoch establishes the impact of vernacular biblical literature: *The Medieval Popular Bible: Expansions of Genesis in the Middle Ages* (Cambridge, MA: D. S. Brewer, 2003).

20. Clark develops a cogent post-structuralist theoretical position from which to analyze patristic exegesis, and I am indebted to her formulation at every point in this book: *Reading Renunciation*, 3–13.

21. "The Order of Discourse," trans. Ian McLeod, in *Untying the Text: A Post-Structuralist Reader,* ed. Robert Young (Boston, London, Henley: Routledge and Kegan Paul, 1981), 58.

22. McCarthy is not commenting specifically on exegetes, but his formulation certainly applies to them: "Critique of Impure Reason," in *Rethinking Power,* ed. Wartenberg, 122.

23. *The Past as Text: The Theory and Practice of Medieval Historiography* (Baltimore and London: Johns Hopkins University Press, 1997), respectively 24 and 25, quoting Carroll Smith-Rosenberg; discussion 3–28.

24. Ralph Hanna brings new insight to this old complaint against so-called exegetical criticism: "Donaldson and Robertson: An Obligatory Conjunction," *Chaucer Review* 41 (2007): 240–49.

25. Berlinerblau, *The Secular Bible*, 81.

26. For the contradictions and discontinuities of scripture, see Jack Miles, *God: A Biography* (New York: Vintage, 1995); and Berlinerblau, *The*

Secular Bible, 17–53. For medieval attitudes, see Smalley on Carolingian exegesis, *The Study of the Bible in the Middle Ages,* 37–46.

27. Jacques Derrida, *Of Grammatology,* trans. Gayatri Chakravorty Spivak (Baltimore and London: Johns Hopkins University Press, 1976), 145. Berlinerblau develops an accessible, cogent account of exegesis as supplementation: *The Secular Bible,* 62–68. Eric Jager likewise points out that exegetes' attempts to "'fill in the lacunae' in the scriptural narrative inevitably drew attention to the gaps in the text," *The Tempter's Voice: Language and the Fall in Medieval Literature* (Ithaca, NY: Cornell University Press, 1993), 33.

2 Subversive Feminine Voices: The Reception of 1 Timothy 2 from Jerome to Chaucer

1. Theologians of the University of Paris, as per G. R. Evans, "Exegesis and Authority in the Thirteenth Century," in *Ad Litteram: Authoritative Texts and Their Medieval Readers,* ed. Mark D. Jordan and Kent Emery, Jr. (Notre Dame: University of Notre Dame Press, 1992), 98–99.

2. 1 Tim. 2: 15, Douay-Rheims translation, *The Holy Bible Translated from the Latin Vulgate* (1899; reprinted Rockford: Tan Books, 1989). Jimmy Carter notes the irony of this utterance, for "Timothy himself had been instructed by his mother and grandmother": *Our Endangered Values: America's Moral Crisis* (New York: Simon and Schuster, 2005), 92.

3. I adapt Sarah J. Tanzer's approach to "Ephesians," in *Searching the Scriptures. Vol. 2: A Feminist Commentary,* ed. Elisabeth Schüssler Fiorenza, 2 vols. (New York: Crossroad, 1994), 2: 328–32. For the prescriptive aspect of the text, see Linda M. Maloney, "The Pastoral Epistles," in *Searching the Scriptures,* ed. Schüssler Fiorenza, 2: 361–74. For an introduction to the pseudonymous Pauline letters, see Harry Gamble, "The Formation of the New Testament Canon and Its Significance for the History of Biblical Interpretation," in *A History of Biblical Interpretation. Vol. 1. The Ancient Period,* ed. Alan J. Hauser and Duane F. Watson (Grand Rapids: William B. Eerdmans, 2003), 411–14.

4. I intend this as a formalist rather than historical assessment. David M. Scholer points to a local heresy as the likely context for this prohibition of women teaching: "1 Timothy 2.9–15 and the Place of Women in the Church's Ministry" (1986), rpt. in *A Feminist Companion to the Deutero-Pauline Epistles,* ed. Amy-Jill Levine with Marianne Blickenstaff (London: Continuum, 2003), 98–121.

5. My analysis is informed by M. M. Bakhtin's theory of heteroglossia and "voice," *The Dialogic Imagination: Four Essays,* ed. Michael Holquist, trans. Caryl Emerson and Holquist (Austin: University of Texas Press, 1981), 259–422. I refer to the author as "Paul," in order to recognize at once questions about the attribution in modern scholarship and the medieval acceptance of the attribution.

6. *In Memory of Her: A Feminist Theological Reconstruction of Christian Origins* (1983; rpt. New York: Crossroad, 1987), 285–342. Mieke Bal develops a perceptive feminist analysis of 1 Timothy: *Lethal Love: Feminist Literary Readings of Biblical Love Stories* (Bloomington: Indiana University Press, 1987), 109–30. First Timothy 2 is of course not the only biblical text reflecting on women's leadership in the early church: the contemporary Gospels of Mark and John as clearly validate women's authority, depicting women as esteemed disciples, apostles, prophets, deacons, preachers, and teachers. These texts and others respect precisely the feminine authority that 1 Timothy 2 seeks to discredit (see Schüssler Fiorenza, *In Memory of Her*, 315–334). Schüssler Fiorenza argues that an original stratum of Christian egalitarianism (preserved fossil-like in Mark and John) was gradually buried beneath the increasing weight of patriarchalization: *In Memory of Her*, 245–342. See also Jane Schaberg's deployment of this idea: "New Testament: The Case of Mary Magdalene," in *Feminist Approaches to the Bible* (Washington, DC: Biblical Archaeology Society, 1995), 77, 81. The biblical canon reveals the same gendered contest apparent in the prescriptive exhortations of 1 Timothy 2—and not resolved for many centuries, if then. Women continue to be ordained into the twelfth century: see the fascinating study by Gary Macy, *The Hidden History of the Ordination of Women: Female Clergy in the Medieval West* (Oxford: Oxford University Press, 2008). Mark, John, and 1 Timothy 2 witness to cross-currents within early Christianity and to the historical reality of diverse religious communities advocating disparate ideas about women's roles and ecclesiastical order.

7. *Epistola Pauli ad Timotheum I, PL* 29, col. 799–800. Elizabeth A. Clark brilliantly explicates these reading strategies (atomization, translation): *Reading Renunciation: Asceticism and Scripture in Early Christianity* (Princeton, NJ: Princeton University Press, 1999), 111–14. For a study of Jerome's textual criticism, the conceptual context for such editorial choices, see Dennis Brown, *Vir Trilinguis: A Study in the Biblical Exegesis of Saint Jerome* (Kampen, The Netherlands: Kok Pharos, 1992), 21–54. Jerome probably did not translate the New Testament beyond the Gospels, so he is correcting a "defective" text. For details about Jerome's translations, see Catherine Brown Tkacz, " 'Labor Tam Utilis': The Creation of the Vulgate," *Vigiliae Christianae* 50 (1996): 42–72; and Dennis Brown, "Jerome and the Vulgate," in *A History of Biblical Interpretation. Vol. 1*, ed. Hauser and Watson, 359–60. For other translations of 1 Timothy, see Clark, *Reading Renunciation*, 113–14.

8. *Against Jovinianus*, in *The Principal Works of St. Jerome*, trans. W. H. Fremantle, A Select Library of Nicene and Post-Nicene Fathers of the Christian Church, 2d series (rpt. Grand Rapids: William B. Eerdmans, 1989), vol. 6: Book I, chapt. 1, pp. 346, 347. Hereafter cited as I.1.346, 347. The Latin: "Epicurum Christianorum" "quod hesternam crapulam ructans, ita," *Adversus Jovinianum, PL*, 23, cols. 211, 212. Hereafter cited *Adversus Jovinianum*, cols. 211, 212.

9. "Nonne vel per febrem somniare eum putes, vel arreptum morbo phrenetico, Hippocratis vinculis alligandum?" *Adversus Jovinianum,* col. 212.

10. "Nunc restat ut Epicurum nostrum, subantem in hortulis suis inter adolescentulos et mulierculas, alloquamur," *Adversus Jovinianum,* cols. 333–34.

11. "Hic adversarius tota exsultatione bacchatur: hoc velut fortissimo ariete, virginitatis murum quatiens," *Adversus Jovinianum,* col. 227.

12. "quodque errorem veterem illa quae semel connubio copulata est, et redacta in conditionem Evae, filiorum procreatione deleret: Ita tamen, si ipsos filios erudiret in fide et dilectione Christi, et in sanctificatione et pudicitia: non enim (ut male habetur in Latinis codicibus) *sobrietas* est legenda, sed *castitas,* id est, σωφροσυνη.... Tunc ergo salvabitur mulier, si illos genuerit filios, qui virgines permansuri sunt: si quod ipsa perdidit, acquirat in liberis, et damnum radicis et cariem, flore compenset et pomis," *Adversus Jovinianum,* cols. 248–49. Translation corrected.

13. J. N. D. Kelly's conclusion, *Jerome: His Life, Writings, and Controversies* (New York: Harper and Row, 1975), 186.

14. See Clark on ascetic reading strategies, *Reading Renunciation,* 104–52.

15. "'For I say, through the grace that was given me, to every man that is among you, not to think of himself more highly than he ought to think; but to think according to chastity' (not soberly as the Latin versions badly render), but 'think,' he says, 'according to chastity,' for the Greek words are εις το σωφρονειν." *Against Jovinianus* I.37.375. "Dico enim per gratiam quae data est mihi, omnibus qui sunt inter vos: non plus sapere quam oportet sapere, sed sapere ad pudicitiam (non ad sobrietatem, ut male in Latinis codicibus legitur), sed sapere, inquit, ad pudicitiam (Rom. XII, 1, et Phil. IV, 18). Siquidem Graece scriptum est, εις το σωφρονειν." *Adversus Jovinianum,* col. 262.

16. Elaine Pagels, *Adam, Eve, and the Serpent* (New York: Random House, 1988), 94–96.

17. John Oppel emphasizes this positive aspect of Jerome's asceticism: "Saint Jerome and the History of Sex," *Viator* 24 (1993): 1–22.

18. See Andrew S. Jacobs, "Writing Demetrias: Ascetic Logic in Ancient Christianity," *Church History* 69 (2000): 728–31.

19. Peter Brown, *The Body and Society: Men, Women and Sexual Renunciation in Early Christianity* (New York: Columbia University Press, 1988), 378. For an introduction to the controversy, see Kelly, *Jerome,* 187–89.

20. Warren S. Smith persuasively analyzes how Chaucer confronts the disagreement between Jerome and Augustine: "The Wife of Bath Debates Jerome," *Chaucer Review* 32 (1997): 129–45.

21. For social-historical changes in the later Roman empire affecting family structure, social order, and definitions of masculinity, see Mathew Kuefler, *The Manly Eunuch: Masculinity, Gender Ambiguity, and Christian Ideology in Late Antiquity* (Chicago: University of Chicago Press, 2001). Kuefler argues that Jerome's contemporary appeal among bishops, and ultimate triumph over Jovinian, lies in his ability to provide Roman men

with a pious rationale for renouncing marriage and public office, both of which held little appeal for contemporary aristocrats (178–81).

22. "apud Judaeos gloria erat in partubus et parturitionibus"; "Rursumque ad Galatas: Ex operibus, inquit, Legis, non justificabitur omnis caro," *Adversus Jovinianum,* respectively cols. 241, 264.

23. "nec detrahere his qui in Lege praecesserint, sed servisse eos temporibus et conditionibus suis, et illam Domini implesse sententiam: Crescite, et multiplicamini, et replete terram…Nobis autem, quibus dicitur: Tempus in collecto est, superest, ut qui habent uxores, sic sint, quasi non habeant, aliud praecipi, et virginitatem…dedicari," *Adversus Jovinianum,* col. 243.

24. My conclusion agrees with Clark's, *Reading Renunciation,* 154.

25. "Cum enim essemus in carne, nostri passiones peccatorum quae per Legem erant, operabantur in membris nostris, ut fructificarent morti. Nunc autem soluti sumus a Lege mortis," *Adversus Jovinianum,* col. 261. For the rationale and dissemination of these stereotypes, see Anna Sapir Abulafia, "Jewish Carnality in Twelfth-Century Renaissance Thought," *Studies in Church History* 29 (1992): 59–75; Abulafia, *Christians and Jews in the Twelfth-Century Renaissance* (New York: Routledge, 1995), 103–22; Jeremy Cohen, *Living Letters of the Law: Ideas of the Jew in Medieval Christianity* (Berkeley: University of California Press, 1999), e.g., 43–64, 80.

26. "in vetustate litterae," *Adversus Jovinianum,* col. 261.

27. "Tactus autem alienorum corporum, et feminarum ardentior appetitus, vicinus insaniae est. Ob hunc sensum, cupimus, irascimur, gestimus, invidemus, aemulamur, solliciti sumus, et expleta voluptate per quamdam poenitudinem, rursus accendimur: quaerimusque facere, quod cum fecerimus, iterum poeniteamus." *Adversus Jovinianum,* cols. 297–98.

28. "qui repugnantem carnem, et ad libidinum incentiva rapientem, inedia subjugamus," *Adversus Jovinianum,* col. 297. Michel Foucault's study of this idea is illuminating, "The Battle for Chastity," in *Western Sexuality: Practice and Precept in Past and Present Times,* ed. Philippe Ariès and André Béjin, trans. Anthony Forster (Oxford: Basil Blackwell, 1985), 14–25.

29. "maxime cum tactus depingat sibi etiam praeteritas voluptates, et recordatione vitiorum cogat animam compati, et quodammodo exercere quod non agit," *Adversus Jovinianum,* col. 298.

30. See, e.g., his discussion of Lucretia, I.46.382.

31. Brown, *The Body and Society,* 376.

32. The thoughtful argument of Stefan Rebenich about another context in Jerome's life, *Jerome* (London: Routledge, 2002), 20.

33. "Sed quid faciam, cum mihi mulieres nostri temporis, Apostoli ingerant auctoritatem; et necdum elato funere prioris viri, memoriter digamiae praecepta decantent?" *Adversus Jovinianum,* col. 276.

34. "Ut quae Christianae pudicitiae despiciunt fidem, discant saltem ab Ethnicis castitatem," *Adversus Jovinianum,* col. 276.

35. David S. Wiesen, *St. Jerome as a Satirist: A Study in Christian Latin Thought and Letters* (Ithaca, NY: Cornell University Press, 1964), respectively 154, 160.

36. For later academic uses of Jerome, see Robert A. Pratt, "Jankyn's 'Book of Wikked Wyves': Medieval Anti-Matrimonial Propaganda in the Universities," *Annuale Mediaevale* 3 (1962): 5–27.

37. Clark, *Reading Renunciation,* 155.

38. Lisa Lampert demonstrates the pervasiveness of the link between carnality, women, and Jews: *Gender and Jewish Difference from Paul to Shakespeare* (Philadelphia: University of Pennsylvania Press, 2004).

39. This suggestion derives from theory that argues masculine gender formation requires differentiation from the feminine, creating a fear of internalized "feminine" traits: see Pierre Bourdieu, *Masculine Domination,* trans. Richard Nice (Cambridge, MA: Polity Press, 2001), 49–53; and Rachel Alsop, Annette Fitzsimons, Kathleen Lennon, and Ros Minsky, *Theorizing Gender* (Cambridge, MA: Polity Press, 2002), 44, 54, 55, 59, 155–59.

40. I borrow from Bourdieu's concept of "embodied social law," *Masculine Domination,* 50.

41. Jacyln L. Maxwell, *Christianization and Communication in Late Antiquity: John Chrysostom and His Congregation in Antioch* (Cambridge: Cambridge University Press, 2006), 81. Women's dress is a recurrent concern in his work: see J. N. D. Kelly, *Golden Mouth: The Story of John Chrysostom— Ascetic, Preacher, Bishop* (London: Duckworth, 1995), 97, 122.

42. Homily 8, in *Chrysostom: Homilies on Galatians, Ephesians, Philippians, Colossians, Thessalonians, Timothy, Titus, and Philemon,* ed. Philip Schaff, Nicene and Post-Nicene Fathers, 1st series (1889; rpt. Peabody: Hendrickson Publishers, 1995), 13: 433.

43. On Chrysostom's attitude toward theater, see Kelly, *Golden Mouth,* 15, 97; and Maxwell, *Christianization and Communication,* 51–54.

44. Kelly, *Golden Mouth,* 28.

45. Elizabeth A. Clark notes the contradiction between Chrysostom's "woman as temptress" theme and his belief in men's responsibility for their sexual sins: "Ideology, History, and the Construction of 'Woman' in Late Ancient Christianity" (1994), rpt. in *A Feminist Companion to Patristic Literature,* ed. Amy-Jill Levine with Maria Mayo Robbins (London: T and T Clark, 2008), 122.

46. I am indebted for this logic to Gerda Lerner, who argues that archaic sumptuary laws ("veiling the woman") demonstrate how patriarchal classifications of women are institutionalized: *The Creation of Patriarchy* (New York: Columbia University Press, 1986), 123–40.

47. Quoting Bourdieu, *Masculine Domination,* 34.

48. Homily 9, in *Chrysostom: Homilies,* ed Schaff.

49. Maxwell establishes his practice of addressing the questions and concerns of the congregation, including women, and their occasional disagreements with him: *Christianization and Communication,* 65–117.

50. Supplying the "authorial intention" is a common hermeneutic strategy in this and later eras: see A. J. Minnis, *Medieval Theory of Authorship: Scholastic*

Literary Attitudes in the later Middle Ages, 2nd ed. (Philadelphia: University of Pennsylvania Press, 1988), e.g., 15, 19–21.

51. Neil Adkin, ed., comments similarly on this homily: *Jerome on Virginity: A Commentary on the "Libellus de Virginitate Servanda" (Letter 22)* (Cambridge, MA: Francis Cairns, 2003), 325.

52. For detailed analysis, see Elizabeth A. Clark, *Jerome, Chrysostom, and Friends: Essays and Translations* (New York: Edwin Mellen, 1979), 1–34.

53. Clark's analysis informs my conclusion: *Reading Renunciation,* 156–62.

54. Interpretive diversity has limits. J. Kevin Coyle's evidence suggests that misogyny is the thread unifying patristic writings on this passage: "The Fathers on Women and Women's Ordination," *Église et théologie* 9 (1978): 51–101.

55. See Frances M. Young's rejection of "literal" and other conventional labels, together with her account of the fathers' reading strategies: *Biblical Exegesis and the Formation of Christian Culture* (Cambridge: Cambridge University Press, 1997), 29–45, 97–213; and Clark's rejection of "literal/figural" categories, together with her analysis of actual hermeneutic strategies, *Reading Renunciation,* 70–152.

56. This is a common development in biblical and exegetical literature; for a particularly vivid example, see Schaberg, "New Testament: The Case of Mary Magdalene," in *Feminist Approaches to the Bible,* 82–84.

57. I quote Robert Young out of context: Introduction to Michel Foucault, "The Order of Discourse," trans. Ian McLeod, in *Untying the Text: A Post-Structuralist Reader,* ed. Robert Young (Boston: Routledge and Kegan Paul, 1981), 51.

58. Éric Rebillard, "A New Style of Argument in Christian Polemic: Augustine and the Use of Patristic Citations," *Journal of Early Christian Studies* 8 (2000): 559–78. Henry Chadwick offers useful general background on exegetical disagreements and the ideal of church unity, extending beyond Augustine: "Disagreement and the Early Church" (1996), rpt. *Studies in Ancient Christianity* (Aldershot: Ashgate, 2006), XXIII, 557–66.

59. Rebillard, "A New Style of Argument," 560. This strategy does not argue that Augustine on principle rejected diversity of interpretation; quite the contrary is true: see Stephen L. Wailes, *Medieval Allegories of Jesus' Parables* (Berkeley: University of California Press, 1987), 11.

60. David A. Wells similarly proposes that "a coherent and sustained context [in exegesis], rather than an isolated reference, is desirable for the identification of exegetical allegory," "Friedrich Ohly and Exegetical Tradition: Some Aspects of Medieval Interpretation," *Forum for Modern Language Studies* 41 (2005): 49.

61. Interpretations—particularly allegories—can undergo sudden, radical transformations. For example, the biblical Absolom gathers a great deal of negative anti-Semitic commentary before the fourteenth century, when he unexpectedly appears as a figure of Christ: see Wells, "Friedrich Ohly

and Exegetical Tradition," 51–52. See also Wailes, *Medieval Allegories of Jesus' Parables,* 22–57.

62. For the classic introduction to the *Gloss,* see Beryl Smalley, *The Study of the Bible in the Middle Ages,* 3rd ed. (Oxford: Basil Blackwell, 1983), x–xi, 46–66; see also the invaluable Introduction to the facsimile of the work's first print edition, Margaret T. Gibson and Karlfried Froehlich, eds., *Biblia Latina cum Glossa Ordinaria, Facsimile Reprint of the Editio Princeps Adolph Rusch of Strassburg 1480/81,* 4 vols. (Turnhout: Brepols, 1992), 1: vii–xxxvi. Margaret T. Gibson surveys the development of the *Gloss's* form and method before 1130, "The Place of the *Glossa Ordinaria* in Medieval Exegesis," in *Ad Litteram,* ed. Jordan and Emery, 6–19. E. Ann Matter's careful study of patristic sources in the *Gloss* demonstrates variations among books, the wide range of sources drawn upon by many compilers, and the need for further manuscript study: "The Church Fathers and the *Glossa Ordinaria,*" in *The Reception of the Church Fathers in the West: From the Carolingians to the Maurists,* ed. Irena Backus, 2 vols. (Leiden: E. J. Brill, 1997), 1: 83–111.

63. E.g., Rachel remains ambiguous in relation to the Slaughter of Innocents: see chapter 4.

64. Smalley's concise judgment, *Study of the Bible in the Middle Ages,* 56; see also Gibson and Froehlich, *Biblia cum Glossa,* 1: xxv–xxvi.

65. C. F. R. de Hamel offers an exemplary analysis of the work's development, *Glossed Books of the Bible and the Origins of the Paris Booktrade* (Woodbridge: D. S. Brewer, 1984), 1–13. Mark Zier examines the manuscript evidence for the work's complex stages of development and persuasively establishes changing emphases: "The Manuscript Tradition of the *Glossa Ordinaria* for Daniel and Hints at a Method for a Critical Edition," *Scriptorium, Revue Internationale des Etudes Relative aux Manuscrits* 47 (1993): 3–25; Zier, "The Development of the Glossa Ordinaria to the Bible in the Thirteenth Century: The Evidence from the Bibliothèque Nationale, Paris," in *La Bibbia del XIII Secolo: Storia del Testo, Storia dell'Esegesi,* ed. Giuseppe Cremascoli and Francesco Santi (Firenze: Sismel edizioni del Galluzzo, 2004), 155–84; and Zier, "Peter Lombard and the *Glossa Ordinaria*: A Missing Link?" in *Pietro Lombardo,* ed. E. Menestò (Spoleto: Centro Italiano de Studi Sull'Alto Medioevo, 2007), 361–409.

66. "Gloss or Analysis? A Crisis of Exegetical Method in the Thirteenth Century," in *La Bibbia del XIII Secolo,* ed. Cremascoli and Santi, 110.

67. "The Development of the Glossa Ordinaria to the Bible in the Thirteenth Century," in *La Bibbia del XIII Secolo,* ed. Cremascoli and Santi, 170.

68. "From Contemplation to Action: The Role of the Active Life in the *Glossa Ordinaria* on the Song of Songs," *Speculum* 82 (2007): 54–69.

69. Mark Zier painstakingly demonstrates that Rusch presents an expanded version of early *Gloss* manuscripts on Romans. Comparing *Gloss* manuscripts, Peter Lombard's twelfth-century *Collectanea in epistolas Pauli,* and Rusch, Zier outlines a likely compositional sequence for the works: Peter probably expands on the contemporary *Gloss* and is in turn most

likely excerpted in Rusch. Put most simply, the twelfth-century *Gloss* is embedded in Rusch along with later supplements: "Peter Lombard and the *Glossa Ordinaria*," in *Pietro Lombardo*, ed. Menestò, 361–409. The danger of oversimplification looms large here, for, as Zier remarks, intermediary or common sources cannot be ruled out and would complicate this sequence (370, 374, 379–81). My own comparison of Peter's *Collectanea* and Rusch discovers a similar pattern for our passage from 1 Timothy 2: Rusch contains a shortened form of Peter's commentary, which probably likewise elaborates on the contemporary *Gloss*. See Peter Lombard, *Collectanea in epistolas Pauli*, PL 192, cols. 340–42; and Gibson and Froehlich, *Biblia cum Glossa*, 4: 487–88. It is worth noting also that the works vary in method: Peter composes a continuous gloss, whereas the *Gloss* combines interlinear and marginal commentary.

70. See Smalley's definitive argument on Anselm, *Study of the Bible in the Middle Ages*, 46–66.

71. This model usefully clarifies the monastic reading practice characteristic of the *Gloss*, though twelfth- and thirteenth-century manuscript page layouts differ substantially from each other and from this model: see J. P. Gumbert, "The Layout of the Bible Gloss in Manuscript and Early Print," in *The Bible as Book: The First Printed Editions*, ed. Paul Saenger and Kimberly Van Kampen (London: British Library and Oak Knoll Press, 1999), 7–13.

72. In point of fact, the *lemmata* do not always match the biblical text cited, mostly because the biblical text varies in the period of the work's compilation: see Gibson, Introduction, *Biblia cum Glossa*, 1: x.

73. "Gloss or Analysis?," in *La Bibbia del XIII Secolo*, ed. Cremascoli and Santi, 94.

74. "[verse 11] Mulier in silentio.... Nunc dicit quod docendi officium solis viris conveniat et quales ad illud debeant ordinari determinat. In silentio.... Si loquitur mage ad luxuriam irritatur et irritat. [verse 12] Docere autem etc.... Ecce non solum habitum humilem et honestum habere mulierem docuit verum etiam auctoritatem docendi ei negavit et subjciendam viro praecepit ut tam habitu quam obsequiis sub potestate sit viri ex quo trahit originem," *Biblia cum Glossa*, 4: 487. I take the liberty of silently expanding the printer's abbreviations.

75. "[verse 15] *Salvabitur autem*. Etsi mulier fuit causa peccati tamen salvabitur non solum virgo et continens sed etiam nupta etsi nunquam ab opera nuptiarum cessans si per generationem filiorum incedens ab hoc mundo exierit. Si permanserit in fide et dilectione et sanctificatione ut praeter proprium virum alterum non cognoscat. Cum sobrietate id est temperantia ut proprio etiam viro," *Biblia cum Glossa*, 4: 487.

76. *Biblia cum Glossa*, 4: 488.

77. For the compilation form, see Malcolm Beckwith Parkes, "The Influence of the Concepts of *Ordinatio* and *Compilatio* on the Development of the Book," in *Medieval Learning and Literature: Essays Presented to Richard William Hunt*, ed. J. J. G. Alexander and M. T. Gibson (Oxford: Clarendon, 1976), 115–41.

78. See, e.g., Clark, *Reading Renunciation,* 153–74, 177–203, 353–70; and Kuefler, *Manly Eunuch,* 161–205.
79. For women preaching and teaching, see Macy, *Hidden History of the Ordination of Women,* 23–87; and Barbara Newman, *Sister of Wisdom: St. Hildegard's Theology of the Feminine* (Berkeley: University of California Press, 1987).
80. See Alcuin Blamires, "Women and Preaching in Medieval Orthodoxy, Heresy, and Saints' Lives," *Viator* 26 (1995): 138–39.
81. This accords with the work's general bias toward institutions: see Zier, "The Manuscript Tradition of the *Glossa Ordinaria* for Daniel," 13. On the "safe" character of the compilation, see Gillian Rosemary Evans, "Gloss or Analysis? A Crisis of Exegetical Method in the Thirteenth Century," in *La Bibbia del XIII Secolo,* ed. Cremascoli and Santi, 94.
82. Macy, *Hidden History of the Ordination of Women,* 23–48, 74–80, 89–113, 117–23.
83. G. R. Evans offers a fascinating account of how this process begins, "Exegesis and Authority in the Thirteenth Century," in *Ad Litteram,* ed. Jordan and Emery, 93–111. See also Minnis on changes in exegesis between the twelfth and fourteenth centuries: *Medieval Theory of Authorship,* 40–117.
84. Evans, "Gloss or Analysis?," in *La Bibbia del XIII Secolo,* ed. Cremascoli and Santi, 100. Scripture glosses on scripture may seem unpromising, but the strategy can be powerful, as Phyllis Trible demonstrates in *Texts of Terror: Literary-Feminist Readings of Biblical Narratives* (Philadelphia: Fortress Press, 1984).
85. See Laura Light, "The New Thirteenth-Century Bible and the Challenge of Heresy," *Viator* 18 (1987): 275–88.
86. Resistance nonetheless occurs: see Macy on Abelard, *Hidden History of the Ordination of Women,* 93–96.
87. Highly negative opinions about Alison's "carnal" exegesis were for decades fueled by D. W. Robertson, Jr., *A Preface to Chaucer: Studies in Medieval Perspectives* (Princeton, NJ: Princeton University Press, 1962), 317–36. Robertson extends his historical analysis and confirms his conclusions about the Wife's exegesis, " 'And for my land thus hast thou mordred me?': Land Tenure, the Cloth Industry, and the Wife of Bath," *Chaucer Review* 14 (1980): 403–20. Comparable judgments appear in Edmund Reiss, "Biblical Parody: Chaucer's 'Distortions' of Scripture," in *Chaucer and Scriptural Tradition,* ed. David Lyle Jeffrey (n.p.: University of Ottawa Press, 1984), 57–58; Chauncey Wood, "Artistic Intention and Chaucer's Use of Scriptural Allusion," in *Chaucer and Scriptural Tradition,* ed. Jeffrey, 37–38, 41; Sarah Disbrow, "The Wife of Bath's Old Wives' Tale," *SAC* 8 (1986): 71; John A. Alford, "The Wife of Bath versus the Clerk of Oxford: What Their Rivalry Means," *Chaucer Review* 21 (1986): 108–32; Susan Schibanoff, "The New Reader and Female Textuality in Two Early Commentaries on Chaucer," *SAC* 10 (1988): 83; Priscilla Martin, *Chaucer's Women: Nuns, Wives, and Amazons* (Iowa

City: University of Iowa Press, 1990), 37–39; Catherine S. Cox, "Holy Erotica and the Virgin Word: Promiscuous Glossing in the *Wife of Bath's Prologue*," *Exemplaria* 5 (1993): 222; Katherine Heinrichs, "Tropological Woman in Chaucer: Literary Elaborations of an Exegetical Tradition," *English Studies* 3 (1995): 212–14; Ann W. Astell, *Chaucer and the Universe of Learning* (Ithaca, NY: Cornell University Press, 1996), 152–67. Many scholars have articulated compellingly nuanced counterarguments to this long tradition, and I am indebted to their insights: Mary Carruthers, "The Wife of Bath and the Painting of Lions" (1979), rpt. with an "Afterword," in *Feminist Readings in Middle English Literature: The Wife of Bath and All Her Sect,* ed. Ruth Evans and Lesley Johnson (London: Routledge, 1994), 22–53; David Aers, *Chaucer, Langland, and the Creative Imagination* (London: Routledge and Kegan Paul, 1980), 83–88; Stephen Knight, *Geoffrey Chaucer* (Oxford: Basil Blackwell, 1986), 98; Peggy A. Knapp, "'Wandrynge by the Weye': On Alisoun and Augustine," in *Medieval Texts and Contemporary Readers,* ed. Laurie A. Finke and Martin B. Shichtman (Ithaca, NY: Cornell University Press, 1987), 142–57; Ralph Hanna III, "*Compilatio* and the Wife of Bath: Latin Backgrounds, Ricardian Texts" (1989), rpt. in *Pursuing History: Middle English Manuscripts and Their Texts* (Stanford: Stanford University Press, 1996), 247–57; Peggy A. Knapp, "Alisoun of Bathe and the Reappropriation of Tradition," *Chaucer Review* 24 (1989): 45–52; Peggy A. Knapp, *Chaucer and the Social Contest* (New York: Routledge, 1990), 114–28; Lisa J. Kiser, *Truth and Textuality in Chaucer's Poetry* (Hanover, NH: University Press of New England, 1991), 136–42; Lee Patterson, *Chaucer and the Subject of History* (Madison: University of Wisconsin Press, 1991), 280–321; Susan Crane, "The Writing Lesson of 1381," in *Chaucer's England: Literature in Historical Context,* ed. Barbara Hanawalt (Minneapolis: University of Minnesota Press, 1992): 201–21; Smith, "The Wife of Bath Debates Jerome," 129–45; Lawrence Besserman, *Chaucer's Biblical Poetics* (Norman: University of Oklahoma Press, 1998), 138–59; Robert Longsworth, "The Wife of Bath and the Samaritan Woman," *Chaucer Review* 34 (2000): 372–87; Thomas C. Kennedy, "The Wife of Bath on St. Jerome," *Mediaevalia* 23 (2002): 75–97; Alastair Minnis, *Fallible Authors: Chaucer's Pardoner and the Wife of Bath* (Philadelphia: University of Pennsylvania Press, 2008), 246–348.

88. Peter Robinson, ed., *The Wife of Bath's Prologue on CD-Rom* (Cambridge: Cambridge University Press, 1996), 346–47 of the base text (Aberystwyth, National Library of Wales, Hengwrt 154). I take the liberty of silently deleting interlinear virgules. All citations of text and glosses are to this edition of the work.

89. Several illuminating discussions of Chaucer and Jerome inform my argument: Smith, "The Wife of Bath Debates Jerome," 129–45; Kennedy, "The Wife of Bath on St. Jerome," 75–97; John V. Fleming, "The Best Line in Ovid and the Worst," in *New Readings of Chaucer's Poetry,* ed. Robert G. Benson and Susan J. Ridyard (Cambridge, MA: D. S. Brewer,

2003), 62–70. Minnis grants Jerome more hermeneutic/cultural authority than I do: *Fallible Authors*, 253–57.

90. For the complicated history of women preaching and discourses on the
topic, see Alcuin Blamires, *The Case for Women in Medieval Culture* (Oxford:
Clarendon, 1997), 184–98; the essays collected by Beverly Wayne Kienzle
and Pamela J. Walker, eds., *Women Preachers and Prophets through Two
Millennia of Christianity* (Berkeley: University of California Press, 1998);
Alcuin Blamires, "Beneath the Pulpit," in *The Cambridge Companion to
Medieval Women's Writing*, ed. Carolyn Dinshaw and David Wallace
(Cambridge: Cambridge University Press, 2003), 141–58; Macy, *Hidden
History of the Ordination of Women*; Minnis, *Fallible Authors*, 170–245.

91. For Chaucer's immediate context, see Knapp, *Chaucer and the Social Contest*,
63–76; for the "grey area" between orthodoxy and heterodoxy in the age
of the Lollards, see the essays in Helen Barr and Ann M. Hutchison, eds.,
Text and Controversy From Wyclif to Bale: Essays in Honour of Anne Hudson
(Turnhout: Brepols, 2005). Gail McMurray Gibson establishes the vigor of
both "nonconformist thought" and "old-style Catholicism" in fifteenth-
century East Anglia, which fertile combination produces a remarkable
flowering of religious literature: *The Theater of Devotion: East Anglian
Drama and Society in the Late Middle Ages* (Chicago: University of Chicago
Press, 1989), esp. 19–43. For a complementary historical perspective, see
Margaret Aston and Colin Richmond, eds., "Introduction," in *Lollardy
and the Gentry in the Later Middle Ages* (Stroud: Sutton Publishing; New
York: St. Martin's Press, 1997), 1–27; and J. A. F. Thomson, "Knightly
Piety and the Margins of Lollardy," 95–111 in the same volume.

92. The *Prologue*'s delicate connection with Lollardy is teased out by Alcuin
Blamires, "The Wife of Bath and Lollardy," *Medium Aevum* 58 (1989):
224–42; and Besserman, *Chaucer's Biblical Poetics*, 159. I am influenced
as well by broader treatments of Chaucer's relationship with Wyclif and
Lollardy: David Lyle Jeffrey, "Chaucer and Wyclif: Biblical Hermeneutic and
Literary Theory in the XIVth Century," in *Chaucer and Scriptural Tradition*,
ed. Jeffrey, 109–40; Knapp, *Chaucer and the Social Contest*, 61–94; Paul
Strohm, "Chaucer's Lollard Joke: History and the Textual Unconscious,"
SAC 17 (1995): 23–42; Lawrence Besserman, "'Priest' and 'Pope,' 'Sire'
and 'Madame': Anachronistic Diction and Social Conflict in Chaucer's
Troilus," *SAC* 23 (2001): 181–224; Katherine Little, "Chaucer's Parson
and the Specter of Wycliffism," *SAC* 23 (2001): 225–53; Alan J. Fletcher,
"Chaucer the Heretic," *SAC* 25 (2003): 53–121; Fletcher, "The Criteria for
Scribal Attribution: Dublin, Trinity College, MS 244, Some Early Copies
of the Works of Geoffrey Chaucer, and the Canon of Adam Pynkhurst
Manuscripts," *The Review of English Studies*, n.s. 58, no. 237 (2007): 597–
632; Craig T. Fehrman, "Did Chaucer Read the Wycliffite Bible?" *Chaucer
Review* 42 (2007): 111–38. I disagree with Minnis's position that Chaucer
adheres to scholastic positions and assumes an unambiguous anti-Wycliffite
stance, *Fallible Authors*, 135, 145, 210–245, 247, 249, 259–82.

93. For detailed argument, see Smith, "The Wife of Bath Debates Jerome," 138–41. Kennedy also finds her in essential agreement with Jerome, "The Wife of Bath on St. Jerome," 75–97.

94. Carolyn Dinshaw's idea of parodic mimicry influences my argument: *Chaucer's Sexual Poetics* (Madison: University of Wisconsin Press, 1989), 115–16.

95. My reading is indebted to critics who emphasize the desacralized, gendered voices that deliver exegesis in this text: see Aers, *Chaucer, Langland, and the Creative Imagination*, 83–88; Robert Hanning, " 'I Shal Finde It in a Maner Glose': Versions of Textual Harassment in Medieval Literature," in *Medieval Texts and Contemporary Readers*, ed. Finke and Shichtman, 27–50; Knapp, " 'Wandrynge by the Weye,' " in *Medieval Texts and Contemporary Readers*, ed. Finke and Shichtman, 142–57; Dinshaw, *Chaucer's Sexual Poetics*, 113–31; Hanna, "*Compilatio* and the Wife of Bath," 247–57; Knapp, "Alisoun of Bathe and the Reappropriation of Tradition," 45–52; Kiser, *Truth and Textuality*, 136–42; Jill Mann, *Geoffrey Chaucer* (Atlantic Highlands: Humanities Press International, 1991), 70–73; Longsworth, "The Wife of Bath and the Samaritan Woman," 372–87.

96. Knapp argues, I think rightly, that such ideas are not exclusively Wycliffite but rather evidence a "dialogically agitated, unsettled area of social life," *Chaucer and the Social Contest*, 65.

97. For Wyclif on dominion, see Margaret Deanesley, *The Lollard Bible and Other Medieval Biblical Versions* (1920; rpt. Eugene: Wipf and Stock, 2002), 226–27; David Luscombe, "Wyclif and Hierarchy," in *From Ockham to Wyclif*, ed. Anne Hudson and Michael Wilks (Oxford: Basil Blackwell, for The Ecclesiastical History Society, 1987), 233–44; Knapp, *Chaucer and the Social Contest*, 63–76; Kantik Ghosh, *The Wycliffite Heresy: Authority and the Interpretation of Texts* (Cambridge: Cambridge University Press, 2002), 22–23; Elemér Boreczky, *John Wyclif's Discourse on Dominion in Community* (Leiden: Brill, 2008).

98. Alan J. Fletcher's apt conclusion about a comparable interrogation of clerical idealism in the *Miller's Tale, Preaching, Politics, and Poetry in Late-Medieval England* (Dublin and Portland: Four Courts Press, 1998), 248.

99. Robertson's influential analysis concentrates on the first 162 lines of the Prologue, which excludes this passage: *Preface to Chaucer*, 317–31. Negative evidence is difficult to establish, and I may have missed an outraged comment or two in the medieval or modern record, in which case my conclusions would have to be qualified. Having searched diligently through manuscripts, modern criticism, and Caroline F. E. Spurgeon's historical records, however, I discover no comments on this issue, which suggests that at the least there has been no sustained outcry against the Wife on this score, though she certainly inspires it at other points. See Spurgeon, *Five Hundred Years of Chaucer Criticism and Allusions, 1357–1900* (1925; rpt., New York: Russell and Russell, 1960), 3 vols.

100. Cambridge, McClean 181, Fitzwilliam Museum (Fi) abbreviates the passage and removes the apostolic authority, so Alison explicitly rejects only her spouses' teaching. Latin source notes may be found in British Library, Additional 5140 (Ad1), Additional 35286 (Ad3), Egerton 2864 (En3); San Marino, Henry E. Huntington Library, Ellesmere 26 C 9 (El); Oxford, Bodleian Library, Rawlinson poet. 141 (Ra1); Cambridge, Trinity College R.3.15 (595) (Tc2). For manuscript sigils, see John M. Manly and Edith Rickert, *The Text of the Canterbury Tales Studied on the Basis of All Known Manuscripts*, 8 vols. (Chicago: University of Chicago Press, 1940), 1: xix–xxi. Schibanoff, "The New Reader and Female Textuality," 81–82 reads one source note as bearing the weight of scribal disapproval, but this is arguable.

101. For orthodox reactions to rebellious lay exegesis, see Deanesley, *Lollard Bible*, 268–97, 351–73.

102. Davis's argument, "Women on Top," 124–51.

103. The work's tension between misogyny and pro-feminine implications is skillfully explored by Susan Crane, "Alison's Incapacity and Poetic Instability in the Wife of Bath's Tale," *PMLA* 102 (1987): 20–28; Patterson, *Chaucer and the Subject of History*, 288–307, 313; Blamires, *The Case for Women*, 219.

104. Peter Brown, *The Rise of Western Christendom: Triumph and Diversity, A.D. 200–1000*, 2nd ed. (Malden: Blackwell, 2003), 15.

105. Kuefler argues this is the social appeal of Christian hierarchies, *Manly Eunuch*.

106. Nicholas Watson illuminates the flowering of vernacular theology/literature 1340–1410: "Censorship and Cultural Change in Late-Medieval England: Vernacular Theology, the Oxford Translation Debate, and Arundel's Constitutions of 1409," *Speculum* 70 (1995): 822–64.

107. My reflections on power are indebted to Richard Valantasis, "Constructions of Power in Asceticism," *Journal of the American Academy of Religion*, 63 (1995): 775–821.

108. E.g., Bourdieu, *Masculine Domination*.

109. Michael Camille analyzes conventional images of hierarchical order: "The Image and the Self: Unwriting Late Medieval Bodies," in *Framing Medieval Bodies*, ed. Sarah Kay and Miri Rubin (Manchester: Manchester University Press, 1994), 62–87.

3   Gender Trouble in Augustine's *Confessions*

1. "…ipsum fecit patrem, ipsum fecit matrem. Pater est, quia condidit, quia uocat, quia iubet, quia regit; mater, quia fouet, quia nutrit, quia lactat, quia continet," Augustine, *Enarrationes in Psalmos*, Corpus Christianorum, Series Latina (Turnhout: Brepols, 1956), vol. 38, p. 164, on Psalm 26: 18.

2. Henry Chadwick situates *Confessions* in relation to a skeptical historical audience composed of both Christians who knew Augustine as a Manichean and pagans who viewed Christianity as a "low" religion: "On Rereading the *Confessions*," 1994, rpt. in *Studies in Ancient Christianity* (Aldershot: Ashgate, 2006), VII, 139–60. Peter Brown suggests Augustine's self-doubts about becoming a bishop and establishing his authority in that position: *Augustine of Hippo, A Biography*, new ed. (Berkeley: University of California Press, 2000), 155–58, 445–55, 491–92.

3. Gerald Bonner underscores the importance of Augustine's ordination to his sense of himself as a Christian: "Augustine's Understanding of the Church as a Eucharistic Community," in *Saint Augustine the Bishop: A Book of Essays*, ed. Fannie LeMoine and Christopher Kleinhenz (New York: Garland, 1994), 40.

4. I am influenced by Brian Stock, who approaches *Confessions* as a project of literary "self-definition": *Augustine the Reader: Meditation, Self-Knowledge, and the Ethics of Interpretation* (Cambridge, MA: Belknap Press, 1996), 16; and by James J. O'Donnell, who reads Augustine's pose in *Confessions* as "an astonishing act of self-presentation and self-justification," *Augustine, A New Biography* (New York: Ecco, 2005), 36. I use the term "self-fashioning" in part to contest Stephen Greenblatt's exclusion of Augustine from self-conscious literary manipulations of identity: *Renaissance Self-Fashioning from More to Shakespeare* (Chicago: University of Chicago Press, 1980), 2. Scholars of *Confessions* once divided into two camps: historicists (all details are historically accurate) and fictionalists (the details are at least in part literary invention). Ironically, a historian, Peter Brown, appreciated Augustine's literary innovations: *Augustine of Hippo*, 160–65. For a well-reasoned defense of the fictionalists' position, see Leo C. Ferrari, "Saint Augustine on the Road to Damascus," *Augustinian Studies* 13 (1982): 151–70.

5. Gillian Clark also emphasizes the work's unity, reading it as a "spiritual autobiography": *Augustine: The Confessions* (Exeter: Bristol Phoenix Press, 2005), 39–40. Margaret R. Miles points out the downside of turning particular experiences into universal truths: "The Body and Human Values in Augustine of Hippo," in *Grace, Politics and Desire: Essays on Augustine*, ed. H. A. Meynell (Calgary: University of Calgary Press, 1990), 55–61.

6. "pro nobis tibi victor et victima, et ideo victor quia victima, pro nobis tibi sacerdos et sacrificium, et ideo sacerdos quia sacrificium, faciens tibi nos de servis filios de te nascendo, nobis serviendo" (10.43.69). All citations of *Confessions* refer to James J. O'Donnell's magisterial edition: *Augustine: Confessions*, 3 vols. (Oxford: Clarendon, 1992), 1. Translations are based on Henry Chadwick, altered at points to capture literal sense: *Confessions* (Oxford: Oxford University Press, 1992).

7. Jennifer A. Herdt explicates the enduring contrast between pagan *dominium* (pride, pursuit of glory, desire to impose one's will on others) and Christian humility in Augustine's thought: *Putting on Virtue: The Legacy of the Splendid Vices* (Chicago: University of Chicago Press, 2008), 45–71. See

also G. I. Bonner's study of the desire to dominate in Augustine's works: "*Libido* and *Concupiscentia* in St. Augustine," *Studia Patristica* 6 (1962): 303–14.

8. My argument is informed by Mathew Kuefler's perceptive analysis of late antique Christian redefinitions of manliness: *The Manly Eunuch: Masculinity, Gender Ambiguity, and Christian Ideology in Late Antiquity* (Chicago: University of Chicago Press, 2001), 37–102, 117–24, 139–48.

9. "infirmitas mea tibi nota est. parvulus sum" (10.4.6).

10. "ut infantiae nostrae lactesceret sapientia tua" (7.18.24).

11. "aut quid sum, cum mihi bene est, nisi sugens lac tuum aut fruens te" (4.1.1).

12. "quibus iussisti ut serviam, si volo tecum de te vivere." (10.4.6) Augustine could have taken a hint from Philo, whose exegesis reveals similar inversions: see Kerstin Aspergren, *The Male Woman: A Feminine Ideal in the Early Church*, ed. Renée Kieffer (Stockholm: Almquist and Wiksell, 1990), 95–98.

13. Hence William E. Connolly discovers familiar gender codes: "Augustine enacts the traditional code of a devout woman [i.e., passive, obedient] with respect to this god and the traditional code of an authoritative male [active, authoritative, powerful] with respect to human believers and nonbelievers below him," *The Augustinian Imperative: A Reflection on the Politics of Morality* (Newbury Park: Sage Publications, 1993), 58. This is one of the most original books on Augustine in recent years, and this analysis has proven influential (e.g., Kuefler, *Manly Eunuch,* 140–47). From my perspective, Connolly's binary gender oppositions are inapposite for *Confessions,* as are his assumptions about a father god. The idea that Augustine feminizes himself as a gesture of humility is not original to Connolly: see, e.g., John M. Bowers, "Augustine as Addict: Sex and Texts in the *Confessions,*" *Exemplaria* 2 (1990): 420–21, 424, 431–32.

14. "non erubuerit esse puer Christi tui et infans fontis tui" (8.2.3).

15. Caroline Walker Bynum, commenting on a later tradition: "...'And Woman His Humanity': Female Imagery in the Religious Writing of the Later Middle Ages," in *Gender and Religion: On the Complexity of Symbols*, ed. Bynum, Stevan Harrell, and Paula Richman (Boston: Beacon Press, 1986), 273.

16. *Pace* Kari Elisabeth Børresen, who considers the feminine "Godalien," "Gender and Exegesis in the Latin Fathers," *Augustinianum* 40 (2000): 65–76. For earlier (and mostly Gnostic) representations of God as mother, see Elaine Pagels, "What Became of God the Mother?" *Signs* 2 (1976): 293–303.

17. Most recently, *Images of Conversion in St. Augustine's Confessions* (New York: Fordham University Press, 1996), 17–18, 40, 164–67. See also O'Connell's earlier works: *St. Augustine's Early Theory of Man, AD 386–391* (Cambridge, MA: Harvard University Press, 1968), 65–86; "The God of Saint Augustine's Imagination," *Thought* 57 (1982): 30–40; "Isaiah's Mothering God in St. Augustine's *Confessions,*" *Thought* 58

(1983): 188–206; *Imagination and Metaphysics in St. Augustine* (Milwaukee: Marquette University Press, 1986), 19–26; *Soundings in St. Augustine's Imagination* (New York: Fordham University Press, 1994), 95–139. Other scholars also remark on Augustine's feminine deity: e.g., T. J. van Bavel, "Augustine's View on Women," *Augustiniana* 39 (1989): 29; Jennifer Hockenbery, "The He, She, and It of God: Translating Saint Augustine's Gendered Latin God-Talk into English," *Augustinian Studies* 36 (2005): 433–46.

18. See O'Connell, *Images of Conversion,* 9–44, 164–67.

19. For the complex imagery that represents Augustine with his deity, see O'Connell, *Images of Conversion,* 17–44. For bishops as brides of Christ, see Kuefler, *Manly Eunuch,* 125–60.

20. This gender variance sets Augustine apart from the later tradition explored by Bynum, "And Woman His Humanity," 257–88, in which masculine aspects of God are associated with the Father, and feminine aspects with Jesus. Augustine's more fluid gendering of the deity associates authority as well as caring nurturance with both father and mother.

21. "rationis et intellegentiae virtute" (13.32.47).

22. See *On Genesis Against the Manichees (De Genesi contra Manichaeos),* 77–79, 90, 111; *On the Literal Interpretation of Genesis, An Unfinished Book (De Genesi ad litteram imperfectus),* 186, both in *St. Augustine on Genesis. Two Books on Genesis: "Against the Manichees" and "On the Literal Interpretation of Genesis: An Unfinished Book,"* trans. Roland J. Teske, The Fathers of the Church: A New Translation, vol. 84 (Washington, DC: Catholic University of America Press, 1991).

23. Judith Butler, *Gender Trouble: Feminism and the Subversion of Identity* (New York: Routledge, 1990), 33–34.

24. Other scholars point out similar challenges to patristic gender ideology, and I am indebted to their methodologies and insights, particularly to Elizabeth A. Clark, "Ideology, History, and the Construction of 'Woman' in Late Ancient Christianity," *Journal of Early Christian Studies* 2 (1994): 155–84; and Elizabeth Castelli, " 'I Will Make Mary Male': Pieties of the Body and Gender Transformation of Christian Women in Late Antiquity," in *Body Guards: The Cultural Politics of Gender Ambiguity,* ed. J. Epstein and K. Straub (New York: Routledge, 1991), 29–49.

25. Butler defines a "performative" utterance as "that discursive practice that enacts or produces what it names," *Bodies That Matter: On the Discursive Limits of "Sex"* (New York: Routledge, 1993), 13.

26. Indeed, we can interpret the contradiction between life and exegesis outlined above as evidence that his ideology changes in the decade or so that intervenes between books 1–9 and 10–13.

27. "cum ea quae ad litteram perversitatem docere videbantur, remoto mystico velamento, spiritaliter aperire" (6.4.6).

28. This remark applies only to Augustine's rhetorical pose, not to his life. Augustine was apparently influenced by Ambrose's interpretations: see J. Patout Burns, "Creation and Fall According to Ambrose of Milan,"

in *Augustine: Biblical Exegete,* ed. Frederick van Fleteren and Joseph C. Schnaubelt (New York: Peter Lang, 2001), 71–97. Stock fruitfully analyzes Augustine's account of Ambrose in the context of his developing ideas about hermeneutics and illumination, *Augustine the Reader,* 59–64.

29. "et sanari credendo poteram, ut purgatior acies mentis meae dirigeretur aliquo modo in veritatem tuam" (6.4.6).

30. Andrew Louth explicates a similar teaching in *De Doctrina Christiana: Discerning the Mystery: An Essay on the Nature of Theology* (Oxford: Clarendon, 1983), 77–82.

31. "quamvis ea diceret quae utrum vera essent adhuc ignorarem" (6.4.6).

32. "ideoque cum essemus infirmi ad inveniendam liquida ratione veritatem et ob hoc nobis opus esset auctoritate sanctarum litterarum" (6.5.8).

33. See John J. O'Meara on Manichean rationalism, *The Young Augustine: The Growth of St. Augustine's Mind Up to His Conversion* (London: Longmans, Green, 1954), 63–64, 80, 141.

34. "invocat te, domine, fides mea, quam dedisti mihi, quam inspirasti mihi per humanitatem filii tui, per ministerium praedicatoris tui" (1.1.1).

35. "per ipsam [scripturam] tibi credi et per ipsam te quaeri voluisses.... cogitabam haec et aderas mihi" (6.5.8).

36. See, e.g., 13.23.33. See also Henry Chadwick on Augustine's positive attitude toward lay vocation and his tendency (early on) not to clericalize the church: *Augustine* (Oxford: Oxford University Press), 61–64, 85.

37. For Augustine's theory of illumination, see Stock, *Augustine the Reader,* 23–42, 159–61, 190–206; Chadwick, *Augustine,* 48–51; G. R. Evans, *Augustine on Evil* (Cambridge: Cambridge University Press, 1982), 30–49. My analysis differs from theirs in discerning a Neoplatonic influence in Augustine's representation of a transcendent Word.

38. Augustine's representational strategy does not always cohere with his explicit statements about exegesis. Despite his theory of illumination, he is clearly influenced by his rhetorical training and education: see Frances M. Young, *Biblical Exegesis and the Formation of Christian Culture* (Cambridge: Cambridge University Press, 1997), 265–84.

39. For detailed studies of Augustine's Neoplatonism, see Paula Fredriksen, "Augustine on History, the Church, and the Flesh," in *Saint Augustine the Bishop,* ed. LeMoine and Kleinhenz, 109–23; Chadwick, *Augustine,* 1–29; Evans, *Augustine on Evil,* 29–90; O'Meara, *The Young Augustine,* 131–72.

40. "inveneram incommutabilem et veram veritatis aeternitatem supra mentem meam commutabilem" (7.17.23).

41. 7.10.16 anticipates and helps establish the themes of this passage.

42. "ut inveniret quo lumine aspergeretur" (7.17.23); the subject (*ratiocinantem potentiam*) falls earlier in the passage.

43. "et pervenit ad id quod est in ictu trepidantis aspectus. tunc vero invisibilia tua per ea quae facta sunt intellecta conspexi" (7.17.23). For close commentary on this difficult passage, see O'Connell, *Images of Conversion,* 123–28, with 93–203. I agree with O'Connell that the narrative represents how Augustine came to understand an omnipresent God (*pace* the

NOTES 149

Manicheans), rather than, as Pierre Courcelle famously argues, a failed Platonic-mystical vision, *Recherches sur les "Confessions" de Saint Augustin* (Paris: Boccard, 1950), 157–67, 222–26. I am indebted to several scholars' analyses of the ascent narratives, and to their subtle conclusions about Augustine's dependence on and differences from Neoplatonism: John Peter Kenney, *The Mysticism of Saint Augustine: Re-Reading the "Confessions"* (New York: Routledge, 2005), 3–11, 27–86; Frederick van Fleteren, "Augustine's Ascent of the Soul in Book VII of the *Confessions: A Reconsideration*," *Augustinian Studies* 5 (1974): 29–72. I find Stock's account of the passage as a "failed ecstatic experience" an unpersuasive engagement with the text, though I concur with his conclusions about how Augustine revises Neoplatonism, *Augustine the Reader*, 73.

44. "Ego vero aliud putabam tantumque sentiebam de domino Christo meo, quantum de excellentis sapientiae viro...quid autem sacramenti haberet verbum caro factum, ne suspicari quidem poteram" (7.19.25).

45. "et cibum, cui capiendo invalidus eram, miscentem carni, quoniam verbum caro factum est ut infantiae nostrae lactesceret sapientia tua, per quam creasti omnia" (7.18.24).

46. "non enim tenebam deum meum Iesum, humilis humilem, nec cuius rei magistra esset eius infirmitas noveram" (7.18.24).

47. Bonner develops a similar analysis, "Augustine's Understanding of the Church," in *St. Augustine the Bishop*, ed. LeMoine and Kleinhenz, 45–46.

48. "erigentes nos ardentiore affectu in idipsum...ut attingeremus regionem ubertatis indeficientis, ubi pascis Israhel in aeternum veritate pabulo, et ibi vita sapientia est, per quam fiunt omnia ista, et quae fuerunt et quae futura sunt" (9.10.24).

49. "omnis lingua et omne signum, et quidquid transeundo fit si cui sileat omnino...et loquatur ipse solus non per ea sed per se ipsum" (9.10.25).

50. "ut audiamus verbum eius, non per linguam carnis neque per vocem angeli nec per sonitum nubis nec per aenigma similitudinis, sed ipsum quem in his amamus, ipsum sine his audiamus (sicut nunc extendimus nos et rapida cogitatione attingimus aeternam sapientiam super omnia manentem)" (9.10.25).

51. O'Donnell's remarks on Monica inform my conclusions, *Augustine, A New Biography*, 56. I am also indebted to J. Kevin Coyle, who argues the Ostia vision represents Monica as a "true philosopher," "In Praise of Monica: A Note on the Ostia Experience of *Confessions* IX," *Augustinian Studies* 13 (1982): 89, discussion 87–96. Augustine's relationship with his mother is more complex than this thread of his narrative implies. Kim Power perceptively analyzes his ambivalence toward her: *Veiled Desire: Augustine's Writing on Women* (London: Darton, Longman, and Todd, 1995), 71–93.

52. "vidit enim se stantem in quadam regula lignea et advenientem ad se iuvenem splendidum hilarem atque arridentem sibi" (3.11.19). Although homely in detail, the narrative bears resonant symbolic implications: see

Leo C. Ferrari, "Monica on the Wooden Ruler (*Confessions* 3.11.19)," *Augustinian Studies* 6 (1975): 193–205.

53. "quin potius fuisse et futurum esse non est in ea [sapientia], sed esse solum, quoniam aeterna est" (9.10.24).

54. "quae me parturivit et carne, ut in hanc temporalem, et corde, ut in aeternam lucem nascerer" (9.8.17).

55. Respectively, "me parturiebat spiritu" (5.9.16); "sempiternam salute meam carius parturiebat" (1.11.17).

56. "sed non praeteribo quidquid mihi anima parturit de illa famula tua" (9.8.17).

57. "hoc nomen salvatoris mei, filii tui, in ipso adhuc lacte matris tenerum cor meum pie biberat" (3.4.8).

58. "sed inhiabamus ore cordis in superna fluenta fontis tui, fontis vitae" (9.10.23).

59. "quoquo modo rem tantam cogitaremus" (9.10.23); compare "perambulavimus," "ascendebamus," "venimus," etc. (9.10.24).

60. "et adhuc ascendebamus interius cogitando et loquendo et mirando opera tua" (9.10.24).

61. "ibi vita sapientia est, per quam fiunt omnia ista" (9.10.24).

62. Margaret R. Miles illuminates Augustine's conversion of sexual desire into desire for God: *Desire and Delight: A New Reading of Augustine's Confessions* (New York: Crossroad, 1992).

63. E.g., O'Donnell stresses the work's unsatisfying lack of unity: *Augustine, A New Biography,* 78.

64. I am indebted to Robert R. Edwards's perceptive analysis of how Augustine leads all loves back to God: *The Flight from Desire: Augustine and Ovid to Chaucer* (New York: Palgrave Macmillan, 2006), 13–37.

65. Far from unique to Augustine, the paradoxical "rhetoric of vulnerability...was...the classic language of male authority in the early Church," Conrad Leyser, "Vulnerability and Power: The Early Christian Rhetoric of Masculine Authority," *Bulletin of the John Rylands University Library of Manchester* 80 (1998): 160.

66. "nos autem, domine, pusillus grex tuus ecce sumus, tu nos posside. praetende alas tuas, et fugiamus sub eas" (10.36.59). A common image in Augustine's writings, for which see O'Connell, *Soundings in Augustine's Imagination,* 97–98, 112–13, 116–19.

67. "et ego id ago factis et dictis, id ago sub alis tuis nimis cum ingenti periculo, nisi quia sub alis tuis tibi subdita est anima mea" (10.4.6).

68. Brent D. Shaw vividly details the violence of patriarchal domination, against which, I propose, Augustine defines his gender role: "The Family in Late Antiquity: The Experience of Augustine," *Past and Present* 115 (1987): 3–51.

69. Kuefler argues that this kind of rhetoric ultimately has just this effect, *Manly Eunuch,* 125–60, 283–91.

70. "absit enim ut in tabernaculo tuo prae pauperibus accipiantur personae divitum aut prae ignobilibus nobiles, quando potius infirma mundi

elegisti ut confunderes fortia, et ignobilia huius mundi elegisti et contemptibilia" (8.4.9).

71. Peter Brown proposes that Augustine's later works demonstrate a shift from an ancient hierarchical ideal to an "ascetic paradigm" that displaces hierarchy and stresses surrender of the self to God: *Augustine and Sexuality* (Berkeley: The Center for Hermeneutical Studies, University of California, 1983), 6–11. *Confessions* implies that the shift takes place earlier than Brown recognizes, and confirms Margaret Miles' argument that the two paradigms coexist throughout Augustine's works (response to Brown in the same volume, 19).

72. His construction parallels other contemporary ascetic definitions of power as a resistant alternative within dominant culture, for which see Richard Valantasis, "Constructions of Power in Asceticism," *Journal of the American Academy of Religion* 63 (1995): 800–15.

73. "nam illa satagebat ut tu mihi pater esses, deus meus, potius quam ille, et in hoc adiuvabas eam, ut superaret virum, cui melior serviebat, quia et in hoc tibi utique id iubenti serviebat" (1.11.17).

74. Alexandre Leupin comments perceptively on Augustine's collapsing gender hierarchies: *Fiction and Incarnation: Rhetoric, Theology, and Literature in the Middle Ages,* trans. David Laatsch (Minneapolis: University of Minnesota Press, 2003), 53–56, 64.

75. JoAnn McNamara posits that early Christians associate (Christian) women with virtue, (pagan) men with vice, a useful context for Augustine's representation of his parents: "An Unresolved Syllogism: The Search for a Christian Gender System," in *Conflicted Identities and Multiple Masculinities: Men in the Medieval West,* ed. Jacqueline Murray (New York: Garland, 1999), 1–24.

76. "et cuius erant nisi tua verba illa per matrem meam, fidelem tuam, quae cantasti in aures meas?" (2.3.7).

77. "qui mihi monitus muliebres videbantur...et te tacere putabam atque illam loqui per quam mihi tu non tacebas" (2.3.7).

78. "et de sanguine cordis matris meae per lacrimas eius diebus et noctibus pro me sacrificabatur tibi" (5.7.13).

79. "et feretro cogitationis offerebat ut diceres filio viduae, 'iuvenis, tibi dico, surge'" (6.1.1).

80. "muliebri habitu, virili fide" (9.4.8).

81. "et lassi prosternerentur in eam, illa autem surgens levaret eos" (7.18.24).

82. For nuanced accounts of Augustine's attitudes toward and relationships with women, see E. Ann Matter, "Christ, God and Woman in the Thought of St. Augustine," in *Augustine and His Critics: Essays in Honour of Gerald Bonner,* ed. Robert Dodaro and George Lawless (London: Routledge, 2000), 164–75; Bavel, "Augustine's View on Women," 5–53; Elizabeth A. Clark, "Theory and Practice in Late Ancient Asceticism: Jerome, Chrysostom, and Augustine," *Journal of Feminist Studies in Religion* 5 (1989): 31–44.

83. "sed numquid, domine, qui solus sine typho dominaris...numquid hoc quoque tertium temptationis genus cessavit a me aut cessare in hac tota

vita potest, timeri et amari velle ab hominibus, non propter aliud sed ut inde sit gaudium quod non est gaudium" (10.36.59).

84. See 8.6.14–15.

85. Valantasis, "Constructions of Power," 798.

86. See, e.g., Jean Baker Miller, "Women and Power," in *Rethinking Power,* ed. Thomas E. Wartenberg (Albany: State University of New York Press, 1992), 240–48.

87. Augustine's theory of sin ultimately leads him to rationalize a rigidly hierarchical paradigm for church and state: on this, see Elaine Pagels, *Adam, Eve, and the Serpent* (New York: Random House, 1988), 98–126.

88. Caroline Walker Bynum discovers remarkably similar imagery and conceptual import in twelfth-century Cistercian writings, which she describes as something new: *Jesus as Mother: Studies in the Spirituality of the High Middle Ages* (Berkeley: University of California Press, 1982), 1–21, 110–69.

89. "et haec ad tempus facta verba tua nuntiavit auris exterior menti prudenti, cuius auris interior posita est ad aeternum verbum tuum" (11.6.8).

90. "et tamen illa [scriptura] temporaliter dicit, verbo autem meo tempus non accedit, quia aequali mecum aeternitate consistit" (13.29.44).

91. "vera enim dicam te mihi inspirante quod ex eis verbis voluisti ut dicerem" (13.25.38).

92. "num dicetis falsa esse, quae mihi veritas voce forti in aurem interiorem dicit" (12.15.18).

93. Variations in the ancient text could partially explain his approach: see John S. McIntosh, *A Study of Augustine's Versions of Genesis* (Chicago: University of Chicago Press, 1912).

94. "intus utique mihi, intus in domicilio cogitationis, nec hebraea nec graeca nec latina nec barbara, veritas sine oris et linguae organis, sine strepitu syllabarum diceret, 'verum dicit'" (11.3.5). Frederick van Fleteren puts it well: "The purpose of [Augustine's] exegesis is to create circumstances by which God can bring those who hear or read his word beyond themselves and beyond the text itself," "Principles of Augustine's Hermeneutic: An Overview," in *Augustine: Biblical Exegete,* ed. Fleteren and Schnaubelt, 7.

95. At one point, Augustine reconciles the transcendent Word and scriptural words, thereby situating his Neoplatonism unambiguously within Christianity: "in the gospel the Word speaks through the flesh, and this sounded externally in human ears" (11.8.10). When God incarnate speaks, his words are the Word, at once physically present and eternal. Yet even in this case, the Word sounds "through the flesh" only "so that it should be believed and sought inwardly, found in the eternal truth" (11.8.10). Words are consistently heard by the ears, the truth by the heart. The Word is transcendent and cannot be reduced to transient, material words.

96. For cogent comments on how Augustine's exegesis develops in these works, see Susan E. Schreiner, "Eve, the Mother of History: Reaching for the Reality of History in Augustine's Later Exegesis of Genesis," in

Genesis 1–3 in the History of Exegesis: Intrigue in the Garden, ed. Gregory Allen Robbins, Studies in Women and Religion, Vol. 27 (Lewiston: Edwin Mellen Press, 1988), 136–69; Elizabeth A. Clark, "'Adam's Only Companion': Augustine and the Early Christian Debate on Marriage," *Recherches Augustiniennes* 21 (1986): 142–43; E[lizabeth A.] Clark, "Heresy, Asceticism, Adam, and Eve: Interpretations of Genesis 1–3 in the Later Latin Fathers," in *Ascetic Piety and Women's Faith: Essays on Late Ancient Christianity,* Studies in Women and Religion, Vol. 20 (Lewiston: Edwin Mellen Press, 1986), 363–69.

97. *On Genesis Against the Manichees,* in *Augustine on Genesis,* trans. Teske, 71.
98. *On Genesis Against the Manichees,* in *Augustine on Genesis,* trans. Teske, 141.
99. "Introduction," *Augustine on Genesis,* 16.
100. The partly contemporary *De Doctrina Christiana* splits the differences between the early Genesis commentaries and *Confessions. De Doctrina Christiana* emphasizes norms, principles, and rules for exegesis, making it similar to the early commentaries on this point. Unlike the commentaries, however, *De Doctrina Christiana* recognizes divine inspiration as a basis of knowledge, though not one that legitimately replaces learning and respect for the principles of authoritative exegesis: see, e.g., *De Doctrina Christiana,* Prologue to Book 1.
101. "et quid in nobis esset secundum quod essemus et recte in scriptura diceremur ad imaginem dei, prorsus ignorabam" (3.7.12).
102. "mente quippe renovatus et conspiciens intellectam veritatem tuam" (13.22.32).
103. "ita homo renovator in agnitione dei secundum imaginem eius, qui creavit eum" (13.22.32).
104. "dispensator ille tuus generans per evangelium filios, ne semper parvulos haberet quos lacte nutriret et tamquam nutrix foveret" (13.22.32).
105. "videmus terrenis animalibus faciem terrae decorari hominemque ad imaginem et similitudinem tuam cunctis inrationabilibus animantibus ipsa tua imagine ac similitudine, hoc est rationis et intellegentiae virtute, praeponi, et quemadmodum in eius anima aliud est quod consulendo dominator, aliud quod subditur ut obtemperet, sic viro factam esse etiam corporaliter feminam, quae haberet quidem in mente rationalis intellegentiae parem naturam, sexu tamen corporis ita masculino sexui subiceretur, quemadmodum subicitur appetitus actionis ad concipiendam de ratione mentis recte agendi sollertiam. videmus haec et singula bona et omnia bona valde" (13.32.47).
106. See 13.28.43–13.35.50. Maryanne Cline Horowitz situates this interpretation in the context of Augustine's other works, and in relation to prior and subsequent traditions: "The Image of God in Man—Is Woman Included?" *Harvard Theological Review* 72 (1979): 175–206. Much of the scholarly commentary on Augustine's exegesis of Genesis (from *De Genesi contra Manichaeos* forward) focuses on the creation of woman (as well as man) in the image of God, and her social subordination, the latter usually attributed to Augustine's acceptance of dominant

cultural norms: e.g., Constance E. McLeese, "Augustinian Exegesis and Sexist Canon from the New Testament," in *Augustine and the Bible,* ed. and trans. Pamela Bright (Notre Dame: Notre Dame University Press, 1999), 282–300; Power, *Veiled Desire,* 9, 121, 131–57; Eugene TeSelle, "Serpent, Eve, and Adam: Augustine and the Exegetical Tradition," in *Collectanea Augustiniana: Augustine, Presbyter Factus Sum,* ed. Joseph T. Lienhard, Earl C. Muller, and Roland J. Teske (New York: Peter Lang, 1993), 341–61; Bavel, "Augustine's View on Women," 18–24; Schreiner, "Eve, the Mother of History," 136–55; Richard McGowan, "Augustine's Spiritual Equality: The Allegory of Man and Woman with Regard to *Imago Dei*," *Revue des études Augustiniennes* 33 (1987): 255–64; Kari Elisabeth Børresen, *Subordination and Equivalence: The Nature and Role of Woman in Augustine and Thomas Aquinas,* trans. Charles H. Talbot (Washington, DC: University Press of America, 1981), 1–140; John J. O'Meara, *The Creation of Man in St. Augustine's "De Genesi ad Litteram"* (Villanova: Villanova University Press, 1980), 37–85.

107. Several scholars remark cogently on the problem of the divided will: Eugene TeSelle, "Exploring the Inner Conflict: Augustine's Sermons on Romans 7 and 8," in *Augustine: Biblical Exegete,* ed. Fleteren and Schnaubelt, 313–45; Connolly, *The Augustinian Imperative,* 53, 79; Peter Brown, *The Body and Society: Men, Women and Sexual Renunciation in Early Christianity* (New York: Columbia University Press, 1988), 387–427.

108. Perhaps Augustine recognizes this, for his later writings evidence his increasingly skeptical attitude toward self-governance, which parallels his greater reliance on church and state government: see Pagels, *Adam, Eve, and the Serpent,* 98–126.

109. Daniel Boyarin maps conflicts between two of Augustine's major sources, Philo and Paul; his analysis suggests the contradictory influences on Augustine's exegesis: "Paul and the Genealogy of Gender," *Representations* 41 (1993): 1–33.

110. "et deinde fidelium animam vivam per affectus ordinatos continentiae vigore formasti, atque inde tibi soli mentem subditam et nullius auctoritatis humanae ad imitandum indigentem renovasti ad imaginem et similitudinem tuam, praestantique intellectui rationabilem actionem tamquam viro feminam subdidisti" (13.34.49).

111. "et inde accendisti quaedam luminaria in firmamento, verbum vitae habentes sanctos tuos et spiritalibus donis praelata sublimi auctoritate fulgentes" (13.34.49).

112. Gerard J. P. O'Daly aptly remarks that hierarchy is central to Augustine's thought, the problem being to replace "the wrong type of hierarchy by the approved version," "Hierarchies in Augustine's Thought," in *From Augustine to Eriugena: Essays on Neoplatonism and Christianity in Honor of John O'Meara,* ed. F. X. Martin and J. A. Richmond (Washington, DC: Catholic University of America Press, 1991), 151.

113. "solidasti auctoritatem libri tui inter superiores, qui tibi dociles essent, et inferiores, qui ei subderentur" (13.34.49). Augustine presents a similar scenario at 13.23.33.

114. Butler, *Gender Trouble,* 33–34.

115. Adrienne Rich, *Of Woman Born* (New York: Bantam, 1976), 40.

116. E. Ann Matter examines Augustine's later exegesis as socially situated, but purposefully avoids autobiography. This allows her productively to shift the conversation away from what she sees as an overly autobiographical emphasis in Augustine studies: "De cura feminarum: Augustine the Bishop, North African Women, and the Development of a Theology of Feminine Nature," *Augustinian Studies* 36 (2005): 87–98. I take her strategy as corrective rather than an end in itself.

117. Erin Sawyer elucidates Augustine's transformation of desire into discourse: "Celibate Pleasures: Masculinity, Desire, and Asceticism in Augustine," *Journal of the History of Sexuality* 6 (1995): 1–29.

118. Gillian Clark astutely comments on this process, which transforms Augustine "from a controversial theologian to an authority" and bestows "canonical status" on "his writings," *Augustine: The Confessions,* 85.

4 Affective Exegesis in the Fleury *Slaughter of Innocents*

1. Clifford Geertz, *The Interpretation of Cultures* (New York: Basic Books, 1973), 82.

2. Caroline Walker Bynum, *Jesus as Mother: Studies in the Spirituality of the High Middle Ages* (Berkeley: University of California Press, 1982), 1–21, 110–69.

3. Bynum, *Jesus as Mother,* 135.

4. Bynum, *Jesus as Mother,* 129 quote, discussion 1–21.

5. In exegetical methodology and in the idea of a "performative exegesis," this chapter resembles Susan Boynton's "Performative Exegesis in the Fleury *Interfectio Puerorum,*" *Viator* 29 (1998): 39–61. Boynton minimizes precisely what I emphasize: the play's anti-Jewish elements.

6. I take the phrase and inspiration from Steven Mullaney, "Affective Technologies: Toward an Emotional Logic of the Elizabethan Stage," in *Environment and Embodiment in Early Modern England,* ed. Mary Floyd-Wilson and Garrett Sullivan (New York: Palgrave Macmillan, 2006), 71–89.

7. The *Slaughter* is one of ten plays in a manuscript collection (Orléans, Bibliothèque Municipale MS. 201), which was copied in the thirteenth century and was, in the same century, in the Benedictine monastery library at Fleury in northern France (Saint-Benoît-sur-Loire): see the Appendix in *The Fleury Playbook: Essays and Studies,* ed. Thomas P. Campbell and Clifford Davidson (Kalamazoo: Medieval Institute, 1985), 161–64; and Marco Mostert, *The Library of Fleury: A Provisional List of*

Manuscripts (Hilversum: Verloren, 1989), 154. The weight of evidence favors Fleury as the site of composition: Richard B. Donovan, "Two Celebrated Centers of Medieval Liturgical Drama: Fleury and Ripoll," in *The Medieval Drama and Its Claudelian Revival,* ed. E. Catherine Dunn, Tatiana Fotitch, and Bernard M. Peebles (Washington, DC: Catholic University of America Press, 1970), 41–47; and Fletcher Collins, Jr., "The Home of the Fleury *Playbook,*" in *The Fleury Playbook,* ed. Campbell and Davidson, 26–34. A major intellectual and cultural center, Fleury is renowned for its liturgical poetry and literary innovations: see Jean Leclercq, *The Love of Learning and the Desire for God: A Study of Monastic Culture,* trans. Catharine Misrahi (New York: Fordham University Press, 1961), 114–15, 159, 180, 191, 294; and Thomas Head, *Hagiography and the Cult of Saints: The Diocese of Orléans, 800–1200* (Cambridge: Cambridge University Press, 1990), 39, 41, 59, 73, 95, 97–98, 129–32, 236, 246–48, 278–79, 281. The attribution to Fleury has been challenged by Solange Corbin: "Le Manuscrit 201 d'Orléans: Drames liturgiques dits de Fleury," *Romania* 74 (1953): 1–43. Corbin assumes the Playbook was composed at the site of a Nicholas cult, and she favors the abbey of St. Laumer at Blois. Clyde W. Brockett suggests a link between the Nicholas plays and a cult of the saint at Angers: "*Persona* in *Cantilena:* St. Nicholas in Music in Medieval Drama," in *The Saint Play in Medieval Europe,* ed. Clifford Davidson (Kalamazoo: Medieval Institute, 1986), 23–26. The place of composition is probably irrecoverable, in part because cults of saints were celebrated regionally, not just locally, and in part because writers composed for cults in other places. Since the manuscript was in the Fleury library, it likely had a reading audience there at the very least.

8. *Biblia Latina cum Glossa Ordinaria: Facsimile Reprint of the Editio Princeps Adolph Rusch of Strassburg 1480/81,* ed. Karlfried Froehlich and Margaret T. Gibson, 4 vols. (Turnhout: Brepols, 1992), 4: 9–10. When quoting from this work, I take the liberty of expanding Latin contractions and adding punctuation for clarity.

9. Pseudo-Bede, *In Matthaei Evangelium Expositio, PL* 92, col. 14; Thomas Aquinas, *Catena Aurea: Commentary on the Four Gospels Collected out of the Fathers by St. Thomas Aquinas,* ed. John Henry Newman, 4 vols. (Southampton: St. Austin Press, 1997), 1: 82 (henceforth *Commentary on the Four Gospels*).

10. See, e.g., Jeremy Cohen, "The Jews as Killers of Christ in the Latin Tradition, from Augustine to the Friars," *Traditio* 39 (1983): 3–27; John Gilchrist, "The Perceptions of Jews in the Canon Law in the Period of the First Two Crusades," *Jewish History* 3 (1988): 9–24; Gavin I. Langmuir, *Toward a Definition of Antisemitism* (Berkeley: University of California Press, 1990); John A. Watt, "Jews and Christians in the Gregorian Decretals," *Studies in Church History* 29 (1992): 93–105; Anna Sapir Abulafia, *Christians and Jews in the Twelfth-Century Renaissance* (New York: Routledge, 1995); Jeremy Cohen, *Living Letters of the Law: Ideas of the Jew in Medieval Christianity* (Berkeley: University of California Press,

1999); Miri Rubin, *Gentile Tales: The Narrative Assault on Late Medieval Jews* (New Haven, CT: Yale University Press, 1999); Sara Lipton, *Images of Intolerance: The Representation of Jews and Judaism in the "Bible moralisée"* (Berkeley: University of California Press, 1999).

11. I borrow the term from Cohen: the "hermeneutical Jew" is "the Jew as constructed in the discourse of Christian theology, and above all else in Christian theologians' interpretation of Scripture," *Living Letters of the Law*, 3.

12. Léon Poliakov offers a readable history of this charge, *The History of Anti-Semitism, Volume 1: From the Time of Christ to the Court Jews,* trans. Richard Howard, 4 vols. (New York: Vanguard Press, 1965), 1: 56–64. Jeremy Cohen demonstrates the myth's potential to unify local Christian communities: "The Flow of Blood in Medieval Norwich," *Speculum* 79 (2004): 26–65. William Chester Jordan brilliantly studies royal policy in *The French Monarchy and the Jews: From Philip Augustus to the Last Capetians* (Philadelphia: University of Pennsylvania Press, 1989), 17–19, 136, 146–48, 153, 190–91, 219–22, 236. For analysis of the myth in a later age, see R. Po-Chia Hsia, *Myth of Ritual Murder: Jews and Magic in Reformation Germany* (New Haven, CT: Yale University Press, 1988). Various theories partially explain the genesis and dissemination of the myth; they are well represented in Alan Dundes, ed., *The Blood Libel Legend: A Casebook in anti-Semitic Folklore* (Madison: University of Wisconsin Press, 1991).

13. Robert Michael documents Church complicity with the myth: *A History of Catholic Antisemitism: The Dark Side of the Church* (New York: Palgrave Macmillan, 2008), esp. 69–70, 90, 166–69.

14. Jordan, *The French Monarchy and the Jews,* 18–19.

15. Langmuir studies this case: *Toward a Definition of Antisemitism,* 237–62.

16. George Bornstein, citing Tzvetan Todorov, "T. S. Eliot and the Real World," *Michigan Quarterly Review* 36 (1997): 499.

17. I agree with Kenneth R. Stow that medieval anti-Semitism derives from interactions of church and state, not from the church alone: *Alienated Minority: The Jews of Medieval Latin Europe* (Cambridge, MA: Harvard University Press, 1992), e.g., 4–5. See also the essays collected in Anna Sapir Abulafia, ed., *Religious Violence between Christians and Jews: Medieval Roots, Modern Perspectives* (New York: Palgrave Macmillan, 2002).

18. *Saint Caesarius of Arles: Sermons,* trans. Mary Magdeleine Mueller, The Fathers of the Church: A New Translation, vol. 66 (Washington, DC: Catholic University of America Press, 1973), "Sermon 222: On the Feast of the Holy Innocents," 140.

19. This chapter is an analysis of a hypothetical performance, based on the play rubrics, and on David Bevington's reconstruction of likely processional routes and locations of action, "The Staging of Twelfth-Century Liturgical Drama in the Fleury *Playbook*," in *The Fleury Playbook,* ed. Campbell and Davidson, 73–75. I draw also on John Marlin's analysis of the Playbook's use of church spaces and congregation, "Virtual

Ritual: History, Drama, and the Spirit of Liturgy in the Fleury *Playbook*," *American Benedictine Review* 48 (1997): 416–27.

20. Per the rubric, "gaudentes per monasterium," ed. and trans. David Bevington, *Medieval Drama* (Boston: Houghton Mifflin, 1975), p. 67. Further page citations are parenthetical; I occasionally revise Bevington's translations to focus on the literal meaning.

21. "O quam gloriosum est regnum," 67. For identification of the antiphons, see Karl Young, *The Drama of the Medieval Church*, 2 vols. (1933; rpt. Oxford: Clarendon, 1951), 2: 110–114; and Clyde W. Brockett, "Modal and Motivic Coherence in the Music of the Music-Dramas in the Fleury *Playbook*," in *The Fleury Playbook*, ed. Campbell and Davidson, 60, n. 19.

22. Leclercq, *Love of Learning*, 287–308.

23. "Emitte agnum, Domine," 67. The biblical verse applies to Innocents' Day, but this is the responsory for All Saints: see Brockett, "Modal and Motivic Coherence," in *The Fleury Playbook*, ed. Campbell and Davidson, 60, n. 19. Again, preexisting music is given new meaning in the play. For the identification of the 144,000 with Christian martyrs, see C. Clifford Flanigan, "Rachel and Her Children: From Biblical Text to Music Drama," in *Metamorphoses and the Arts: Proceedings of the Second Lilly Conference*, ed. Breon Mitchell (Bloomington: Indiana University Press, 1979), 39–40; Boynton, "Performative Exegesis," 45–46, 50.

24. "Interfectio parvulorum occisionem significat martyrum Christi," *In Matthaeum, PL* 92, col. 14.

25. "Quam cito christus apparuit mundo incepit in eum persecutio, quae figuravit persecutionem sanctorum; et dum infans quaeritur infantes occiduntur, in quibus forma martyrii nascitur, ubi infantia ecclesiae dedicator," *Biblia cum Glossa*, 4:10.

26. The Crucifixion similarly overdetermines interpretation throughout the *Gloss*. E.g., Michael A. Signer argues that the *Gloss* both transmits patristic anti-Jewish themes and "recasts them with a harsher twist": "The *Glossa ordinaria* and the Transmission of Medieval Anti-Judaism," in *A Distinct Voice: Medieval Studies in Honor of Leonard E. Boyle, O. P.*, ed. Jacqueline Brown and William P. Stoneman (Notre Dame: University of Notre Dame Press, 1997), 591–605, quotation at 593.

27. *Commentary on the Four Gospels*, 1: 82; "Et dum insequitur Christum, regi nostro coaevum procuravit exercitum stolis victricibus candidatum," *Catena Aurea in Quatuor Evangelia*, ed. P. Angelici Guarienti, 2 vols. (Turin and Rome: Marietti, 1953), 1: 41 (henceforth *Catena Aurea*).

28. "Ille de vestra corona dubitabit in passione pro Christo," *Catena Aurea*, 1: 41.

29. "In this death of the children the precious death of all Christ's martyrs is figured; that they were infants signifies, that by the merit of humility alone can we come to the glory of martyrdom; that they were slain in Bethlehem and the coasts thereof, that the persecution shall be both in Judaea whence the Church originated, and throughout the world," *Commentary on the Four Gospels*, 1: 83. "In hac autem morte puerorum,

omnium Christi martyrum pretiosa est mors designata: quod parvuli occisi sunt, significat per humilitatis meritum ad martyrii perveniendum gloriam; quod in Bethlehem et in omnibus finibus eius occisi sunt, ostendit in Iudaea, unde Ecclesiae coepit origo, et ubique per orbem persecutionem saevituram," *Catena Aurea,* 1: 41.

30. "Salve, Agnus Dei! Salve, qui tollis peccata mundi" (69).
31. "Why do you not defend our blood, our God?" ("Quare non defendis sanguinem nostrum, Deus noster?"), 69.
32. "Agno sacrato pro nobis mortificato, Splendorem patris splendorem virginitatis / Offerimus Christo sub signo luminis isto. / Multis ira modis ut quos inquirit Herodis / Agno salvemur, cum Christo conmoriemur." (68)
33. Sinanoglou studies a later era, but the imagery is relatively constant and applies as well to the earlier drama: "The Christ Child as Sacrifice: A Medieval Tradition and the Corpus Christi Plays," *Speculum* 48 (1973): 491–509, esp. 501 on the Innocents.
34. "Super solium Dauid, et super regnum eius sedebit in aeternum" (67).
35. For the development of this Christian stereotype, see Abulafia, *Christians and Jews,* 94–106; and see also her "Jewish Carnality in Twelfth-Century Renaissance Thought," *Studies in Church History* 29 (1992): 59–75.
36. "Rex, in aeternum vive!" (68); "O quam gloriosum est regnum" (67).
37. "Herodes vero significat odium Judaeorum, qui nomen Christi delere, et credentes in eum perdere cupiebant," *In Matthaeum, PL* 92, cols. 13–14.
38. Cohen, "The Jews as Killers of Christ," 3–27.
39. See Watt, "Jews and Christians in the Gregorian Decretals," 93–105.
40. Herod is described during the flight into Egypt: "relicto herode id est iudaeorum infidelitate," *Biblia cum Glossa,* 4: 9.
41. John Y. B. Hood's apt description, *Aquinas and the Jews* (Philadelphia: University of Pennsylvania Press, 1995), 74; for contradictions in the *Gloss,* see 73; for dominant influences on Aquinas, see 1–18, 56, 73.
42. Quoted and discussed in Hood, *Aquinas and the Jews,* 74.
43. Aquinas, *Catena Aurea,* 1: 35, 37–38, 41.
44. "Tunc Herodes, quasi corruptus, arrepto gladio, paret seipsum occidere; sed prohibeatur tandem a suis et pacificetur, dicens: Incendium meum ruina restinguam." (68)
45. Skey, "The Iconography of Herod in the Fleury *Playbook* and in the Visual Arts," in *The Fleury Playbook,* ed. Campbell and Davidson, 135–41.
46. For the invention of supersessionism, see Sarah Pearce, "Attitudes of Contempt: Christian Anti-Judaism and the Bible," in *Cultures of Ambivalence and Contempt: Studies in Jewish–Non-Jewish Relations,* ed. Siân Jones, Tony Kushner, and Sarah Pearce (London: Vallentine Mitchell, 1998), 59–68.
47. "Discerne, Domine, vindicare iram tuam, et stricto mucrone jube occidi pueros; forte inter occisos occidetur et Christus" (69).
48. "Figurat mors parvulorum passionem omnium martyrum qui parvuli, humiles et innocentes occisi sunt, qui non in iudaea tantum, sed ubique passi sunt ab impiis, quos significat herodes," *Biblia cum Glossa,* 4: 10.

49. See Terrence G. Kardong, trans., *Benedict's Rule: A Translation and Commentary* (Collegeville: Liturgical Press, 1996), "De Humilitate," 129–68. I am indebted to two studies of this aspect of the Rule: Dom Cuthbert Butler, *Benedictine Monachism: Studies in Benedictine Life and Rule* (1924; rpt. Cambridge, MA: Speculum Historiale; New York: Barnes and Noble, 1961), 46–57; and Bynum, *Jesus as Mother,* 59–81.

50. I allude to R. I. Moore's study, *The Formation of a Persecuting Society: Power and Deviance in Western Europe 950–1250,* 2nd ed. (Malden: Blackwell, 2007).

51. "fili David" (68); "super solium David" (67).

52. See Head, *Hagiography and the Cult of Saints,* 166–67.

53. "Egypte, noli flere, quia Dominator tuus veniet tibi" (68). Flanigan, "Rachel and Her Children," 37 remarks cogently on this typology.

54. "Joseph significat doctores, Maria Ecclesiam; Aegyptus vero, quae tenebrae interpretatur, significat istam gentilitatem; et haec figura Christi in Aegyptum significat transitum ejus cum Ecclesia sua de Israelitico populo per praedicatores ad gentes" Pseudo-Bede, *In Matthaeum, PL* 92, col. 13.

55. "nox vero significat ignorantiam, qua Judaei in errore suo relicti sunt, quando apostoli lucem fidei gentibus intimabant." Pseudo-Bede, *In Matthaeum, PL* 92, col. 14.

56. "Joseph is a figure of the preachers, who carried Christ with his mother, that is, the faith of Christ and of the Church, to all peoples, with Herod left behind, that is, the faithlessness of the Jews. 'At night.' Because he [Joseph] went secretly in flight down to illuminate Egypt, when night was left behind for the Jews" ("Joseph figura praedicatorum qui christum cum matre, id est fidem christi et ecclesiae tulerunt ad gentes, relicto herode id est iudaeorum infidelitate. *Nocte.* Quia occulte per fugam ad illustrandam egyptum descendit, relicta nocte iudaeis"), *Biblia cum Glossa,* 4: 9.

57. "In Joseph is figured the order of preachers, in Mary Holy Scripture; by the child the knowledge of the Saviour; by the cruelty of Herod the persecution which the Church suffered in Jerusalem; by Joseph's flight into Egypt the passing of the preachers to the unbelieving Gentiles, (for Egypt signifies darkness;) by the time that he abode in Egypt the space of time between the ascension of the Lord and the coming of Antichrist; by Herod's death the extinction of jealousy in the hearts of the Jews," *Commentary on the Four Gospels,* 1: 81. ("Per Ioseph autem designatur ordo praedicatorum, per Mariam sacra Scriptura, per puerum notitia Salvatoris, per persecutionem Herodis persecutio quam passa est Ecclesia in Hierosolymis, per fugam Ioseph in Aegyptum transitus praedicatorum ad gentes infideles: Aegyptus enim tenebrae interpretatur; per tempus quo fuit in Aegypto spatium temporis ab ascensione Domini usque ad adventum Antichristi; per obitum Herodis extinctio invidiae in cordibus Iudaeorum," *Catena Aurea,* 1: 40–41.)

58. *Commentary on the Four Gospels,* 1: 79–80 ("ideo mittit Filium suum in eam [Aegyptum] et dat illi magnae reconciliationis signum, ut decem plagas Aegypti una medicina sanaret; ut populus qui ante fuerat persecutor

populi primogeniti, custos fieret Filii unigeniti; ut quia illi violenter dominati sunt, isti cum devotione servirent; ut iam non irent ad mare rubrum demergendi, sed vocarentur ad aquas baptismatis vivificandi," *Catena Aurea,* 1: 40).

59. "Egipte, noli flere, quia Dominator tuus veniet tibi" (68).

60. "Interim, occisoribus venientibus, subtrahatur agnus clam, quem abeuntem salutant Innocentes" (rubric, 69).

61. Aquinas, *Commentary on the Four Gospels,* 1: 83.

62. Flanigan, "Rachel and Her Children," 37.

63. E.g., Jerome, *Commentaria in Evangelium Matthaei, PL* 26, col. 28; Pseudo-Bede, *In Matthaeum, PL* 92, col. 14; Aquinas, *Catena Aurea,* 1: 42.

64. "*Rachel* id est ecclesia suos teneros agnos plorat peremptos," *Biblia cum Glossa,* 4: 10. Pseudo-Bede comments similarly, *In Matthaeum, PL* 92, col. 14.

65. *Commentary on the Four Gospels,* 1: 84–85 ("Rachel Ecclesiae typum praetulit diu sterilis, nunc fecundae. Huius ploratus ex filiis, non idcirco quia peremptos dolebat, auditur, sed quia ab his perimeba[n]tur quos primum genitos filios retinere voluisset," *Catena Aurea,* 1: 42).

66. "Heu! teneri partus, laceros quos cernimus artus! / Heu! dulces nati, sola rabie jugulati!" (69).

67. "Si quae tristaris, exulta quae lacrimaris. / Namque tui nati vivunt super astra beati" (70).

68. "lacrimarum fundite fletus, / Judaeae florem patriae lacrimando dolorem!" (70).

69. "Quid tu, virgo, / mater Rachel, ploras formosa, / cuius vultus Jacob delectat? / Ceu sororis anniculae / lippitudo eum juvat! / Terge, mater, flentes oculos. / Quam te decent genarum rivuli?" (70–71).

70. "Victorinus martir Rachel et lyam in similitudinem ecclesiae et synogogae interpretatus est. Lyam maiorem natu synagogam significare existimat: quia prior populum dei genuit, quae oculis lippa dicitur, quia lex per moysen data cooperata est et signata. Rachel minor et pulchra prius sterilis post fecunda, ecclesiam significant: quae tempore posterior, sed sancta corpore et spiritu. Oculi eius decori quia evangelium videre meruerunt. Sed diu sterilis dum sinagoga populum generavit. Pro rachel iacob servivit, et supponitur ei lya: quia christus ut ecclesiam sibi assumeret, prius sibi synagogam coniunxit," *Biblia cum Glossa,* 1: 75.

71. Schlauch, "Allegory of Church and Synagogue," *Speculum* 14 (1939): 448–64. Michael Camille extends the image patterns: *The Gothic Idol: Ideology and Image-Making in Medieval Art* (Cambridge: Cambridge University Press, 1989), 175–80.

72. "Alas, alas, alas! Why do you find fault with me for having poured forth tears uselessly, / When I have been deprived of my child, who alone would show concern for my poverty, / Who would not yield to enemies the narrow boundaries which Jacob acquired for me, / And who was going to be of benefit to his stolid brethren, of whom many, alas my sorrow, I have buried?" ("Heu, heu, heu! Quid me incusastis fletus incassum fudisse, / Cum sim orbata nato paupertatem meam qui solus

curare, / Qui non hostibus cederet angustos terminus, quos mihi Jacob adquisivit, / Quique stolidis fratribus, quos multos, proh dolor, extuli, esset profuturus?") (71).

73. "Anxiatus est in me spiritus meus; in me turbatum est cor meum" (71).

74. See Butler, *Benedictine Monachism*, 101.

75. See Rubin, *Gentile Tales*, esp. 7–39.

76. Jordan, *The French Monarchy and the Jews*, 18, documents this and other links between the cult of Mary and ritual murder.

77. All of these meanings are established by Flanigan, "Rachel and Her Children," 38, 44–46, 49–50; Boynton, "Performative Exegesis," 50–58.

78. Abulafia illuminates this trend: *Christians and Jews*, 77–93.

79. Aquinas, *Commentary on the Four Gospels*, 1: 87.

80. "Sinite parvulos venire ad me, talium est enim regnum caelorum" (71).

81. "O Christe, quantum patri exercitum, juvenis doctus ad bella maxima...colligis, umbras suggerens cum tantum misereris" (71–72).

82. "Et dum insequitur Christum, regi nostro coaevum procuravit exercitum stolis victricibus candidatum," Aquinas, *Catena Aurea*, 1: 41.

83. P. Alphandéry and A. Dupront (1959) and H. E. Mayer (1972), as reported by Peter Raedts, "The Children's Crusade of 1212," *Journal of Medieval History* 3 (1977): 281–82.

84. I rely on Raedts's account, "Children's Crusade," 292–95.

85. Jonathan Riley-Smith, "The First Crusade and the Persecution of the Jews," *Studies in Church History* 21 (1984): 68.

86. See, e.g., Jerome, *Commentaria in Evangelium Matthaei*, PL 26, col. 29; Pseudo-Bede, *In Matthaeum*, PL 92, col. 14; *Biblia cum Glossa*, 4: 10; Aquinas, *Catena Aurea*, 1: 43.

87. Respectively, *Commentary on the Four Gospels*, 1: 81, 87 ("per obitum Herodis extinctio invidiae in cordibus Iudaeorum [designatur]"; "Iudaei, sopita modernae invidiae flamma, fidem veritatis accipient," *Catena Aurea*, 1: 41, 43).

88. See, e.g., Gilchrist on canon law, "Perceptions of Jews in the Canon Law," 13.

89. "tollatur Herodes et substituatur in loco eius filius eius, Archelaus, et exaltetur in regem" (72).

90. "Contra illum regulum, / contra natum paruulum / iube, pater, filium / hoc inire prelium," *Herodes,* in Young, *Drama of the Medieval Church,* 2: 88.

91. A similar thematic undertow sometimes appears in exegesis. E.g., Pseudo-Bede: "The reign of Archelaus signifies the imperial power of Antichrist in his followers, in whose company the preachers of the true faith fear to join themselves" ("Archelai regnum imperium Antichristi significat in sequacibus suis, quorum se consortio jungere timent verae fidei praedicatores"), *In Matthaeum,* PL 92, col. 15. Compare *Biblia cum Glossa,* 4: 10; Aquinas, *Catena Aurea,* 1: 44.

92. "Joseph, Joseph, Joseph, fili David! Revertere in terram Judam, defuncti sunt enim qui quaerebant animam pueri" (72).

93. Compare Pseudo-Bede, who has Joseph's return signify the end of Jewish hatred: "For Joseph comprises a type of Enoch and Elijah and preachers of the last time, because admonished by God when the Jews' hatred was concluded, after the entrance of all people into the faith, they will preach Christ to the Jewish people" ("Hic namque Joseph, Enochi et Eliae, et praedicatorum novissimi temporis typum tenet, quia a Deo moniti, finito odio Judaeorum, post ingressum gentium ad fidem, Christum Judaico populo praedicabunt"), In Matthaeum, PL 92, cols. 14–15. See also Biblia cum Glossa, 4: 10.

94. "Then let Joseph return with Mary and the boy, withdrawing into the region of Galilee" ("Tunc Joseph revertatur cum Maria et puero, secedens in partes Galilaeae") (72).

95. Pseudo-Bede, In Matthaeum, PL 92, col. 15; Biblia cum Glossa, 4: 10; Aquinas, Catena Aurea, 1: 44.

96. According to Young, Drama of the Medieval Church: "Rejoice, rejoice, rejoice, O Virgin Mary; you alone have purified all heresies in the whole world" ("Gaude, gaude, gaude, Maria uirgo; cunctas haereses sola intemeristi in uniuerso mundo," 2: 113 and note 5).

97. C. Clifford Flanigan, "The Liturgical Context of the Quem Queritis Trope," Comparative Drama 8 (1974): 60.

98. Langmuir, Toward a Definition of Antisemitism, 209–36.

99. McCulloh, "Jewish Ritual Murder: William of Norwich, Thomas of Monmouth, and the Early Dissemination of the Myth," Speculum 72 (1997): 739.

100. I do not mean to exclude the influence of other discourses: see, e.g., Maureen Bolton, "Anti-Jewish Attitudes in Anglo-Norman Religious Texts: Twelfth and Thirteenth Centuries," in Christian Attitudes toward the Jews in the Middle Ages, ed. Michael Frassetto (New York: Routledge, 2007), 151–65.

5   The Wife of Bath's Marginal Authority

1. See chapter 2, pp. 38–44.

2. Considered together, existing studies reveal the diversity in glossing programs: Susan Schibanoff, "The New Reader and Female Textuality in Two Early Commentaries on Chaucer," SAC 10 (1988): 71–108; Christopher Baswell, "Talking Back to the Text: Marginal Voices in Medieval Secular Literature," in The Uses of Manuscripts in Literary Studies: Essays in Memory of Judson Boyce Allen, ed. Charlotte Cook Morse, Penelope Reed Doob, and Marjorie Curry Woods (Kalamazoo: Medieval Institute, 1992), 121–60; Beverly Kennedy, "Contradictory Responses to the Wife of Bath As Evidenced by Fifteenth-Century Manuscript Variants," in The Canterbury Tales Project Occasional Papers, ed. N. Blake and P. Robinson (London: Office for Humanities Communication Publications, 1997), 2: 23–39; Beverly Kennedy,

"The Rewriting of the *Wife of Bath's Prologue* in Cambridge Dd.4.24," in *Rewriting Chaucer: Culture, Authority, and the Idea of the Authentic Text, 1400–1602,* ed. Thomas A. Prendergast and Barbara Kline (Columbus: Ohio State University Press, 1999), 203–33.

3. Lines 26–29 of the Prologue in the New College manuscript (Ne); my emphasis. All citations are from Peter Robinson, ed., *The Wife of Bath's Prologue on CD-Rom* (Cambridge: Cambridge University Press, 1996). I take the liberty of simplifying and modernizing orthography (silently expanding abbreviations, regularizing thorns and yoghs, deleting virgules, etc.) and of supplying modern punctuation to improve readability, particularly of the Latin glosses. All citations refer to the base text unless otherwise noted. For manuscript sigils, see John M. Manly and Edith Rickert, *The Text of the Canterbury Tales Studied on the Basis of All Known Manuscripts* (Chicago: University of Chicago Press, 1940), 1: xix–xxi.

4. Ne; British Library, Additional 5140 (Ad1), Additional 35286 (Ad3), Egerton 2864 (En3), Harley 1758 (Ha2), Lansdowne 851 (La), and Sloane 1685 (Sl1); Oxford, Corpus Christi College 198 (Cp); Bodleian Library, Laud 600 (Ld1), Rawlinson poet. 141 (Ra1), and Arch. Selden B.14 (SC 3360) (Se); San Marino, Henry E. Huntington Library, Ellesmere 26 C 9 (El); Lichfield Cathedral 2 (Lc); Lincoln Cathedral 110 (Ln); Chicago, University of Chicago Library 564 (Mc); Alnwick Castle, Northumberland MS 455 (Nl); Paris, Bibliothèque Nationale, Fonds anglais 39 (Ps); Petworth, Sussex, Petworth House MS 7 (Pw); and Cambridge, Trinity College R.3.15 (595) (Tc2). A number of scholars mention the presence of Chaucer's *Canterbury Tales* in a suspected heretic's library, but consider his work "unexceptionable," as John A. F. Thomson does, *The Later Lollards, 1414–1520* (London: Oxford University Press, 1965), 243. I find the work more provocative than it is sometimes considered: although the fictional Wife would have aural access to scripture, the glossed texts flag Chaucer's citations of scripture as translations. For the vernacular scripture controversy, see Anne Hudson, "Lollardy: The English Heresy?" *Studies in Church History* 18 (1982): 261–83; and Nicholas Watson, "Censorship and Cultural Change in Late-Medieval England: Vernacular Theology, the Oxford Translation Debate, and Arundel's Constitutions of 1409," *Speculum* 70 (1995): 822–64, which should be read with his later remarks, "Cultural Changes," *ELN* 44 (2006): 127–37.

5. E.g., "Poule durst nat commaunden at the leste / A thyng of which his mayster yaf noon heste / The dart is set vpon virgynyte" (73–75, En3); is glossed, "Non enim audeo aliquid loquo eorum que per me non efficit Christi, *Apostolus ad Romanos.* Si [*sic*] currite vt comprehendatus, *Apostolus ad Corinthios*" (74, En3; my emphasis).

6. For typical biblical literature, see Margaret Deanesley, *The Lollard Bible and Other Medieval Biblical Versions* (1920; rpt. Eugene: Wipf and Stock, 2002), 146–87; Brian Murdoch, *The Medieval Popular Bible: Expansions of Genesis in the Middle Ages* (Cambridge, MA: D. S. Brewer, 2003).

7. See Deanesley, *Lollard Bible*, 146–55.
8. That is, "acceptable" to some conservatives. Chaucer elsewhere exposes weaknesses in this standard for lay piety: see Alan J. Fletcher, *Preaching, Politics, and Poetry in Late-Medieval England* (Dublin: Four Courts Press, 1998), 239–46.
9. See, e.g., Henri de Lubac, *Medieval Exegesis: Volume 1, The Four Senses of Scripture*, trans. Mark Sebanc (Grand Rapids: William B. Eerdmans; Edinburgh: T and T Clark, 1998), 1: 12; Deanesley, *The Lollard Bible*, 31, 36–37, 45–46.
10. For preaching, see Beryl Smalley, *The Study of the Bible in the Middle Ages*, 3rd ed. (Oxford: Basil Blackwell, 1983), 281–308, with the qualifications set forth in the Preface to that edition, xiii–xvi; A. J. Minnis, *Medieval Theory of Authorship: Scholastic Literary Attitudes in the Later Middle Ages*, 2nd ed. (Philadelphia: University of Pennsylvania Press, 1988), 73–117; L.-J. Bataillon, O.P., "Early Scholastic and Mendicant Preaching as Exegesis of Scripture," in *Ad Litteram: Authoritative Texts and Their Medieval Readers*, ed. Mark D. Jordan and Kent Emery, Jr. (Notre Dame: University of Notre Dame Press, 1992), 165–98. For exegetes, see Douglas Wurtele, "Chaucer's *Canterbury Tales* and Nicholas of Lyra's *Postillae litteralis et moralis super totam Bibliam*," in *Chaucer and Scriptural Tradition*, ed. David Lyle Jeffrey (Ottawa: University of Ottawa Press, 1984), 89–107; Philip D. W. Krey and Lesley Smith, ed., *Nicholas of Lyra: The Senses of Scripture* (Leiden: Brill, 2000); Deeana Copeland Klepper, *The Insight of Unbelievers: Nicholas of Lyra and Christian Reading of Jewish Text in the Later Middle Ages* (Philadelphia: University of Pennsylvania Press, 2007), 32–43. For the controversial theology of Wyclif, see G. R. Evans, "Wyclif on Literal and Metaphorical," in *From Ockham to Wyclif*, ed. Anne Hudson and Michael Wilks (Oxford: Basil Blackwell, for The Ecclesiastical History Society, 1987), 259–66; Kantik Ghosh, *The Wycliffite Heresy: Authority and the Interpretation of Texts* (Cambridge: Cambridge University Press, 2002), 11–14, 22–66, 101–2, 135. For the various and complex senses of the literal in, e.g., Nicholas of Lyra's works, see Krey and Smith, ed., *Nicholas of Lyra*; Klepper, *The Insight of Unbelievers*, 32–43.
11. Respectively, "The Wife of Bath and Lollardy," *Medium Aevum* 58 (1989): 224–42; *Chaucer's Biblical Poetics* (Norman: University of Oklahoma Press, 1998), 138–59. See also Besserman, "'Glosynge Is a Glorious Thyng': Chaucer's Biblical Exegesis," in *Chaucer and Scriptural Tradition*, ed. Jeffrey, 65–73. For Lollard hermeneutics, see Deanesley, *Lollard Bible*, 268–97, 319–73; Rita Copeland, *Pedagogy, Intellectuals, and Dissent in the Later Middle Ages: Lollardy and Ideas of Learning* (Cambridge: Cambridge University Press, 2001), 99–140.
12. See, e.g., John M. Bowers on two manuscripts of the *Canterbury Tales* produced for high-ranking Lancastrian courtiers, "Two Professional Readers of Chaucer and Langland: Scribe D and the HM 114 Scribe," *SAC* 26 (2004): 113–46.

13. From the official point of view, the problem was not vernacular scripture per se, but rather open challenges to orthodoxy and structures of power; such challenges were associated with the lower class, not the gentry: see Watson, "Censorship and Cultural Change," 831, 847, 857; Margaret Aston and Colin Richmond, eds., "Introduction," *Lollardy and the Gentry in the Later Middle Ages* (Stroud: Sutton Pub.; New York: St. Martin's Press, 1997), 19–21; Shannon McSheffrey, "Heresy, Orthodoxy, and English Vernacular Religion, 1480–1525," *Past and Present* 186 (2005): 47–80.

14. See Aston and Richmond, eds., "Introduction," *Lollardy and the Gentry,* 1–27, quote 18; and, in the same volume, J. A. F. Thomson, "Knightly Piety and the Margins of Lollardy," 95–111.

15. Nicholas Love's *Mirror of the Blessed Life of Jesus Christ,* e.g., explicitly argues against Lollardy; but manuscripts display Latin source notes beside his vernacular biblical citations, exhibiting his own acts of translation and thus turning him into something of a Lollard: as per Ghosh, *The Wycliffite Heresy,* 168–70.

16. I.e., the ms was not copied privately for personal use; it does not embody a merely individual set of values. For a description, see Stephen Partridge, "A Newly Identified Manuscript by the Scribe of the New College *Canterbury Tales,*" *English Manuscript Studies 1100–1700* 6 (1997): 229–36.

17. The subject of manuscript groups is complicated. Manly and Rickert's groups and lines of descent have been partially disproven, partially confirmed by computer analysis: see Peter M. W. Robinson, "An Approach to the Manuscripts of the 'Wife of Bath's Prologue,'" in *Computer-Based Chaucer Studies,* ed. Ian Lancashire (Toronto: Centre for Computing in the Humanities, University of Toronto, 1993), 17–47; Robert O'Hara and Peter Robinson, "Computer-Assisted Methods of Stemmatic Analysis," in *The Canterbury Tales Project Occasional Papers,* ed. N. F. Blake and Peter Robinson (Oxford: Office for Humanities Communication, 1993), 1: 53–74; and Robinson, "A Stemmatic Analysis," 69–132. When I refer to manuscript groups in this chapter, I mean manuscripts connected by Robinson's stemmatic analysis. The glosses present particularly challenging stemmatic issues. For informative arguments on this point, see Stephen Partridge, "The *Canterbury Tales* Glosses and the Manuscript Groups," in *The Canterbury Tales Project Occasional Papers,* ed. Blake and Robinson, 1: 85–94; and Partridge, "Wynkyn de Worde's Manuscript Source for the *Canterbury Tales*: Evidence from the Glosses," *Chaucer Review* 41 (2007): 325–59.

18. Chaucer's authorship of Latin glosses has been the subject of some controversy. Accepting Chaucer's authorship of some glosses are Aage Brusendorff, *The Chaucer Tradition* (London: Oxford University Press, 1925), 82, 127–28; J. S. P. Tatlock, "*The Canterbury Tales* in 1400," *PMLA* 50 (1935): 103–4; Daniel S. Silvia, Jr., "Glosses to *The Canterbury Tales* from St. Jerome's *Epistola adversus Jovinianum,*" *SP* 62 (1965): 28–39. Charles A. Owen, Jr., contends the glosses are part of the editorial finish

added to the work after Chaucer's death, "The Alternative Reading of *The Canterbury Tales:* Chaucer's Text and the Early Manuscripts," *PMLA* 97 (1982): 237–50. To date, the most exhaustive and definitive study inclines toward Chaucerian authorship of some glosses: Stephen Partridge, "Glosses in the Manuscripts of Chaucer's 'Canterbury Tales': An Edition and Commentary," Dissertation, Harvard, 1992, chapter 2. Recent research argues that Chaucer supervised early mss; this evidence would support the possibility that he wrote some glosses. See N. F. Blake, "Geoffrey Chaucer and the Manuscripts of the *Canterbury Tales*," *Journal of the Early Book Society* 1 (1997): 96–122; Peter Robinson, "A Stemmatic Analysis of the Fifteenth-Century Witnesses to the *Wife of Bath's Prologue,*" *The Canterbury Tales Project Occasional Papers,* ed. Blake and Robinson, 2: 126–27; Linne R. Mooney, "Chaucer's Scribe," *Speculum* 81 (2006): 97–138; Estelle Stubbs, "'Here's One I Prepared Earlier': The Work of Scribe D on Oxford, Corpus Christi College, MS 198," *Review of English Studies* n.s. 58, no. 234 (2007): 133–53. Not all manuscripts cohere with the conclusions developed in this chapter. For notable exceptions to the conclusions drawn here, see my "The Wife of Bath's Marginal Authority," *SAC* (Fall 2010).

19. Scholars have established this point: Besserman, *Chaucer's Biblical Poetics*, 138–59; John A. Alford, "Scriptural Testament in *The Canterbury Tales:* The Letter Takes its Revenge," in *Chaucer and Scriptural Tradition,* ed. Jeffrey, 197–203; Robert W. Hanning, "'I Shal Finde It in a Maner Glose': Versions of Textual Harassment in Medieval Literature," in *Medieval Texts and Contemporary Readers,* ed. Finke and Shichtman, 27–50.

20. Ad1, Ad3, El, En3, Mc, Ps, Ra1, Tc2.

21. If the first word of either verse is omitted, source becomes ambiguous. Cp, Ha2, Ld1, Nl, Pw, Ps, and Sl1 clearly quote from Genesis at one point; Lc probably quotes Genesis; En3 quotes from Genesis but misidentifies the quote ("Apostolus ad Philipenses," 28, En3); Ad1 quotes both books and also misidentifies the Ephesians passage.

22. Ad1, Ad3, El, En3, Ra1, Tc2.

23. Ad3, Cp, El, En3, Ha2, La, Lc, Ld1, Nl, Ps, Pw, Ra1, Sl1, Tc2. Several manuscripts also explicitly note the verse's biblical authority ("Apostolus ad Corintheos," 59, Ad3, compare En3; "Secundum Paulum," 60, Tc2), making the Wife's reference to "thapostle seith" (49, base text) more specific.

24. "Fallere nere [*sic*] flere cepit deus in muliere," 401, Ad1. A Latin version appears in Cp, En3, Ha2, La, Lc,Ld1, Nl, Pw, Sl1, Tc2, and in Austin, University of Texas Library 143 (Cn); Manchester, John Rylands Library, English 113 (Ma); and Oxford, Bodleian Library, Rawlinson poet. 223 (Ra3). "Nota" appears in Cambridge, Fitzwilliam Museum, McClean 181 (Fi) and University Library, Mm.ii.5 (Mm), each manuscript's only gloss on the *Prologue.* Another proverb of broad interest in the manuscripts reminds men of their disciplinary role in marriage (632–38). Although the Wife dismisses the "old sawe," many scribes mark it with

a "Nota," "Nota bene," or "Nota prouerbium": Ad3, Cp, El, Ha2, La, Ln, Ma, Nl, Pw, Oxford, Bodleian Library, Bodley 414 (SC 27880) (Bo1); Cambridge, University Library, Dd.iv.24 (Dd) and Gg.iv.27 (1) (Gg); Aberystwyth, National Library of Wales, Hengwrt 154 (Hg); and Philadelphia, Rosenbach Foundation MS f. 1084/1, Phillipps 8137 (Ph3). Two manuscripts (Ad3, El) also identify a biblical source (Ecclesiasticus 25: 34), making the Wife dissent from Scripture itself.

25. Nl reads "Bettir it is to be weddit then to blyn," and Tc2 agrees (52). Both nonetheless include a version of the Latin proverb: "Secundum Paulum Melius est nubere quam vri" (60, Tc2; compare 52, Nl).

26. Ad1, Ad3, El, En3, Mc, Ps, Ra1, Tc2.

27. Ad1, En3.

28. Versions of this gloss appear in Ad1, Cp, En3, Ha2, Lc, Ld1, Ln, Nl, Ps, Pw, Ra1, Sl1. Se marks the passage with "Nota bene."

29. E.g., Robertson, *Preface to Chaucer,* 329; Graham D. Caie, "The Significance of the Early Chaucer Manuscript Glosses (With Special Reference to the *Wife of Bath's Prologue," Chaucer Review* 10 (1976): 354–55; Dinshaw, *Chaucer's Sexual Poetics,* 124; Robert Longsworth, "The Wife of Bath and the Samaritan Woman," *Chaucer Review* 34 (2000): 382.

30. A similar gloss appears in Ad1, Ad3, El, En3, Ha2, La, Lc, Ld1, Ln, Nl, Ps, Pw, Ra1, Se, Sl1, Tc2.

31. Ad1, Ad3, El, En3, Ln, Mc, Ps, Ra1, Tc2.

32. Several other manuscripts similarly exhort men to love their wives: see Ad1, Ad3, El, En3. This gloss does not appear in Ra1 or Tc2, which otherwise follow El closely; the omission is suggestive.

33. With the possible occasional exception of En3 and Ad1, discussed in my "The Wife of Bath's Marginal Authority."

34. For the relevant part of Jerome's diatribe, see *Against Jovinianus,* in *The Principal Works of St. Jerome,* trans. W. H. Fremantle, A Select Library of Nicene and Post-Nicene Fathers of the Christian Church, 2nd series, 14 vols. (rpt. Grand Rapids: William B. Eerdmans, 1989), 6: Book 1, Chapt. 47, pp. 383–84. For the tradition of misogamy, and the contexts of Jankyn's book, see Robert A. Pratt, "Jankyn's 'Book of Wikked Wives': Medieval Anti-Matrimonial Propaganda in the Universities," *Annuale Mediaevale* 3 (1962): 5–27.

35. Jill Mann, *Geoffrey Chaucer* (Atlantic Highlands: Humanities Press International, 1991), 55–70, quotes respectively 51, 56, 58.

36. See chapter 2, note 98.

37. *The Riverside Chaucer,* ed. Larry D. Benson, 3rd edition (Boston: Houghton Mifflin, 1987), 6, 18.

38. Mann, *Geoffrey Chaucer,* 57–58.

39. Cp, Ha2, La, Lc, Ld1, Ln, Mc, Nl, Ps, Pw, Se, Sl1.

40. Mc, Ps.

41. Cp, Ha2, Ld1, Mc, Nl, Ps, Pw.

42. Cp, Ha2, Lc, Ld1, Nl, Ps, Pw, Sl1.

43. Cp, Ha2, La, Lc, Ld1, Nl, Ps, Pw, Sl1.

44. Mc, Ps.
45. Ha2, La, Lc, Ld1, Ln, Nl, Ps, Pw, Se, Sl1.
46. Ln, Mc, Ps.
47. Cp, Ha2, Lc, Ld1, Ln, Mc, Nl, Ps, Pw, Sl1.
48. "Argus habuit mille oculos," 358, Cp (also Nl); compare "Argus habuit .
    C. oculos," 358, Ha2. La reveals a correcting hand at work. Se just marks
    "Argus" (358).
49. "Creta insula," 707, Ha2; also Lc.
50. "Fallere flere nere [*sic*] dedit deus in muliere," 402, Cp; also Ha2, La,
    Lc, Ld1, Nl, Pw, Sl1. "Solo melius est habitare," 748, Cp; also Ha2, Lc,
    Ld1, Mc, Nl, Pw, Se, Sl1. Similarly, "Whoso that buyldeth his hous al
    of salwes" (633) is noted in Cp, Ha2, La, Ln, Nl, Pw. And finally, "Tria
    sunt que expellunt hominem a domo sua . fumus stillicidium et mala
    mulier," 278, Mc; also Ps. The idea that proverbs were considered "a
    source of wisdom" is advanced by Julia Boffey, "Proverbial Chaucer and
    the Chaucer Canon," in *Reading from the Margins: Textual Studies, Chaucer,
    and Medieval Literature,* ed. Seth Lerer (San Marino: Huntington Library,
    1996), 46.
51. By "majority," I mean the thirteen (out of nineteen) manuscripts repre-
    sented in this section of the argument. Since I think Chaucer probably
    wrote the El glosses on the *Prologue,* I exclude El and closely related mss
    from this conclusion, though these mss confirm the historical pattern and
    would further swell the majority.
52. *From Gutenberg to Google: Electronic Representations of Literary Texts*
    (Cambridge: Cambridge University Press, 2006), 49.
53. Warren S. Smith makes this case, "The Wife of Bath Debates Jerome,"
    Chaucer Review 32 (1997): 129–45.
54. See Blamires, "The Wife of Bath and Lollardy," 233–34.

Afterword

1. Tobin Siebers, *Disability Theory* (Ann Arbor: University of Michigan
   Press, 2008), 8.

BIBLIOGRAPHY

Abulafia, Anna Sapir. *Christians and Jews in the Twelfth-Century Renaissance.* New York: Routledge, 1995.

————. "Jewish Carnality in Twelfth-Century Renaissance Thought." *Studies in Church History* 29 (1992): 59–75.

————, ed. *Religious Violence between Christians and Jews: Medieval Roots, Modern Perspectives.* New York: Palgrave Macmillan, 2002.

Adkin, Neil, ed. *Jerome on Virginity: A Commentary on the "Libellus de Virginitate Servanda" (Letter 22).* Cambridge, MA: Francis Cairns, 2003.

Aers, David. *Chaucer, Langland, and the Creative Imagination.* London: Routledge and Kegan Paul, 1980.

Alford, John A. "Scriptural Testament in *The Canterbury Tales:* The Letter Takes Its Revenge." In *Chaucer and Scriptural Tradition,* ed. David Lyle Jeffrey, 197–203. N.p.: University of Ottawa Press, 1984.

————. "The Wife of Bath versus the Clerk of Oxford: What Their Rivalry Means." *Chaucer Review* 21 (1986): 108–32.

Almond, Gabriel A., R. Scott Appleby, and Emmanuel Sivan. *Strong Religion: The Rise of Fundamentalisms around the World.* Chicago: University of Chicago Press, 2003.

Alsop, Rachel, Annette Fitzsimons, Kathleen Lennon, and Ros Minsky. *Theorizing Gender.* Cambridge, MA: Polity Press, 2002.

Aquinas, Thomas. *Catena Aurea: Commentary on the Four Gospels Collected out of the Fathers by St. Thomas Aquinas.* Ed. John Henry Newman. 4 vols. Southampton: St. Austin Press, 1997.

————. *Catena Aurea in Quatuor Evangelia.* Ed. P. Angelici Guarienti. 2 vols. Turin and Rome: Marietti, 1953.

Aspergren, Kerstin. *The Male Woman: A Feminine Ideal in the Early Church.* Ed. Renée Kieffer. Stockholm: Almqvist and Wiksell, 1990.

Astell, Ann W. *Chaucer and the Universe of Learning.* Ithaca, NY: Cornell University Press, 1996.

————. *The Song of Songs in the Middle Ages.* Ithaca, NY: Cornell University Press, 1990.

Aston, Margaret, and Colin Richmond, eds. *Lollardy and the Gentry in the Later Middle Ages.* Stroud: Sutton Publishing; New York: St. Martin's Press, 1997.

Augustine. *Augustine: "Confessions."* Ed. James J. O'Donnell. 3 vols. Oxford: Clarendon, 1992.

Augustine. *Confessions.* Trans. Henry Chadwick. Oxford: Oxford University Press, 1992.

———. *Enarrationes in Psalmos.* Corpus Christianorum, Series Latina, vol. 38. Turnhout: Brepols, 1956.

———. *St. Augustine on Genesis. Two Books on Genesis: "Against the Manichees" and "On the Literal Interpretation of Genesis: An Unfinished Book."* Trans. Roland J. Teske. The Fathers of the Church: A New Translation, vol. 84. Washington, DC: Catholic University of America Press, 1991.

Bakhtin, M. M. *The Dialogic Imagination: Four Essays.* Ed. Michael Holquist. Trans. Caryl Emerson and Holquist. Austin: University of Texas Press, 1981.

Bal, Mieke. *Lethal Love: Feminist Literary Readings of Biblical Love Stories.* Bloomington: Indiana University Press, 1987.

Barr, Helen, and Ann M. Hutchison, eds. *Text and Controversy from Wyclif to Bale: Essays in Honour of Anne Hudson.* Turnhout: Brepols, 2005.

Baswell, Christopher. "Talking Back to the Text: Marginal Voices in Medieval Secular Literature." In *The Uses of Manuscripts in Literary Studies: Essays in Memory of Judson Boyce Allen,* ed. Charlotte Cook Morse, Penelope Reed Doob, and Marjorie Curry Woods, 121–60. Kalamazoo: Medieval Institute, 1992.

Bataillon, L.-J. "Early Scholastic and Mendicant Preaching and Exegesis of Scripture." In *Ad Litteram: Authoritative Texts and Their Medieval Readers,* ed. Mark D. Jordan and Kent Emery, Jr., 165–98. Notre Dame: Notre Dame University Press, 1992.

Bavel, T. J. van. "Augustine's View on Women." *Augustiniana* 39 (1989): 5–53.

Benedict's Rule: A Translation and Commentary. Trans. Terrence G. Kardong. Collegeville: Liturgical Press, 1996.

Berlinerblau, Jacques. *The Secular Bible: Why Nonbelievers Must Take Religion Seriously.* New York: Cambridge University Press, 2005.

Besserman, Lawrence. *Chaucer's Biblical Poetics.* Norman: University of Oklahoma Press, 1998.

———. "'Glosynge Is a Glorious Thyng': Chaucer's Biblical Exegesis." In *Chaucer and Scriptural Tradition,* ed. Jeffrey, 65–73.

———. "'Priest' and 'Pope,' 'Sire' and 'Madame': Anachronistic Diction and Social Conflict in Chaucer's *Troilus.*" *SAC* 23 (2001): 181–224.

Bevington, David, ed. *Medieval Drama.* Boston: Houghton Mifflin, 1975.

———. "The Staging of Twelfth-Century Liturgical Drama in the Fleury *Playbook.*" In *The Fleury Playbook: Essays and Studies,* ed. Thomas P. Campbell and Clifford Davidson, 62–81. Kalamazoo: Medieval Institute, 1985.

Biblia Latina cum Glossa Ordinaria. Facsimile Reprint of the Editio Princeps Adolph Rusch of Strassburg 1480/81. Ed. Karlfried Froehlich and Margaret T. Gibson. 4 Vols. Turnhout: Brepols, 1992.

Bitel, Lisa M., and Felice Lifshitz, eds. *Gender and Christianity in Medieval Europe: New Perspectives.* Philadelphia: University of Pennsylvania Press, 2008.

Blake, N. F. "Geoffrey Chaucer and the Manuscripts of the *Canterbury Tales.*" *Journal of the Early Book Society* 1 (1997): 96–122.

Blamires, Alcuin. "Beneath the Pulpit." In *The Cambridge Companion to Medieval Women's Writing*, ed. Carolyn Dinshaw and David Wallace, 141–58. Cambridge: Cambridge University Press, 2003.

———. *The Case for Women in Medieval Culture*. Oxford: Clarendon, 1997.

———. "The Wife of Bath and Lollardy." *Medium Aevum* 58 (1989): 224–42.

———. "Women and Preaching in Medieval Orthodoxy, Heresy, and Saints' Lives." *Viator* 26 (1995): 135–52.

Boffey, Julia. "Proverbial Chaucer and the Chaucer Canon." In *Reading from the Margins: Textual Studies, Chaucer, and Medieval Literature*, ed. Seth Lerer, 37–47. San Marino: Huntington Library, 1996.

Bonner, G. I. "*Libido* and *Concupiscentia* in St. Augustine." *Studia Patristica* 6 (1962): 303–14.

Bonner, Gerald. "Augustine's Understanding of the Church as a Eucharistic Community." In *Saint Augustine the Bishop: A Book of Essays*, ed. Fannie LeMoine and Christopher Kleinhenz, 39–63. New York: Garland, 1994.

Boreczky, Elemér. *John Wyclif's Discourse on Dominion in Community*. Leiden: E. J. Brill, 2008.

Bornstein, George. "T. S. Eliot and the Real World." *Michigan Quarterly Review* 36 (1997): 494–505.

Børresen, Kari Elisabeth. "Gender and Exegesis in the Latin Fathers." *Augustinianum* 40 (2000): 65–76.

———. *Subordination and Equivalence: The Nature and Role of Woman in Augustine and Thomas Aquinas*. Trans. Charles H. Talbot. Washington, DC: University Press of America, 1981.

Boulton, Maureen. "Anti-Jewish Attitudes in Anglo-Norman Religious Texts: Twelfth and Thirteenth Centuries." In *Christian Attitudes toward the Jews in the Middle Ages*, ed. Michael Frassetto, 151–65. New York: Routledge, 2007.

Bourdieu, Pierre. *Masculine Domination*. Trans. Richard Nice. Cambridge, MA: Polity Press, 2001.

Bowers, John M. "Augustine as Addict: Sex and Texts in the *Confessions*." *Exemplaria* 2 (1990): 403–48.

———. "Two Professional Readers of Chaucer and Langland: Scribe D and the HM 114 Scribe." *SAC* 26 (2004): 113–46.

Boyarin, Daniel. "Paul and the Genealogy of Gender." *Representations* 41 (1993): 1–33.

Boynton, Susan. "Performative Exegesis in the Fleury *Interfectio Puerorum*." *Viator* 29 (1998): 39–61.

Brockett, Clyde W. "Modal and Motivic Coherence in the Music of the Music-Dramas in the Fleury *Playbook*." In *The Fleury Playbook*, ed. Campbell and Davidson, 35–61.

———. "*Persona* in *Cantilena*: St. Nicholas in Music in Medieval Drama." In *The Saint Play in Medieval Europe*, ed. Clifford Davidson, 11–29. Kalamazoo: Medieval Institute, 1986.

Brown, Dennis. "Jerome and the Vulgate." In *A History of Biblical Interpretation. Vol. 1: The Ancient Period*, ed. Alan J. Hauser and Duane F. Watson, 355–79. Grand Rapids, MI: William B. Eerdmans, 2003.

Brown, Dennis. *Vir Trilinguis: A Study in the Biblical Exegesis of Saint Jerome.* Kampen, The Netherlands: Kok Pharos, 1992.

Brown, Peter. *Augustine and Sexuality.* Berkeley: The Center for Hermeneutical Studies, University of California, 1983.

———. *Augustine of Hippo: A Biography.* New ed. Berkeley: University of California Press, 2000.

———. *The Body and Society: Men, Women, and Sexual Renunciation in Early Christianity.* New York: Columbia University Press, 1988.

———. *The Rise of Western Christendom: Triumph and Diversity, A. D. 200–1000.* 2nd ed. Malden, MA: Blackwell, 2003.

Brusendorff, Aage. *The Chaucer Tradition.* London: Oxford University Press, 1925.

Burns, J. Patout. "Creation and Fall According to Ambrose of Milan." In *Augustine: Biblical Exegete,* ed. Frederick van Fleteren and Joseph C. Schnaubelt, 71–97. New York: Peter Lang, 2001.

Butler, Dom Cuthbert. *Benedictine Monachism: Studies in Benedictine Life and Rule.* 1924; rpt. Cambridge, MA: Speculum Historiale; New York: Barnes and Noble, 1961.

Butler, Judith. *Bodies That Matter: On the Discursive Limits of "Sex."* New York: Routledge, 1993.

———. *Gender Trouble: Feminism and the Subversion of Identity.* New York: Routledge, 1990.

———. *Precarious Life: The Powers of Mourning and Violence.* London and New York: Verso, 2004.

Bynum, Caroline Walker. *Jesus as Mother: Studies in the Spirituality of the High Middle Ages.* Berkeley: University of California Press, 1982.

———. "'…And Woman His Humanity': Female Imagery in the Religious Writing of the Later Middle Ages." In *Gender and Religion: On the Complexity of Symbols,* ed. Caroline Walker Bynum, Stevan Harrell, and Paula Richman, 257–88. Boston: Beacon Press, 1986.

Caesarius of Arles. *Saint Caesarius of Arles: Sermons.* Trans. Mary Magdeleine Mueller. The Fathers of the Church: A New Translation, vol. 66. Washington, DC: Catholic University of America Press, 1973.

Caie, Graham D. "The Significance of the Early Chaucer MS Glosses (With Special Reference to the *Wife of Bath's Prologue*)." *Chaucer Review* 10 (1976): 350–60.

Camille, Michael. *The Gothic Idol: Ideology and Image-Making in Medieval Art.* Cambridge: Cambridge University Press, 1989.

———. "The Image and the Self: Unwriting Late Medieval Bodies." In *Framing Medieval Bodies,* ed. Sarah Kay and Miri Rubin, 62–99. Manchester: Manchester University Press, 1994.

Campbell, Thomas P., and Clifford Davidson, ed. *The Fleury Playbook: Essays and Studies.* Kalamazoo: Medieval Institute, 1985.

Carruthers, Mary. "The Wife of Bath and the Painting of Lions." 1979; rpt. with "Afterword." In *Feminist Readings in Middle English Literature: The Wife of Bath and All Her Sect,* ed. Ruth Evans and Lesley Johnson, 22–53. London: Routledge, 1994.

Carter, Jimmy. *Our Endangered Values: America's Moral Crisis.* New York: Simon and Schuster, 2005.

Castelli, Elizabeth. " 'I Will Make Mary Male': Pieties of the Body and Gender Transformation of Christian Women in Late Antiquity." In *Body Guards: The Cultural Politics of Gender Ambiguity,* ed. J. Epstein and K. Straub, 29–49. New York: Routledge, 1991.

Cerquiglini, Bernard. *In Praise of the Variant: A Critical History of Philology.* Trans. Betsy Wing. Baltimore and London: Johns Hopkins University Press, 1999.

Chadwick, Henry. *Augustine.* Oxford: Oxford University Press, 1986.

———. "Disagreement and the Early Church." 1996; rpt. in *Studies in Ancient Christianity,* XXIII, 557–66. Aldershot: Ashgate, 2006.

———. "On Re-Reading the *Confessions.*" 1994; rpt. in *Studies in Ancient Christianity,* VII, 139–60. Aldershot: Ashgate, 2006.

Chaucer, Geoffrey. *The Riverside Chaucer.* Ed. Larry D. Benson. 3rd ed. Boston: Houghton Mifflin, 1987.

———. *The Text of the "Canterbury Tales" Studied on the Basis of All Known Manuscripts.* Ed. John M. Manly and Edith Rickert. 8 vols. Chicago: University of Chicago Press, 1940.

———. *The "Wife of Bath's Prologue" on CD-ROM.* Ed. Peter Robinson. Cambridge: Cambridge University Press, 1996.

Chrysostom, John. *Chrysostom: Homilies on Galatians, Ephesians, Philippians, Colossians, Thessalonians, Timothy, Titus, and Philemon.* Ed. Philip Schaff, Nicene and Post-Nicene Fathers, 1st series, vol. 13. 1889; rpt. Peabody: Hendrickson Publishers, 1995.

Clark, Elizabeth A. " 'Adam's Only Companion': Augustine and the Early Christian Debate on Marriage." *Recherches Augustiniennes* 21 (1986): 139–62.

———. "Heresy, Asceticism, Adam, and Eve: Interpretations of Genesis 1–3 in the Later Latin Fathers." In *Ascetic Piety and Women's Faith: Essays on Late Ancient Christianity.* Studies in Women and Religion, vol. 20, 353–85. Lewiston: Edwin Mellen Press, 1986.

———. "Ideology, History, and the Construction of 'Woman' in Late Ancient Christianity." 1994; rpt. in *A Feminist Companion to Patristic Literature,* ed. Amy-Jill Levine with Maria Mayo Robbins, 101–24. London: T and T Clark, 2008.

———. *Jerome, Chrysostom, and Friends: Essays and Translations.* New York: Edwin Mellen, 1979.

———. *Reading Renunciation: Asceticism and Scripture in Early Christianity.* Princeton, NJ: Princeton University Press, 1999.

———. "Theory and Practice in Late Ancient Asceticism: Jerome, Chrysostom, and Augustine." *Journal of Feminist Studies in Religion* 5 (1989): 25–46.

Clark, Gillian. *Augustine: "The Confessions."* Exeter: Bristol Phoenix Press, 2005.

Cohen, Jeremy. "The Flow of Blood in Medieval Norwich." *Speculum* 79 (2004): 26–65.

———. "The Jews as Killers of Christ in the Latin Tradition, from Augustine to the Friars." *Traditio* 39 (1983): 3–27.

———. *Living Letters of the Law: Ideas of the Jew in Medieval Christianity.* Berkeley: University of California Press, 1999.

Collins, Fletcher, Jr. "The Home of the Fleury *Playbook*." In *The Fleury Playbook*, ed. Campbell and Davidson, 26–34.

Connolly, William E. *The Augustinian Imperative: A Reflection on the Politics of Morality.* Morality and Political Thought, vol. 1. Newbury Park: Sage Publications, 1993.

Copeland, Rita. *Pedagogy, Intellectuals, and Dissent in the Later Middle Ages: Lollardy and Ideas of Learning.* Cambridge: Cambridge University Press, 2001.

Corbin, Solange. "Le Manuscrit 201 d'Orléans: Drames liturgiques dits de Fleury." *Romania* 74 (1953): 1–43.

Courcelle, Pierre. *Recherches sur les "Confessions" de Saint Augustin.* Paris: Boccard, 1950.

Coyle, J. Kevin. "The Fathers on Women and Women's Ordination." *Église et théologie* 9 (1978): 51–101.

———. "In Praise of Monica: A Note on the Ostia Experience of *Confessions* IX." *Augustinian Studies* 13 (1982): 87–96.

Crane, Susan. "Alison's Incapacity and Poetic Instability in the *Wife of Bath's Tale*." *PMLA* 102 (1987): 20–28.

———. "The Writing Lesson of 1381." In *Chaucer's England: Literature in Historical Context*, ed. Barbara Hanawalt, 201–21. Minneapolis: University of Minnesota Press, 1992.

Davis, Natalie Zemon. *Society and Culture in Early Modern France: Eight Essays.* Stanford: Stanford University Press, 1975.

Deanesley, Margaret. *The Lollard Bible and Other Medieval Biblical Versions.* 1920; rpt. Eugene: Wipf and Stock, 2002.

Derrida, Jacques. *Of Grammatology.* Trans. Gayatri Chakraverty Spivak. Baltimore: Johns Hopkins University Press, 1976.

Dinshaw, Carolyn. *Chaucer's Sexual Poetics.* Madison: University of Wisconsin Press, 1989.

Disbrow, Sarah. "The Wife of Bath's Old Wives' Tale." *SAC* 8 (1986): 59–71.

Donovan, Richard B. "Two Celebrated Centers of Medieval Liturgical Drama: Fleury and Ripoll." In *The Medieval Drama and Its Claudelian Revival*, ed. E. Catherine Dunn, Tatiama Fotitch, and Bernard M. Peebles, 41–51. Washington, DC: Catholic University of America, 1970.

Dundes, Alan, ed. *The Blood Libel Legend: A Casebook in anti-Semitic Folklore.* Madison: University of Wisconsin Press, 1991.

Edwards, Robert R. *The Flight from Desire: Augustine and Ovid to Chaucer.* New York: Palgrave Macmillan, 2006.

Evans, G. R. *Augustine on Evil.* Cambridge: Cambridge University Press, 1982.

———. "Exegesis and Authority in the Thirteenth Century." In *Ad Litteram*, ed. Jordan and Emery, 93–111.

———. "Gloss or Analysis? A Crisis of Exegetical Method in the Thirteenth Century." In *La Bibbia del XIII Secolo: Storia del Testo, Storia dell'Esegesi*, ed. Giuseppe Cremascoli and Francesco Santi, 93–111. Firenze: Sismel edizioni del Galluzzo, 2004.

―――. "Wyclif on Literal and Metaphorical." In *From Ockham to Wyclif*, ed. Anne Hudson and Michael Wilks, 259–66. Oxford: Basil Blackwell, for The Ecclesiastical History Society, 1987.

Fehrman, Craig T. "Did Chaucer Read the Wycliffite Bible?" *Chaucer Review* 42 (2007): 11–38.

Ferrari, Leo C. "Monica on the Wooden Ruler (*Confessions* 3.11.19)." *Augustinian Studies* 6 (1975): 193–205.

―――. "Saint Augustine on the Road to Damascus." *Augustinian Studies* 13 (1982): 151–70.

Flanigan, C. Clifford. "The Liturgical Context of the *Quem Queritis* Trope." *Comparative Drama* 8 (1974): 45–62.

―――. "Rachel and Her Children: From Biblical Text to Music Drama." In *Metamorphoses and the Arts, Proceedings of the Second Lilly Conference*, ed. Breon Mitchell, 31–52. Bloomington: Indiana University Press, 1979.

Fleming, John V. "The Best Line in Ovid and the Worst." In *New Readings of Chaucer's Poetry*, ed. Robert G. Benson and Susan J. Ridyard, 51–74. Cambridge, MA: D. S. Brewer, 2003.

Fletcher, Alan J. "Chaucer the Heretic." *SAC* 25 (2003): 53–121.

―――. "The Criteria for Scribal Attribution: Dublin, Trinity College, MS 244, Some Early Copies of the Works of Geoffrey Chaucer, and the Canon of Adam Pynkhurst Manuscripts." *Review of English Studies*, n.s. 58, no. 237 (2007): 597–632.

―――. *Preaching, Politics, and Poetry in Late-Medieval England*. Dublin: Four Courts Press, 1998.

Fleteren, Frederick van. "Augustine's Ascent of the Soul in Book VII of the *Confessions*: A Reconsideration." *Augustinian Studies* 5 (1974): 29–72.

―――. "Principles of Augustine's Hermeneutic: An Overview." In *Augustine: Biblical Exegete*, ed. Fleteren and Schnaubelt, 1–32.

Foucault, Michel. *The Archaeology of Knowledge and The Discourse on Language*. Trans. A. M. Sheridan Smith. New York: Pantheon, 1972.

―――. "The Battle for Chastity." In *Western Sexuality: Practice and Precept in Past and Present*, ed. Philippe Ariès and André Béjin, trans. Anthony Forster, 14–25. Oxford: Basil Blackwell, 1985.

―――. "The Order of Discourse." Trans. Ian McLeod. In *Untying the Text: A Post-Structuralist Reader*, ed. Robert Young, 48–78. Boston: Routledge and Kegan Paul, 1981.

Fredriksen, Paula. "Augustine in History, the Church, and the Flesh." In *Saint Augustine the Bishop*, ed. LeMoine and Kleinhenz, 109–23.

Gamble, Harry. "The Formation of the New Testament Canon and Its Significance for the History of Biblical Interpretation." In *History of Biblical Interpretation*, ed. Hauser and Watson, 409–29.

Geertz, Clifford. *The Interpretation of Cultures*. New York: Basic Books, 1973.

Ghosh, Kantik. *The Wycliffite Heresy: Authority and the Interpretation of Texts*. Cambridge: Cambridge University Press, 2002.

Gibson, Gail McMurray. *The Theater of Devotion: East Anglian Drama and Society in the Late Middle Ages*. Chicago: University of Chicago Press, 1989.

Gibson, Margaret T. "The Place of the *Glossa Ordinaria* in Medieval Exegesis." In *Ad Litteram*, ed. Jordan and Emery, 5–27.

Gilchrist, John. "The Perceptions of Jews in the Canon Law in the Period of the First Two Crusades." *Jewish History* 3 (1988): 9–24.

Greenblatt, Stephen. *Renaissance Self-Fashioning from More to Shakespeare.* Chicago: University of Chicago Press, 1980.

Gumbert, J. P. "The Layout of the Bible Gloss in Manuscript and Early Print." In *The Bible as Book: The First Printed Editions*, ed. Paul Saenger and Kimberly van Kampen, 7–13. London: British Library and Oak Knoll Press, 1999.

Hamel, C. F. R. de. *Glossed Books of the Bible and the Origins of the Paris Booktrade.* Woodbridge: D. S. Brewer, 1984.

Hanna, Ralph. "Donaldson and Robertson: An Obligatory Conjunction." *Chaucer Review* 41 (2007): 240–49.

———. *Pursuing History: Middle English Manuscripts and Their Texts.* Stanford: Stanford University Press, 1996.

Hanning, Robert W. "'I Shal Finde It in a Maner Glose': Versions of Textual Harassment in Medieval Literature." In *Medieval Texts and Contemporary Readers*, ed. Laurie A. Finke and Martin B. Shichtman, 27–50. Ithaca, NY: Cornell University Press, 1987.

Head, Thomas. *Hagiography and the Cult of Saints: The Diocese of Orléans, 800–1200.* Cambridge: Cambridge University Press, 1990.

Heinrichs, Katherine. "Tropological Woman in Chaucer: Literary Elaborations of an Exegetical Tradition." *English Studies* 3 (1995): 209–14.

Herdt, Jennifer A. *Putting on Virtue: The Legacy of the Splendid Vices.* Chicago: University of Chicago Press, 2008.

Hockenbery, Jennifer. "The He, She, and It of God: Translating Saint Augustine's Gendered Latin God-Talk into English." *Augustinian Studies* 36 (2005): 433–46.

Hood, John Y. B. *Aquinas and the Jews.* Philadelphia: University of Pennsylvania Press, 1995.

Horowitz, Maryanne Cline. "The Image of God in Man—Is Woman Included?" *Harvard Theological Review* 72 (1979): 175–206.

Hsia, R. Po-Chia. *Myth of Ritual Murder: Jews and Magic in Reformation Germany.* New Haven, CT: Yale University Press, 1988.

Hudson, Anne. "Lollardy: The English Heresy?" *Studies in Church History* 18 (1982): 261–83.

Jacobs, Andrew S. "Writing Demetrius: Ascetic Logic in Ancient Christianity." *Church History* 69 (2000): 719–48.

Jager, Eric. *The Tempter's Voice: Language and the Fall in Medieval Literature.* Ithaca, NY: Cornell University Press, 1993.

Jeffrey, David Lyle. "Chaucer and Wyclif: Biblical Hermeneutic and Literary Theory in the XIVth Century." In *Chaucer and Scriptural Tradition*, ed. Jeffrey, 109–40.

Jerome. *Adversus Jovinianum. PL* 23, cols. 205–338.

———. *Against Jovinianus.* In *The Principal Works of St. Jerome*, trans. W. H. Fremantle, A Select Library of Nicene and Post-Nicene Fathers of the

Christian Church, 2nd series, vol. 6, 346–416. Grand Rapids, MI: William B. Eerdmans, 1989.

———. *Commentaria in Evangelium Mattaei. PL* 26, cols. 15–218.

———. *Epistola Pauli ad Timotheum I. PL* 29, cols. 797–802.

Jordan, William Chester. *The French Monarchy and the Jews: From Philip Augustus to the Last Capetians*. Philadelphia: University of Pennsylvania Press, 1989.

Kelly, Henry Ansgar. *Satan: A Biography*. Cambridge: Cambridge University Press, 2006.

Kelly, J. N. D. *Golden Mouth: The Story of John Chrysostom—Ascetic, Preacher, Bishop*. London: Duckworth, 1995.

———. *Jerome: His Life, Writings, and Controversies*. New York: Harper and Row, 1975.

Kennedy, Beverly. "Contradictory Responses to the Wife of Bath as Evidenced by Fifteenth-Century Manuscript Variants." In *The Canterbury Tales Project Occasional Papers*, ed. N. Blake and P. Robinson, 2: 23–39. London: Office for Humanities Communication Publications, 1997.

———. "The Rewriting of the *Wife of Bath's Prologue* in Cambridge Dd.4.24." In *Rewriting Chaucer: Culture, Authority, and the Idea of the Authentic Text, 1400–1602*, ed. Thomas A. Prendergast and Barbara Kline, 203–33. Columbus: Ohio State University Press, 1999.

Kennedy, Thomas C. "The Wife of Bath on St. Jerome." *Mediaevalia* 23 (2002): 75–97.

Kenney, John Peter. *The Mysticism of Saint Augustine: Re-Reading the "Confessions."* New York: Routledge, 2005.

Kienzle, Beverly Wayne, and Pamela J. Walker, eds. *Women Preachers and Prophets through Two Millennia of Christianity*. Berkeley: University of California Press, 1998.

Kiser, Lisa J. *Truth and Textuality in Chaucer's Poetry*. Hanover: University Press of New England, 1991.

Klepper, Deeana Copeland. *The Insight of Unbelievers: Nicholas of Lyra and Christian Reading of Jewish Text in the Later Middle Ages*. Philadelphia: University of Pennsylvania Press, 2007.

Knapp, Peggy A. "Alisoun of Bathe and the Reappropriation of Tradition." *Chaucer Review* 24 (1989): 45–52.

———. *Chaucer and the Social Contest*. New York: Routledge, 1990.

———. " 'Wandrynge by the Weye': On Alisoun and Augustine." In *Medieval Texts and Contemporary Readers*, ed. Finke and Shichtman, 142–57.

Knight, Stephen. *Geoffrey Chaucer*. Oxford: Basil Blackwell, 1986.

Krey, Philip D. W., and Lesley Smith. *Nicholas of Lyra: The Senses of Scripture*. Leiden: E. J. Brill, 2000.

Kuefler, Mathew. *The Manly Eunuch: Masculinity, Gender Ambiguity, and Christian Ideology in Late Antiquity*. Chicago: University of Chicago Press, 2001.

Lampert, Lisa. *Gender and Jewish Difference from Paul to Shakespeare*. Philadelphia: University of Pennsylvania Press, 2004.

Langmuir, Gavin I. *Toward a Definition of Antisemitism*. Berkeley: University of California Press, 1990.

La Vere, Suzanne. "From Contemplation to Action: The Role of the Active Life in the *Glossa Ordinaria* on the Song of Songs." *Speculum* 82 (2007): 54–69.

Leclercq, Dom Jean. *The Love of Learning and the Desire for God: A Study of Monastic Culture.* Trans. Catharine Misrahi. New York: Fordham University Press, 1961.

Leupin, Alexandre. *Fiction and Incarnation: Rhetoric, Theology, and Literature in the Middle Ages.* Trans. David Laatsch. Minneapolis: University of Minnesota Press, 2003.

Leyser, Conrad. "Vulnerability and Power: The Early Christian Rhetoric of Masculine Authority." *Bulletin of the John Rylands University Library of Manchester* 80 (1998): 159–73.

Light, Laura. "The New Thirteenth-Century Bible and the Challenge of Heresy." *Viator* 18 (1987): 275–88.

Lipton, Sara. *Images of Intolerance: The Representation of Jews and Judaism in the "Bible moralisée."* Berkeley: University of California Press, 1999.

Little, Katherine. "Chaucer's Parson and the Specter of Wycliffism." *SAC* 23 (2001): 225–53.

Lombard, Peter. *Collectanea in epistolas Pauli. PL* 192, cols. 335–42.

Longsworth, Robert. "The Wife of Bath and the Samaritan Woman." *Chaucer Review* 34 (2000): 372–87.

Louth, Andrew. *Discerning the Mystery: An Essay on the Nature of Theology.* Oxford: Clarendon, 1983.

Lubac, Henri de. *Medieval Exegesis: Volume 1, The Four Senses of Scripture.* Trans. Mark Sebanc. Grand Rapids, MI: William B. Eerdmans; Edinburgh: T and T Clark, 1998.

———. *Medieval Exegesis: Volume 2, The Four Senses of Scripture.* Trans. E. M. Macierowski. Grand Rapids, MI: William B. Eerdmans; Edinburgh: T and T Clark, 2000.

Luscombe, David. "Wyclif and Hierarchy." In *From Ockham to Wyclif,* ed. Hudson and Wilks, 233–44.

Macy, Gary. *The Hidden History of the Ordination of Women: Female Clergy in the Medieval West.* Oxford: Oxford University Press, 2008.

Maloney, Linda M. "The Pastoral Epistles." In *Searching the Scriptures. Vol. 2: A Feminist Commentary,* ed. Elisabeth Schüssler Fiorenza, 361–80. New York: Crossroad, 1994.

Mann, Jill. *Geoffrey Chaucer.* Atlantic Highlands: Humanities Press International, 1991.

Marlin, John. "Virtual Ritual: History, Drama, and the Spirit of the Liturgy in the Fleury Playbook." *American Benedictine Review* 48 (1997): 396–427.

Martin, Priscilla. *Chaucer's Women: Nuns, Wives, and Amazons.* Iowa City: University of Iowa Press, 1990.

Matter, E. Ann. "Christ, God and Woman in the Thought of St. Augustine." In *Augustine and the Critics: Essays in Honour of Gerald Bonner,* ed. Robert Dodaro and George Lawless, 164–75. London: Routledge, 2000.

————. "The Church Fathers and the *Glossa Ordinaria.*" In *The Reception of the Church Fathers in the West: From the Carolingians to the Maurists*, ed. Irena Backus, Vol. 1, 83–111. Leiden: E. J. Brill, 1997.

————. "De cura feminarum: Augustine the Bishop, North African Women, and the Development of a Theology of Female Nature." *Augustinian Studies* 36 (2005): 87–98.

————. *The Voice of My Beloved: The Song of Songs in Western Medieval Christianity.* Philadelphia: University of Pennsylvania Press, 1990.

Maxwell, Jacyln L. *Christianization and Communication in Late Antiquity: John Chrysostom and His Congregation in Antioch.* Cambridge: Cambridge University Press, 2006.

McCarthy, Thomas. "The Critique of Impure Reason: Foucault and the Frankfurt School." In *Rethinking Power*, ed. Thomas E. Wartenberg, 121–48. Albany: State University of New York Press, 1992.

McCulloh, John M. "Jewish Ritual Murder: William of Norwich, Thomas of Monmouth, and the Early Dissemination of the Myth." *Speculum* 72 (1997): 698–740.

McGowan, Richard. "Augustine's Spiritual Equality: The Allegory of Man and Woman with Regard to *Imago Dei.*" *Revue des Études Augustiniennes* 33 (1987): 255–64.

McIntosh, John S. *A Study of Augustine's Versions of Genesis.* Chicago: University of Chicago Press, 1912.

McLeese, Constance E. "Augustinian Exegesis and Sexist Canon from the New Testament." In *Augustine and the Bible*, ed. and trans. Pamela Bright, 282–300. Notre Dame: Notre Dame University Press, 1999.

McNamara, JoAnn. "An Unresolved Syllogism: The Search for a Christian Gender System." In *Conflicted Identities and Multiple Masculinities: Men in the Medieval West*, ed. Jacqueline Murray, 1–24. New York: Garland, 1999.

McSheffrey, Shannon. "Heresy, Orthodoxy, and English Vernacular Religion, 1480–1525." *Past and Present* 186 (2005): 47–80.

Michael, Robert. *A History of Catholic Antisemitism: The Dark Side of the Church.* New York: Palgrave Macmillan, 2008.

Miles, Jack. *God: A Biography.* New York: Vintage, 1995.

Miles, Margaret R. "The Body and Human Values in Augustine of Hippo." In *Grace, Politics and Desire: Essays on Augustine*, ed. H. A. Meynell, 55–67. Calgary: University of Calgary Press, 1990.

————. *Desire and Delight: A New Reading of Augustine's "Confessions."* New York: Crossroad, 1992.

Miller, Jean Baker. "Women and Power." In *Rethinking Power*, ed. Wartenberg, 240–48.

Minnis, A. J. *Fallible Authors: Chaucer's Pardoner and the Wife of Bath.* Philadelphia: University of Pennsylvania Press, 2008.

————. *Medieval Theory of Authorship: Scholastic Literary Attitudes in the later Middle Ages.* 2nd ed. Philadelphia: University of Pennsylvania Press, 1988.

Mooney, Linne R. "Chaucer's Scribe." *Speculum* 81 (2006): 97–138.

Moore, R. I. *The Formation of a Persecuting Society: Power and Deviance in Western Europe 950–1250.* 2nd ed. Malden, MA: Blackwell, 2007.

Mostert, Marco. *The Library of Fleury: A Provisional List of Manuscripts.* Hilversum: Verloren, 1989.

Mullaney, Steven. "Affective Technologies: Toward an Emotional Logic of the Elizabethan Stage." In *Environment and Embodiment in Early Modern England,* ed. Mary Floyd-Wilson and Garrett Sullivan, 71–89. New York: Palgrave Macmillan, 2006.

Murdoch, Brian. *The Medieval Popular Bible: Expansions of Genesis in the Middle Ages.* Cambridge, MA: D. S. Brewer, 2003.

Murray, Jacqueline. "One Flesh, Two Sexes, Three Genders?" In *Gender and Christianity in Medieval Europe: New Perspectives,* ed. Lisa M. Bitel and Felice Lifshitz, 34–51. Philadelphia: University of Pennsylvania Press, 2008.

Newman, Barbara. *Sister of Wisdom: St. Hildegard's Theology of the Feminine.* Berkeley: University of California Press, 1987.

O'Connell, Robert J. "The God of Saint Augustine's Imagination." *Thought* 57 (1982): 30–40.

———. *Images of Conversion in St. Augustine's "Confessions."* New York: Fordham University Press, 1996.

———. *Imagination and Metaphysics in St. Augustine.* Milwaukee: Marquette University Press, 1986.

———. "Isaiah's Mothering God in St. Augustine's *Confessions.*" *Thought* 58 (1983): 188–206.

———. *Soundings in St. Augustine's Imagination.* New York: Fordham University Press, 1994.

———. *St. Augustine's Early Theory of Man, A.D. 386–391.* Cambridge, MA: Harvard University Press, 1968.

O'Daly, Gerard J. P. "Hierarchies in Augustine's Thought." In *From Augustine to Eriugena: Essays on Neoplatonism and Christianity in Honor of John O'Meara,* ed. F. X. Martin and J. A. Richmond, 143–54. Washington, DC: Catholic University of America Press, 1991.

O'Donnell, James J. *Augustine: A New Biography.* New York: Ecco, 2005.

O'Hara, Robert, and Peter Robinson. "Computer-Assisted Methods of Stemmatic Analysis." In *The Canterbury Tales Project Occasional Papers,* ed. N. F. Blake and Peter Robinson, 1: 53–74. Oxford: Office for Humanities Communication, 1993.

O'Meara John J. *The Creation of Man in St. Augustine's "De Genesi ad Litteram."* Villanova: Villanova University Press, 1980.

———. *The Young Augustine: The Growth of St. Augustine's Mind up to His Conversion.* London: Longmans, Green, 1954.

Oppel, John. "Saint Jerome and the History of Sex." *Viator* 24 (1993): 1–22.

Owen, Charles A., Jr. "The Alternative Reading of *The Canterbury Tales:* Chaucer's Text and the Early Manuscripts." *PMLA* 97 (1982): 237–50.

Pagels, Elaine. *Adam, Eve, and the Serpent.* New York: Random House, 1988.

———. "What Became of God the Mother?" *Signs* 2 (1976): 293–303.

Pagels, Elaine, and Karen L. King. *Reading Judas: The Gospel of Judas and the Shaping of Christianity.* New York: Viking, 2007.

Parkes, Malcolm Beckwith. "The Influence of the Concepts of *Ordinatio* and *Compilatio* on the Development of the Book." In *Medieval Learning and Literature: Essays Presented to Richard William Hunt,* ed. J. J. G. Alexander and M. T. Gibson, 115–41. Oxford: Clarendon, 1976.

Partridge, Stephen. "The *Canterbury Tales* Glosses and the Manuscript Groups." In *The Canterbury Tales Project Occasional Papers,* ed. N. F. Blake and Peter Robinson, 1: 85–94. Oxford: Office for Humanities Communication, 1993.

———. "Glosses in the Manuscripts of Chaucer's *Canterbury Tales:* An Edition and Commentary." Dissertation, Harvard University, 1992.

———. "A Newly Identified Manuscript by the Scribe of the New College *Canterbury Tales.*" *English Manuscript Studies 1100–1700* 6 (1997): 229–36.

———. "Wynkyn de Worde's Manuscript Source for the *Canterbury Tales:* Evidence from the Glosses." *Chaucer Review* 41 (2007): 325–59.

Patterson, Lee. *Chaucer and the Subject of History.* Madison: University of Wisconsin Press, 1991.

Pearce, Sarah. "Attitudes of Contempt: Christian Anti-Judaism and the Bible." In *Cultures of Ambivalence and Contempt: Studies in Jewish–Non-Jewish Relations,* ed. Siân Jones, Tony Kushner, and Sarah Pearce, 50–71. London: Vallentine Mitchell, 1998.

Poliakov, Léon. *The History of Anti-Semitism, Volume 1: From the Time of Christ to the Court Jews.* Trans. Richard Howard. 4 vols. New York: Vanguard Press, 1965.

Power, Kim. *Veiled Desire: Augustine's Writing on Women.* London: Darton, Longman, and Todd, 1995.

Pratt, Robert A. "Jankyn's 'Book of Wikked Wyves': Medieval Anti-Matrimonial Propaganda in the Universities." *Annuale Mediaevale* 3 (1962): 5–27.

Pseudo-Bede. *In Matthaei Evangelium Expositio. PL* 92, cols. 9–132.

Raedts, P. "The Children's Crusade of 1212." *Journal of Medieval History* 3 (1977): 279–323.

Rebenich, Stefan. *Jerome.* London: Routledge, 2002.

Rebillard, Éric. "A New Style of Argument in Christian Polemic: Augustine and the Use of Patristic Citations." *Journal of Early Christian Studies* 8 (2000): 559–78.

Reiss, Edmund. "Biblical Parody: Chaucer's 'Distortions' of Scripture." In *Chaucer and Scriptural Tradition,* ed. Jeffrey, 47–61.

Rich, Adrienne. *Of Woman Born.* New York: Bantam, 1976.

Riley-Smith, Jonathan. "The First Crusade and the Persecution of the Jews." *Studies in Church History* 21 (1984): 51–72.

Robertson, D. W., Jr. "'And for my land thus hast thou murdred me?': Land Tenure, the Cloth Industry, and the Wife of Bath." *Chaucer Review* 14 (1980): 403–20.

———. *A Preface to Chaucer: Studies in Medieval Perspectives.* Princeton, NJ: Princeton University Press, 1962.

Robinson, Peter M. W. "An Approach to the Manuscripts of the 'Wife of Bath's Prologue.'" In *Computer-Based Chaucer Studies*, ed. Ian Lancashire, 17–47. Toronto: Centre for Computing in the Humanities, University of Toronto, 1993.

———. "A Stemmatic Analysis of the Fifteenth-Century Witnesses to the *Wife of Bath's Prologue*." In *The Canterbury Tales Project Occasional Papers*, ed. N. Blake and P. Robinson, 2: 69–132. London: Office for Humanities Communication Publications, 1997.

Rubin, Miri. *Gentile Tales: The Narrative Assault on Late Medieval Jews*. New Haven, CT: Yale University Press, 1999.

Sawyer, Erin. "Celibate Pleasures: Masculinity, Desire, and Asceticism in Augustine." *Journal of the History of Sexuality* 6 (1995): 1–29.

Schaberg, Jane. "New Testament: The Case of Mary Magdalene." In *Feminist Approaches to the Bible: Symposium at the Smithsonian Institute, September 24, 1994*, 75–91. Washington, DC: Biblical Archaeology Society, 1995.

Schibanoff, Susan. "The New Reader and Female Textuality in Two Early Commentaries on Chaucer." *SAC* 10 (1988): 71–108.

Schlauch, Margaret. "Allegory of Church and Synagogue." *Speculum* 14 (1939): 448–64.

Scholer, David M. "I Timothy 2.9–15 and the Place of Women in the Church's Ministry." 1986; rpt. in *A Feminist Companion to the Deutero-Pauline Epistles*, ed. Amy-Jill Levine with Marianne Blickenstaff, 98–121. London: Continuum, 2003.

Schottroff, Luise, Silvia Schroer, and Marie-Theres Wacker. *Feminist Interpretation: The Bible in Women's Perspective*. Trans. Martin and Barbara Rumscheidt. Minneapolis: Fortress Press, 1998.

Schreiner, Susan E. "Eve, the Mother of History; Reaching for the Reality of History in Augustine's Later Exegesis of Genesis." In *Genesis 1–3 in the History of Exegesis: Intrigue in the Garden*, ed. Gregory Allen Robbins, 136–69. Studies in Women and Religion, vol. 27. Lewiston: Edwin Mellen Press, 1988.

Schüssler Fiorenza, Elisabeth. *Bread Not Stone: The Challenge of Feminist Biblical Interpretation*. Boston: Beacon Press, 1984.

———. *In Memory of Her: A Feminist Theological Reconstruction of Christian Origins*. 1983; rpt. New York: Crossroad, 1987.

Shaw, Brent D. "The Family in Late Antiquity: The Experience of Augustine." *Past and Present* 115 (1987): 3–51.

Shillingsburg, Peter L. *From Gutenberg to Google: Electronic Representations of Literary Texts*. Cambridge: Cambridge University Press, 2006.

Siebers, Tobin. *Disability Theory*. Ann Arbor: University of Michigan Press, 2008.

Signer, Michael A. "The *Glossa ordinaria* and the Transmission of Medieval Anti-Judaism." In *A Distinct Voice: Medieval Studies in Honor of Leonard E. Boyle, O.P.*, ed. Jacqueline Brown and William P. Stoneman, 591–605. Notre Dame: Notre Dame University Press, 1997.

Silvia, Daniel S., Jr. "Glosses to the *Canterbury Tales* from St. Jerome's *Epistola adversus Jovinianum*." *SP* 62 (1965): 28–39.

Sinanoglou, Leah. "The Christ Child as Sacrifice: A Medieval Tradition and the Corpus Christi Plays." *Speculum* 48 (1973): 491–509.

Skey, Miriam Anne. "The Iconography of Herod in the Fleury *Playbook* and in the Visual Arts." In *The Fleury Playbook*, ed. Campbell and Davidson, 120–43.

Smalley, Beryl. *The Gospels in the Schools, c. 1100–c. 1280.* London and Ronceverte: Hambledon, 1985.

———. *The Study of the Bible in the Middle Ages.* 3rd ed. Oxford: Basil Blackwell, 1983.

Smith, Warren S. "The Wife of Bath Debates Jerome." *Chaucer Review* 32 (1997): 129–45.

Southern, R. W. "Beryl Smalley and the Place of the Bible in Medieval Studies, 1927–84." In *The Bible in the Medieval World: Essays in Memory of Beryl Smalley*, ed. Katherine Walsh and Diana Wood, 1–16. Oxford: Blackwell, for the Ecclesiastical History Society, 1985.

Spiegel, Gabrielle M. *The Past as Text: The Theory and Practice of Medieval Historiography.* Baltimore: Johns Hopkins University Press, 1997.

Spurgeon, Caroline F. E. *Five Hundred Years of Chaucer Criticism and Allusion, 1357–1900.* 1925; rpt. New York: Russell and Russell, 1960. 3 vols.

Stock, Brian. *Augustine the Reader: Meditation, Self-Knowledge, and the Ethics of Interpretation.* Cambridge, MA: Belknap Press of Harvard University Press, 1996.

Stow, Kenneth R. *Alienated Minority: The Jews of Medieval Latin Europe.* Cambridge, MA: Harvard University Press, 1992.

Strohm, Paul. "Chaucer's Lollard Joke: History and the Textual Unconscious." *SAC* 17 (1995): 23–42.

Stubbs, Estelle. "'Here's One I Prepared Earlier': The Work of Scribe D on Oxford, Corpus Christi College, MS 198." *Review of English Studies,* n.s. 58, n. 234 (2007): 133–53.

Tatlock, J. S. P. "The *Canterbury Tales* in 1400." *PMLA* 50 (1935): 100–39.

TeSelle, Eugene. "Exploring the Inner Conflict: Augustine's Sermons on Romans 7 and 8." In *Augustine: Biblical Exegete*, ed. Fleteren and Schnaubelt, 313–45.

———. "Serpent, Eve, and Adam: Augustine and the Exegetical Tradition." In *Collectanea Augustiniana: Augustine, Presbyter Factus Sum*, ed. Joseph T. Lienhard, Earl C. Muller, and Roland J. Teske, 341–61. New York: Peter Lang, 1993.

Thomson, J. A. F. "Knightly Piety and the Margins of Lollardy." In *Lollardy and the Gentry in the Later Middle Ages*, ed. Margaret Aston and Colin Richmond, 95–111. Stroud: Sutton Publishing; New York: St. Martin's Press, 1997.

———. *The Later Lollards, 1414–1520.* London: Oxford University Press, 1965.

Tinkle, Theresa. "The Wife of Bath's Marginal Authority." *SAC,* Fall 2010.

Tkacz, Catherine Brown. "'Labor Tam Utilis': The Creation of the Vulgate." *Vigiliae Christianae* 50 (1996): 42–72.

Trible, Phyllis. *Texts of Terror: Literary-Feminist Readings of Biblical Narratives.* Philadelphia: Fortress Press, 1984.

Valantasis, Richard. "Constructions of Power in Asceticism." *Journal of the American Academy of Religion* 63 (1995): 775–821.

Vander Stichele, Caroline, and Todd Penner. "Mastering the Tools or Retooling the Masters? The Legacy of Historical-Critical Discourse." In *Her Master's Tools? Feminist and Postcolonial Engagements of Historical-Critical Discourse*, ed. Vander Stichele and Penner, 1–29. Leiden: E. J. Brill, 2005.

Wailes, Stephen L. *Medieval Allegories of Jesus' Parables*. Berkeley: University of California Press, 1987.

Warhol, Tamara. "Gender Constructions and Biblical Exegesis: Lessons from a Divinity School Seminar." In *Language and Religious Identity: Women in Discourse*, ed. Allyson Jule, 50–72. New York: Palgrave Macmillan, 2007.

Wartenburg, Thomas E. "Situated Social Power." In *Rethinking Power*, ed. Wartenburg, 79–101.

Watson, Nicholas. "Censorship and Cultural Change in Late-Medieval England: Vernacular Theology, the Oxford Translation Debate, and Arundel's Constitutions of 1409." *Speculum* 70 (1995): 822–64.

———. "Cultural Changes." *ELN* 44 (2006): 127–37.

Watt, John A. "Jews and Christians in the Gregorian Decretals." *Studies in Church History* 29 (1992): 93–105.

Wells, David A. "Friedrich Ohly and Exegetical Tradition: Some Aspects of Medieval Interpretation." *Forum for Modern Language Studies* 41 (2005): 43–70.

Wiesen, David S. *St. Jerome as a Satirist: A Study in Christian Latin Thought and Letters*. Ithaca, NY: Cornell University Press, 1964.

Wood, Chauncey. "Artistic Intention and Chaucer's Use of Scriptural Allusion." In *Chaucer and Scriptural Tradition*, ed. Jeffrey, 35–46.

Wurtele, Douglas. "Chaucer's *Canterbury Tales* and Nicholas of Lyre's *Postillae litteralis et moralis super totam Bibliam*." In *Chaucer and Scriptural Tradition*, ed. Jeffrey, 89–107.

Young, F. M. *Biblical Exegesis and the Formation of Christian Culture*. Cambridge: Cambridge University Press, 1997.

Young, Karl. *The Drama of the Medieval Church*. 2 vols. 1933; rpt. Oxford: Clarendon, 1951.

Zier, Mark. "The Development of the *Glossa Ordinaria* to the Bible in the Thirteenth Century: The Evidence from the Bibliothèque Nationale, Paris." In *La Bibbia del XIII Secolo*, ed. Cremascoli and Santi, 155–84.

———. "The Manuscript Tradition of the *Glossa Ordinaria* for Daniel and Hints at a Method for a Critical Edition." *Scriptorium, Revue Internationale des etudes relative aux manuscrits* 47 (1993): 3–25.

———. "Peter Lombard and the *Glossa Ordinaria*: A Missing Link?" In *Pietro Lombardo*, ed. E. Menestò, 361–409. Spoleto: Centro Italiano de Studi Sull'Alto Medioevo, 2007.

INDEX